MW01253024

DIGITAL INDIA

DIGITAL INDIA

UNDERSTANDING INFORMATION, COMMUNICATION AND SOCIAL CHANGE

Pradip Ninan Thomas

 SAGE

www.sagepublications.com

Los Angeles • London • New Delhi • Singapore • Washington DC

First published in 2012 by

SAGE Publications India Pvt Ltd
B1/I-1 Mohan Cooperative Industrial Area
Mathura Road, New Delhi 110 044, India
www.sagepub.in

SAGE Publications Inc
2455 Teller Road
Thousand Oaks, California 91320, USA

SAGE Publications Ltd
1 Oliver's Yard
55 City Road
London EC1Y 1SP, United Kingdom

SAGE Publications Asia-Pacific Pte Ltd
33 Pekin Street
#02-01 Far East Square
Singapore 048763

Published by Vivek Mehra for SAGE Publications India Pvt Ltd, typeset in 10/12 Minion by Tantla Composition Pvt Ltd, Chandigarh, and printed at Yash Printographics, Noida

Library of Congress Cataloging-in-Publication Data Available

ISBN: 978-81-321-0904-4 (HB)

The SAGE Team: Shambhu Sahu, Shreya Chakraborti, Nand Kumar Jha

*To Prem, Beena, Sneha, Mathew and
Shruthi—with love, lots
of it*

Contents

List of Abbreviations

ANT	Actor Network Theory
ARPU	Average Revenues per User
AYUSH	Department of Ayurveda, Yoga and Naturopathy, Unani, Siddha and Homoeopathy
BJP	Bharatiya Janata Party
BOO	Build-Own-Operate
BOSS	Bharat Operating System Solutions
BOT	Build-Operate-Transfer (Model)
BPO	Business Process Outsourcing
BSNL	Bharat Sanchar Nigam Limited
BTEF	Bharatiya Telecom Employees Federation
CAG	Comptroller and Auditor General
CAGR	Compound Annual Growth Rate
C-DAC	Centre for Development of Advanced Computing
C-DoT	Centre for Development of Telematics
CIRP	Committee on Internet-Related Policies
COA	Cellular Operators Association
CR	Community Radio
CRTs	Cathode Ray Tubes
CSIR	Council of Scientific and Industrial Research
DIT	Department of Information Technology
DMCA	Digital Millennium Copyright Act
DoT	Department of Telecommunications
DRM	Digital Rights Management
DTH	Direct-to-Home
ELCOT	Electronics Corporation of Tamil Nadu Limited
ENTEL	La Empresa Nacional de Telecomunicaciones
EOI	Export-oriented Industrialisation
EPO	European Patent Office
EXIM	Export–Import
F/OSS, FOSS	Free and Open Source Software
FDI	Foreign Direct Investment
FERA	Foreign Exchange Regulation Act
FICCI	Federation of Indian Chambers of Commerce and Industry

FII	Foreign Institutional Investors
FNTO	Federation of National Telecom Organisations
FYP	Five Year Plan
GAO	Government Accountability Office
GATT	General Agreement on Tariffs and Trade
GDP	Gross Domestic Product
GIS	Geographic Information System
GSM	Groupe Spécial Mobile (Global System for Mobile Communications)
GSP	Generalized System of Preferences
IBM	International Business Machines
ICANN	Internet Corporation for Assigned Names and Numbers
ICSIR	Indian Council of Scientific and Industrial Research
ICT	Information and Communication Technology
ICT4D	Information and Communication Technologies for Development
IFIS	Integrated Financial Information System
IIPA	International Intellectual Property Alliance
IIT	Indian Institute of Technology
IK	Indigenous Knowledge
IMF	International Monetary Fund
IP	Intellectual Property
IPC	International Patent Classification
IPR	Intellectual Property Rights
IT	Information Technology
ITI	Indian Telephone Industries
ITU	International Telecommunication Union
KIADB	Karnataka Industrial Areas Development Board
KSITM	Kerala State IT Mission
LAA	Land Acquisition Act, 1894
MAIT	Manufacturing Association of IT Industry
MGNREGA	Mahatma Gandhi National Rural Employment Guarantee Act
MNC	Multinational Corporation
MRTP	Monopolies and Restrictive Trade Practices
MSSRF	M.S. Swaminathan Research Foundation
MTNL	Mahanagar Telephone Nigam Ltd.
NASDAQ	National Association of Securities Dealers Automated Quotations
NASSCOM	National Association for Software and Services Companies

NCP	New Computer Policy
NeGP	National e-Governance Plan
NFTE	National Federation of Telecom Employees
NGO	Non-governmental Organisation
NIC	National Informatics Centre
NISCAIR	National Institute of Science Communication and Information Resources
NIT	National Institute of Technology
NLRMP	National Land Records Modernisation Programme
NLT	Nokia Life Tools
NRCFOSS	National Resource Centre for Free and Open Source Software
NTP	New Telecoms Policy, 1999
NWICO	New World Information and Communication Order
OCR	Optical Character Recognition
OLPC	One Laptop Per Child
OLTP	Online Transaction Processing
OSYU	Open Source Yoga Unity
PPP	Public–Private Partnership
RAND	Reasonable and Non-Discriminatory
RAX	Rural Automatic Exchange
RML	Reuters Market Light
RTC	Rights, Tenancy and Crops
RTI	Right to Information
SAARC	South Asian Association for Regional Cooperation
SAPs	Structural Adjustment Policies
SARI	Sustainable Access in Rural India
SEZ	Special Economic Zone
SIM	Subscriber Identity Module/Subscriber Identification Module
TCIL	Telecommunications Consultants of India
TCS	Tata Consultancy Services
TEMA	Telecom Equipment Manufacturers' Association
TK	Traditional Knowledge
TKDL	Traditional Knowledge Digital Library
TKRC	Traditional Knowledge Resource Classification (System)
TRAI	Telecom Regulatory Authority of India
TRIPS	Trade-related Aspects of Intellectual Property Rights
UAS	Universal Access Service Provider
UASL	Unified Access Services Licensing
UIDAI	Unique Identification Authority of India

UKPTO	United Kingdom Patent and Trademark Office
UN	United Nations
UNESCO	United Nations Educational, Scientific and Cultural Organization
USIBC	US–India Business Council
USO	Universal Service Obligation
USOF	Universal Service Obligation Fund
USPTO	US Patent and Trademark Office
USTR	United States Trade Representative
VA	Village Accountant
VPT	Village Public Telephone
VRS	Voluntary Redundancy Scheme
VSNL	Videsh Sanchaar Nigam Limited
WB	World Bank
WCT	WIPO Copyright Treaty
WEEE	Waste Electrical and Electronic Equipment (Directive)
WIPO	World Intellectual Property Organization
WLL	Wireless Local Loop
WPPT	WIPO Performances and Phonograms Treaty
WTO	World Trade Organization

Foreword

The Kenyan writer and cultural critic Ngugi wa Thiong'o seeks to develop what he calls 'poor theory'. This concept does more than merely recognize that poor people think—though in itself this remains crucially important. Shorn of scholasticism and other excesses, poor theory also carries the incendiary idea that society's processes of knowing themselves need to be reorganized in light of those who, decades ago, Fanon called 'the wretched of the earth'.[1]

Digital India makes major contributions to poor theory. It does so by delivering us to a concept of the digital that is determinedly different from the one that brays through cellphone advertisements and news features about the latest Internet service. Herein the digital is stripped down to its societal essentials. Self-satisfied consumers stand revealed as only one part of the picture. This is not just another prolix celebration of consumers' subjectivity, of the sort that has so confused and diverted communications scholarship, but also an honest and creative engagement with the social and political forces that shape our modernity.

In the United States, nowadays India is often presented as a rising commercial power—and, at the same time, as an ineffable blend of poverty and high-tech entrepreneurship, perhaps filtered through a supposedly timeless caste system. Pradip Thomas reveals a more coherent, contingent, and historically grounded reality. In the India that he scrupulously depicts, the digital is a volatile mix of commodification initiatives and attempts to push back. If, on one hand, the political economy of information is being generalized so that it encompasses not only familiar media and network services but also software and biotechnology and e-government programs of public sector commodification, then, on the other hand, *Digital India* is also deeply attentive to the social agency of resistance movements. Each of the two moments requires equally careful scrutiny.

From Free and Open Source Software to mobilizations around a 'right to know'; from anti-GMO protests, to community radio—Professor Thomas shows us a society rife with social struggle. Drawing on his years of engagement with the accumulating experience of activists contesting poverty, domination, and exclusion, he depicts a *Digital India* that goes beyond the banalities of 'business process outsourcing' and the talents of Indian engineers. Here at last the study of communications is opened to India's farmers and urban poor, its participants in a grey economy, its under-represented and despised—in other words, its majority—as a shaping force. The result is both a tribute to poor theory and a yardstick with which to measure the world.

Dan Schiller
Professor, Graduate School of Library and Information Science
Department of Communication, University of Illinois
Urbana-Champaign, USA
February 2012

Note

1. Ngugi wa Thiong'o, *Globalectics: Theory and the Politics of Knowing*. New York: Columbia University Press, 2012: 2.

Preface

Trying to account for the digital in India is a close-to-impossible task. The viral imprint of the digital is shaping both the formal and informal sectors in India, and I believe that we are yet to witness the full impact of the information revolution on our society and in our lives. To a certain extent, media scholars have had little choice but to deal with the digital, given its ubiquitous, shaping presence in and through the many cross-sectoral convergences that continue to redefine production and reproduction in the 21st century. The digital is the common language that has enabled marriages between previously separate technologies, and is the basis for a variety of applications—from consumer and media technologies to telecommunications, computing, the life sciences, artificial intelligence, nanotechnology, military technology, etc. Information processing is the key to the digital. The informational logic of cybernetics, characterised by information and feedback, and expressed via flows and networks, is the basis for a whole range of productive processes across multiple sectors—biotechnology laboratories, just-in-time manufacturing, clerical work, classrooms, military strategies, public surveillance, the health industry, agriculture, seed production, national and global governance, investments and financial networks, transport, not forgetting the cultural industries. The informational mode of production, in turn, is located within, and sustained by neo-liberalism and the free market.

In the previous two SAGE volumes—*Political Economy of Communications in India: The Good, the Bad and the Ugly* (2010) and *Negotiating Communication Rights: Case Studies from India* (2011)—I had highlighted upon the issues linked to India's tryst with 'information' as technology, process, product, and the opportunities and contestations this had given rise to, in the context of uneven, capitalist development. These included chapters on the 'informationalisation of life processes', and the Free and Open Source and Citizen Journalism movements in India. I see this volume as a natural postscript to the two previous volumes and, in a sense, the completion of an integrated three-volume project. The chapters in this volume deepen the engagement with the digital and explore a range of issues related to India's embrace of informational futures. There are many aspects to the digital and this volume highlights *some* of these aspects. In particular, it deals with the relationship between the digital and social change; the role played by structures, policies and products such as the mobile phone in the change processes; the gaps between principle and practice; the many contested contexts of the digital in India and the reasons behind why a key actor—the state—in the context of both external and internal pressures aimed at privileging the market as the key arbiter of access and growth in matters related to new technologies, is investing in public sector digital initiatives. The state in India has not withered away in the context of the march of capitalism. On the contrary, it remains a formidable entity that is playing an active role as a midwife to the information revolution, continuously adapting to the challenges posed by Gov.2.0. At an international level, for example, the Indian government at the 2011 UN General Assembly proposed the establishment of a U.N. Committee on Internet-Related Policies (CIRP) as an alternative to the US-controlled Internet Corporation for Assigned Names and Numbers (ICANN).

The chapters in this volume are mainly grounded in a critical political economy approach to understand the digital moment, and, as such, the frameworks of domination resistance and agency structure have been used as pegs to construct the argument. The digital cannot be understood in isolation from the political economy that has shaped it and continues to give meaning to it. The story of the digital in India is not just about the successes of India's software industries and should not be limited to an appreciation of the revenues earned from the business process outsourcing (BPO) projects, important as they are. There is much more that can be attributed to this revolution as more and more people in India experience their digital moments and encounter the enveloping presence of the digital in their everyday lives. What makes the digital fascinating is that it is both structure and anti-structure, meaning that the 'dominant' digital in India is complemented with a multitude of subversive digitalities—from counterfeit mobile phones to pirate software. And it is this broad spectrum of digital practices in India that make it an interesting project for study. Technologies, however, are not neutral. They shape and are shaped by human interventions. Technological shaping is a complex process—be it in the contexts of telecommunications, e-governance, public sector software, mobile telephony, digital piracy, Information and Communication Technologies (ICTs) in development, and this volume highlights some ways in which the 'information revolution' is shaping lives, opportunities and processes in India. This 'shaping' involves contestations and power plays, advocacy and mobilisations, policy and politics, and the involvement of civil society and the private sector along with the State.

There is a conspicuous lack of critical material on the various ways by which the language of the digital is shaping *all* productive sectors in its image. Research on the social impact of the digital in India remains fragmented. The tradition of administrative research predominates, and the industry has played a key role in investing in ICTs research. There is a need for detailed, independent research on the informational economy and most definitely the need for evidence-based research on the worth or otherwise of the multi-billion dollar investments in e-government, ICTs for development and other connectivity projects in India. I have used the acronyms IT (Information Technology) and ICT in an interchangeable fashion throughout the text, despite the fact that the term ICTs is used to describe convergent technologies.

As a coordinator of courses on communication and social movements, and ICTs and social change at the University of Queensland, I have had numerous opportunities to debate and discuss issues related to the digital with a number of students, including research higher degree candidates, in particular, Ellen Strickland and Bambang Budiwiranto. In my journey towards trying to make sense of the digital, I have been privileged to have had the occasional conversation with critical theorists of information, including Professors Dan Schiller, Cees Hamelink, Hopeton Dunn, Bruce Girard along with information activists like Roberto Verzola, Sylvia Cadena, Frederick Noronha, Sunil Abraham and Lawrence Liang who share deeply grounded views on the information revolution, the Internet and the role of information as property. To them and many others, my thanks for freely sharing knowledge on the contested nature of information politics and processes.

I have been fortunate to have been through a 3-year period characterised by a writing surge and have been surprised at my own willingness to be driven to write and complete a series of books on communications in India. Apart from the two books that I had written between 2009 and 2011, I had also written a couple of journal articles on issues related to the digital in *Info*, 9, 23 (Telecom Musings: Public Service Issues in India, 2007), *Telematics & Informatics*, 26, 1 (Bhoomi, Gyan Ganga, E-Governance and the Right to Information, 2009), *Media Development*, 4 (Cyanide for Gold: Dealing with E-Waste, 2009), the *International Communications Gazette* (Traditional Knowledge and the Traditional Knowledge Digital Library: Digital Quandaries and Other Concerns, 2010), the *Nordicom Review* (The Role of Public Sector Software in Development in India: Contested Futures, 2012) along with assorted book chapters on issues such as the digital divide and citizen journalism. While the chapters in this book allude to some of these writings, the material in this book is based on the research that I have been involved in during the last five years. India, for my money, is the most exciting terrain for the denouement of the digital in all its variety, complexity and contestability. In this project, I have been privileged to have had SAGE as my publishers, and would like to thank Rekha Natarajan in particular along with Shambhu Sahu and others at SAGE who have supported my writings. Finally, my thanks to my family—Preetha, Nitin and Prianka who are now reconciled to the fact that I am, alas, no JK Rowling!! This book is dedicated to my brother Prem, and Beena, Shruthi, Sneha and Sannu who have played an extraordinary role in shaping the dreams of an academic.

Namaskaram.

Brisbane
October 2011

1

An Introduction to the Digital Moment in India

Evidence of growth and productivity are the standard means used to highlight the developments in any given sector. In India, the business press and the television generate and manufacture data on the Information Technology (IT) industry on a daily basis. Apex bodies such as National Association for Software and Services Companies (NASSCOM) also churn out such data and taken together, there is information that suggests that a number of sectors associated with IT are thriving in India.

The contribution made by the informational mode of production to the Indian Gross Domestic Product (GDP) has risen steadily over the last two decades and reached around 4 per cent in 2009, within which, 1.5 per cent is directly attributed to the telecoms sector (see Cybermedia News 2009). The estimates for the year 2010, put together by the Central Statistical Organisation, place this figure at a much higher level. A report in the *Hindu* by C. P. Chandrasekhar (2010) reveals:

> Estimated GDP (at 2-digit level of the National Industrial Classification) generated in the ICT sector has increased from Rs. 656 billion in 2000–01 to Rs. 2530 billion in 2007–08, which amounts to a compound annual growth rate of 21.3 per cent. The CSO estimates that the share of the ICT sector in total GDP has risen from 3.4 per cent in 2000–01 to 5.9 per cent in 2007–08. ICT services dominate the ICT industry and over time the share of ICT services in total GDP has increased from 3.1 per cent in 2000–01 to 5.5 per cent in 2007–08. This compares with the fact that the contribution of the ICT Manufacturing sector to GDP remains more or less constant at about 0.35 per cent during 2000–01 to 2007–08.

These figures take into account, manufacturing of a range of equipment and devices, telecommunication services, trade in services, the provision of services and repairs.

Similar statistical information on growth is available in a number of IT-related sectors, the Business Process Outsourcing (BPO) sector, the animation industries, biotechnology, telecommunications and taken together, they suggest that India is firmly grounded in a global network economy, that the services sector's contribution to employment and growth is increasing on an annual basis and that the issues and concerns associated with the knowledge economy and network societies highlighted by Castells (1996, 1997, 1998) in his three-volume analysis of the information age and network society, from money laundering to networked terrorism are realities in contemporary India. The deployments of digital solutions at functional levels include initiatives such as e-government, e-ticketing and e-education and vast investments on IT parks. The launch of a prototype US$35 tablet computer 'Aakash' in October 2011 suggests that the government is committed towards finding solutions to the digital divide. The IT companies have changed the landscapes of cities such as Hyderabad which now has an enclave known as Cyberabad that is dotted with global banks, business schools and software companies enveloped in what can be described as an ambience resembling Silicon Valley. This knowledge economy, however, is complemented with other economies that feed off this dominant economy via the recycling of grayware and through a variety of pirate solutions that enable those on the margins, to access, use and by doing so, contribute to the domestication of the digital, often in novel ways.

While the share of the IT sector in the national GDP may not amount to much in comparison to the contributions made by agriculture and manufacturing, this sector has seen extraordinary growth over the last two decades and is the face of Brand India. This aspect of the 'new' India has global cache and the country is routinely referred to in the global media as an IT superpower. A number of books and articles have been written on the turnaround—from what was derisively referred to as the 'Hindu' rate of growth of about 3 per cent per annum to a consistent annual growth rate of up to 10 per cent witnessed over the last two decades (see Baghwati and Calomiris 2008; Eichengreen et al. 2010; McCartney 2009; Richter and Banerjee 2003; Sjerps 2002). Prominent Western journalists such as *New York Times*-based Thomas Friedman (1999, 2005) have played a key role in celebrating this image of India as a knowledge superpower. Many among the major Indian software companies, inclusive of Infosys, Wipro, TCS and a host of other companies, are listed on the National Association of Securities Dealers Automated Quotations (NASDAQ) index. The BPO sector too in India is a major revenue earner, and the impact of the global economic downturn on the software industry in India seems to have had only a minimal effect. While the software industry and the BPO sector need to be seen as the important aspects of the digital in India, the imprint of the digital, however, is much larger than any given informational sector. It really needs to be seen not simply as products per se such as software but as products that are deeply embedded in cultures of use and as significantly, in terms of processes that are slowly, but surely, invading every sector linked to production and consumption—from education to buying train tickets online to biotechnology, convergent media, inventories, citizen journalism, e-government, social networking, flexible production, crowd sourcing, collaborative design and development of Free and Open Source Software and new consumer media practices associated with products such as iPods and the ubiquitous mobile phone. There is, in this connection, the need to highlight the role played by web 2.0 in social change—in particular, the facilitation of information sharing and collaborative work best illustrated by projects such as Wikipedia. While web 2.0 has certainly contributed to new thinking and new possibilities for solutions related to social change, we do need to be careful when ascribing causality to prosumers of web 2.0, given that change, more often than not, is a consequence of a number of factors, including considerations stemming from political economy. Manuel Castells (1989: 15) has observed that the ubiquity of information processing makes this revolution like no other:

> A fundamental consequence is derived from the essential process-orientation of technological innovation because processes, unlike products enter into all spheres of human activity, their transformation by such technologies, focussing on omnipotent flows of information, leads to modification in the material basis for the entire social organisation.

Even as it is right to celebrate the successes of the IT industry in India, there is more to this story. While one can certainly argue that the software industry and the BPO sectors have resulted in spillover effects and that the mobile revolution has begun to transcend some of the barriers that have hitherto acted as a break on information access and use, the benefits of this revolution have accrued, on most occasions, to the already privileged segments of the Indian population. In this sense, what is required is an honest review and assessment of this sector, warts and all. What I have tried to cover in this book are not only the success stories—software, telecommunications, etc., but also the emerging initiatives such as public sector software, the challenges faced by e-governance and issues related to digital intellectual property that are as significant as the story of software exports in the shaping of India's information economy. These latter initiatives reveal the shaping of the future of information for all in India and point towards the fact that it is not just the business sector which is involved in shaping this future. The role of supra-national agencies such as the International Telecommunication Union (ITU), the World Trade Organization (WTO) and the Internet Corporation for Assigned Names and Numbers (ICANN), along with the state and civil society are also critical. While the state is involved in regulation, it is also keenly involved in the planning of information futures in India. Civil society too, on a much smaller scale, is involved in enabling access via a myriad of projects and rather critically, plays a key role in experimenting with the possibilities of the digital in development and social change.

Arguably, many of these are top-down initiatives, although this veritable plethora of initiatives related to access is being complemented by a shaping from below—including by those who are often derisorily dismissed as cultural pirates. These software, CD and DVD pirates, ought to be seen not merely as exploiters of the digital 'copy', but also as innovators who, in addition to profiting from work in 'grey zones', are also providing opportunities for the otherwise marginalised to take part in their digital moments and in that process, contribute towards globalisation. Ravi Sundaram's *Pirate Modernity: Delhi's Media Urbanism* (2009) is among the most erudite and elegant readings of piracy as a complex phenomenon that is today a feature of most, if not all, global capital cities. These pirate cultures in Delhi are the means by which, poorer populations connect to and are sustained by, the global. In Sundaram's words:

> The mixing of technology and urban life was also an enabling moment for subaltern populations to access media. Low-cost technologies of mechanical and digital reproduction often blurred the distinctions between producers and consumers of media, adding to the diffusion of both media infrastructures (video stores, photocopy and design shops, bazaars, cable networks, piracy) and media forms (images, video, phone sms/txt, sounds). In the past, such "informal" networks were more vulnerable for incorporation by the state or large capital. Since the 1980s these networks have often taken on a life of their own, refusing to follow the mandates of legal accumulation. (2009: 3–4)

In other words, the digital is making itself present and felt in intended and unintended ways as innovation and creativity are unleashed in both formal and informal environments. Rangasamy and Nair (2010: 63), in an article on the mobile phone store within a Mumbai slum community, highlight the features of this ecology that is possibly replicated in the numerous low-income neighbourhoods throughout the country.

> The mobile phone store business relies heavily on information business practices and social networking to find its way around infrastructural hardships. The 'archetypical' mobile phone store is a bricolage of gray real estate (space), infrastructure (electricity) and hardware. The latter is a motley collection of SIM cards; recharge coupons; branded, spurious, used, recycled, and stolen handsets; batteries; chips; memory cards; and other accessories.

It is this presence of thriving digital *economies*—legal, illegal and emergent, that makes up the story of India's digital moment. The digital thrives on leakage—as the intellectual property policy-makers and the dominant cultural industries, who are trying every trick up their sleeves to enclose knowledge, are finding out, to their discomfort. There is also, in addition to these 'shapings', the role played by the ordinary consumers of digital technologies celebrated in books such as Henry Jenkin's *Convergence Culture* (2006). These millions of Internet users, broadband customers and mobile phone junkies are now part of a growing tribe of digital natives in India, who are deeply embedded in the digital market not merely as customers, but also as users and shapers of technology. The digital is part of the story of globalising India. It is also a story of localising India and of the role of the artefacts in the making of what de Certeau famously described as, 'the practice of everyday life'. These practices of everyday life have begun to disrupt 'traditions' of inherited discourses, although it has been argued that the mediated forms of consumption have, rather ironically, merely resulted in 'Marginality ... becoming universal'. Everyday practices feed into the making of contested cultures. As de Certeau (1984: xvii) describes:

> Culture articulates conflicts and alternatively legitimises, displaces or controls the superior force. It develops in an atmosphere of tensions, and often of violence, for which it provides symbolic balances, contracts of compatability and compromises, all more or less temporary. The tactics of consumption, the ingenuous ways in which the weak make use of the strong, thus lend a political dimension to everyday practices.

Contextualising This Volume

These contestations, however, need to be seen as an aspect of larger contestations in India over meanings, identities, access to resources and struggles to live life with dignity. I have, in the previous two SAGE volumes, *Political Economy of Communication in India: The Good, the Bad and the Ugly* (2010) and *Negotiating Communication Rights in India* (2011), dealt with some of these contestations and on some of the key battles over India's communication futures such as the community radio and Free and Open Source Software (F/OSS) movements. There indeed are grey areas where the lines of struggle are not clear-cut, although for the most part these struggles over communication rights and information futures are aspects of larger struggles being fought over in India, linked to access and participation. How to theorise such struggles remains a fraught exercise, given that the apparency of change and evidence of 'India Shining' is undergirded by a deepening crisis in the margins.

European media scholars are fond of employing Chantal Mouffe's concept of an 'agonistic' public sphere to describe open spaces that are continuously shaped by debate and discussion, moves and counter-moves in an elaborate and continuous process of meaning-making and in which there are no winners and losers, thus, resulting in a society that is shaped by such rational debates. While the upsurge of people's movements in India around initiatives such as the Right to Information (RTI) and Lokpal Bills and their links to legislative politics does seem to indicate the victory of deliberativeness and debate over the dull weight of a dominant politics, reality suggests the coexistence of a variety of public spheres—antagonistic, agonistic and countervailing. In fact, in Europe too, that ideal of an agonistic public sphere seems to look like an impossibly romantic ideal in the context of the Islamaphobia that has unsettled even the liberal states such as the Netherlands in which, rational debate over immigration is no longer an option and France where the forced deportations of Roma (Gypsies) back to Romania has been fuelled by exclusionary mindsets. One can argue that in our over-technologised worlds, the informational mode of production privileges the making of dominant public spheres. In spite of the valorisations of 'consumer power' and a celebration of the levelling enabled by 'interactive' technologies, the exercise of 'substantive' power remains largely in the hands of the dominant power brokers, linked to the state, business sectors and civil society. The possibilities for deliberativeness in this context are, to a large extent, determined by the boundaries set by these forces.

Given that the digital is emerging as an important productive force in India and around which key discourses on the ideal of the 'good society' are being shaped, it is necessary to deal with the digital as both theory and practice and assess its strengths and limitations.

Assessing the Digital

It would, of course, be foolhardy to claim that a comprehensive and holistic assessment of the digital is possible, given its many manifestations and the fact that it is characterised by frantic innovations across multiple sectors. The viral nature of the digital is impossible to apprehend or even make sense of. Barry Sandywell (2003: 112), in an essay on the works of the information theorist Scott Lash, describes the nature of the digital thus:

As everyday life has become digitalised, every sphere of society is increasingly mediated: politics, culture, education, ethics, and morality are not entangled in information/disinformation 'economies' and the new relations of power that emerge with the information mode of production.

What I have tried to do in this volume is to highlight the specific instances in which the story of the digital has reflected the story of India as it grapples with the 'New' in the context of the tenacity and persistence of the 'Old' in all its variety. India beats any other country in the world for its sheer diversity—the layers upon layers of history and culture, tradition and technology which are also reflected in contemporary India and its many ways of 'seeing' and 'doing'. The informational mode of production coexists with older modes of production and while the mobile phone in agricultural India is breaking the barrier between the agricultural and informational mode of production, it also remains a tantalising symbol of the gaps that currently exist in Indian society. So, while it is right to celebrate projects such as CGNet Swara in Chhattisgarh that has, through mobile telephony, validated the voices of the 'tribal' citizen journalists, such projects, on their own, cannot bring about lasting, sustainable change in the contexts in which these largely forgotten people live, pressured as they are, by mining interests, a corrupt state bureaucracy, Maoists and a largely indifferent media. How to factor in this larger context in stories of the digital moment in India is absolutely critical towards coming to an honest understanding of the reality of and possibilities for the digital in India. Journalist P. Sainath, in an article on rural reporting in the magazine *Himal Asia* (2010), attempts to distinguish media hype from the reality. He says:

> There may be cyber-cafes in small towns, but that doesn't mean villagers are accessing the Internet. They talk about how farmers are using cell phones, checking up on prices in other markets. They make it sound as though the cell phone was invented for use only by poor people. The first people to get a cell phone in a village are the moneylender and the trader. If a peasant is given a cell phone, he doesn't have any number to call. The hype makes it sound like the cell phone is a revolutionary instrument invented to liberate poor peasants in India. Nowadays you will find some labourers, particularly migrants, who may have cell phones because it means their contractors can call them to work from the city or town.

While Sainath's analysis does not give any credibility to the 'active' user of mobile phones, it nevertheless does highlight the fact that many new technologies can quite easily become the basis for the reinforcement of old forms of domination.

Observations on the Informational Mode of Production in the Two Indias

Given the key role played by the informational mode of production in the 'New' India—a role that is bound to get even larger in the years to come, it seems fitting to deal with the structures, processes, policies, contestations and the intended and unintended consequences of the unfolding story of the digital in India. It is clear that a lot of hope has been invested in the digital reshaping India in its image, as previous revolutions have tried to do in the past. However, I have argued that this dominant ideal of information-based change is built on a narrow vision that discounts the fact that, as against the two per cent of the working population who are employed in the IT sector, close to seventy per cent work in agriculture and related occupations. Luce (2006: 24), writing in the *New Statesman*, highlights some of the contradictions and disparities between the agricultural and informational economies in India:

> India's agricultural output was roughly $150 billion last year (2005), while India's IT sector produced almost $25 billion, mostly in export earnings. India has almost 400 million farmers. In other words, India's one million IT employees earned roughly 65 times more per head than India's farmer. The phrase 'productivity gap' is far too mild to describe the yawning gulf in output between rural and high tech India.

To this majority, most of whom are small farmers, the information revolution simply has to be of practical benefit to lives and livelihoods lived in the slow lane. The mobile phone has enabled access to connectivity and in some cases, to information that is making a difference in the lives of farmers. However, the challenges are many and whether the IT revolution will make real differences to the lives of the millions of urban and rural poor is anybody's guess, even if laptops are going to be given for free to the poor, as is the case in Tamil Nadu today.

Historian and scholar Ramachandra Guha (2009: 33) in an article entitled 'Two Indias' comments on the complex nation that India is and that poses impossible challenges for government and governance. 'India is both an *unnatural nation* as well as an *unlikely democracy*. Never before has a territory so disparate and diverse been constructed as a single political unit' (emphasis added). Is it possible for the information revolution to help meld a disparate nation? Given the major disparities in wealth and opportunities, can we expect this revolution to deliver when others have failed? In the context of the fervent hopes invested in this technology, what really is the nature of access and interactivity? To what extent is this revolution controlled by industry and the state as opposed to the citizens? And what is the role of the state in this revolution? In the case of the Indian state, its role really is a fascinatingly ambivalent one where on the one hand, it seems to be beholden to IT lobby groups and national and multinational players, while on the other, it is seen to be playing an active role in developing policies supportive of the public interest. This would seem to indicate that the state in India is indeed a multifaceted entity involved in an elaborate dance of development that has implications both at macro and micro levels. While there are occasions when the sovereignty of India as a nation has been compromised, as for instance, the pressure to harmonise its legislations with international laws in the context of its accession to the WTO, for the most part, the Indian government has been able to negotiate agreements that largely have been in the interests of its people. While there is pressure on the Indian state to deal with food security and to open up to agricultural imports, the state is not oblivious to voices from within, who support the more sustainable project associated with food sovereignty.

At the end of the day, the digital revolution will be judged according to the extent to which it benefits the majority of Indians. Jean Dreze and Amartya Sen (2002: 333), while acknowledging the contributions being made by the services sector, observe the larger role this sector needs to be playing. As they have observed: 'What is less clear, however, is the extent to which the rapid growth of the service sector as a whole contributes to the generation of widely shared employment, the elimination of poverty and the enhancement of the quality of life.' The Marxian economist Prabhat Patnaik (2000: 204), who is the vice chairperson of the Planning Commission in Kerala and professor at the Centre for Economic Studies and Planning, Jawaharlal Nehru University, New Delhi, qualifies the priorities of development in India in the following words:

> The alternative economic strategy must be built on the basis of four elements: egalitarian land reforms which, apart from their economic effects in terms of releasing productive forces in agriculture and expanding the domestic market would mobilise the rural masses behind the new strategy; a revival of public investment especially in infrastructure which is designed to promote agricultural growth as a means to expand domestic food availability as well as the domestic market; vastly increased public expenditures on education, sanitation and health which would eliminate illiteracy, provide free and compulsory primary education to every child, and ensure minimum health standards for all; and much greater accountability of the state which can be ensured *inter alia* through the devolution of decision making and resources to elected bodies functioning under direct popular scrutiny.

While the revenues generated from software and services have certainly contributed to the strengthening of the informational economy in India and to the country's GDP, such successes have reinforced a technocratic vision of development and growth in India and a belief in the inevitability of an 'information' trickle down. The informational mode of production, like previous modes of production, is deeply implicated in a political economy that is based on a singular vision of technocratic growth and progress. While this trickling down may or may not materialise, the larger issue relates to the need for IT policies that factor in existing disparities and that take into account, the need for solutions beyond the technological fix.

In the following sections of this introductory chapter, I highlight key moments, trajectories and issues linked to India's tryst with the digital. While it can certainly be argued that this list is idiosyncratic and subjective, the rationale for highlighting these three issues is as follows. The *liberalisation of telecommunications* in many ways, inaugurated India's tryst with the digital. It heralded India's departure from growth which was based on import substitution. It also led to growth across sectors and the strengthening of the service economy and the consumer boom. In hindsight, one can argue that India's eventual development as a software power-house was, to some extent, helped by the exit of IBM in the mid-1970s, which led to a reliance on local capacities. India's inability to build on these local capacities remains one of the unfortunate consequences of deregulation and economic liberalisation. One can argue that the moves to strengthen *indigenous manufacturing capacities and the capacity to shape India's informational futures* are aspects of a resonant, citizen-oriented 'imaginary' in scientific, political and non-governmental organisation (NGO) circles in India, illustrated by many projects such as that supported by C-DoT, the 'Simputer' initiative, F/OSS and more recently, the movement around the creation of Public Sector Software. This countervailing vision and approach is, however, contested by software and hardware lobbies that are firmly rooted in a neo-liberal vision of Indian IT servicing to the global economy. To some extent, both the export and import substitution lobbies are avid supporters of the 'ICTs fix'. This technocratic vision is shared by the state, private sector and some parts of civil society. While this 'fix' looks plausible on paper, we are only too aware that the digital divide is one aspect of other divides in society—social, economic and political. These divides too have to be dealt with. Finally, there is the issue of *governance*. Who should be involved in creating blueprints for information futures in India? It cannot be left to the private sector, given their core commitment to their share holders and profit above everything else, nor can it be left to the government of the day. While it makes sense to involve the civil society in digital governance, the government has had an ambivalent approach towards involving it in information/communications governance.

The Early Years: The Liberalisation of Telecoms

One of the fascinating aspects of the digital is its impact on society. What is clear is that the exponential increase in broadband access, mobile phone penetration, investments in rural access centres and social networking is the consequence of a number of productive forces—from hardware and software manufacturers to business lobby groups, regulatory agencies, policy initiatives and the civil society. From the perspective of industry, the digital moment has been India's finest hour—the moment when the country was catapulted from a life lived in the 'bullock cart' lane to a life in the era of broadband flows. However, this change was not just initiated by the private sector, as we are often led to believe, but is also a direct consequence of a gradual change in state policies supportive of economic liberalisation that began in the late 1980s and that has continued since then. Deregulation, privatisation and liberalisation were core tenets in India's New Economic Policy that laid the foundations for tumultuous changes to the Indian economy and led to the opening up of sectors, hitherto reserved for the public sector, to private investments. The liberalisation of telecommunications via the New Telecommunication Policy (1994) led to the entry of foreign and domestic players in the telecoms market and changes to the structure and objectives of the local public sector telecommunications behemoth directly under the Department of Telecommunications (DoT). Dasgupta (2005: 232) describes the corporatisation of the public sector telecommunications firm VSNL:

> Forty seven per cent of the shares of VSNL were disinvested to institutional investors and industrial shareholders in March 1999. Of the remaining shares, the government decided that it would sell 25 per cent to a strategic partner and 1.97 per cent to employees. On 5 February 2002, Panatone Finvest, a company belonging to the Tata Group purchased 25 per cent of the VSNL for Rs. 14.39 billion against the reserve price of Rs. 12–18 billion.

VSNL has since then been renamed as Tata Communications Services.

Telecommunications was one of the first industries slated for liberalisation, following the Indian government's agreement to Structural Adjustment Policies in the aftermath of its taking of loans from both the International Monetary Fund (IMF) and World Bank. Nikhil Sinha (1996: 30) refers to some of these early policy-based changes that laid the foundations for both telecoms and the digital in India.

> The liberalisation of telecommunications equipment had already begun in the 1980s and 1990s with the licensing of equipment providers in the customer premises and switching and transmission segments. In 1992, the government initiated the gradual liberalisation of value-added services such as electronic mail, voice mail, information services, audiotext and videotext services, videoconferencing and paging. The government also licensed two competing cellular companies in each of the four metropolitan cities of Delhi, Bombay, Calcutta and Madras.... However the most significant step in the liberalisation of Indian telecommunications came in the 1994 policy statement in which the government announced the opening up of cellular services in the rest of the country and, more dramatically, the entry of private companies to provide basic services in competition with the DoT.

This liberalisation has continued unabated, thereby resulting in the availability of a range of competitively priced services for citizens and healthy profit margins for companies in the Indian telecommunications market. An online report (Thakur 2011) on the state of telecommunications in India includes the following projections for growth in the mobile sector:

> According to a report published by Gartner Inc in June 2009, the total mobile services revenue in India is projected to grow at a compound annual growth rate (CAGR) of 12.5 per cent from 2009–2013 to exceed US$ 30 billion. The India mobile subscriber base is set to exceed 771 million connections by 2013, growing at a CAGR of 14.3 per cent in the same period from 452 million in 2009. This growth is poised to continue through the forecast period, and India is expected to remain the world's second largest wireless market after China in terms of mobile connections.

This sector is just one of the many sectors linked to the wireless industry, slated for growth.

The establishment of the Telecom Regulatory Authority of India (TRAI) in 1997, via an act of Parliament—the Telecommunications Regulatory Authority of Indian Act, 1997—established the first regulatory body in India for the era of convergence. In 2004, the regulation of broadcasting and cable television too was brought under the aegis of TRAI, although this has not been favourably received by the broadcast mandarins who would rather wish that the regulation of this sector is left in their hands. Today, telecommunications is a multi-billion dollar sector and the state makes vast amount of money from auctioning spectrum. While it made around ₹90 billion in the auction of 2G Spectrum in 2008, the sale of 3G licenses in 2010 was expected to earn for the government close to

₹6,800 billion (see Mukherjee 2010b). 'The annual license fee and the spectrum charges are the largest non-tax revenue [components] of the government. Till March 2010, the government has collected about ₹77,938 crore under the revenue-sharing regime' (ex-CandIT Minister A. Raja, in an interview with Radhakrishnan 2010). Such large revenue streams have rather unfortunately resulted in scams and issues related to nepotism and corruption, which has dogged spectrum sales and the allocation of telecommunication licenses. The most recent instance (2010) of high-level resignation over alleged corruption was that of the Minister for Communications and Information Technology, Andimuthu Raja. Raja submitted his resignation on 13 November 2010 against allegations by the opposition and Comptroller and Auditor General (CAG) that his preferred policy of spectrum allocation to favoured companies as against spectrum allocations of 2G licenses, had led to a net loss of ₹1,770 billion (US$40 billion) to the national exchequer (see Jacob 2011; Radhakrishnan 2010). The CAG Report (8 November 2010) submitted by the Director General of Audit, Posts and Telecommunications and the CAG of India notes that in spite of advice to the contrary:

> The Department of Telecommunications, in 2008, proceeded to issue 122 new licences for 2G spectrum at 2001 prices, by flouting every cannon of financial propriety, rules and procedures...The Department of Telecommunications also did not do the requisite due diligence in the examination of the applications submitted for the UAS licenses, leading to the grant of 85 out of 122 UAS (Universal Access Service Provider) licences to ineligible applicants. These companies, created barely months ago, deliberately suppressed facts, disclosed incomplete information, submitted fictitious documents and used fraudulent means for getting UAS licences and thereby access to spectrum. Owners of these licences, obtained at unbelievably low price, have in turn sold significant stakes in their companies to the Indian/foreign companies at high premium within a short period of time. (57–58)

Indigenous Capacities and the Making of an Informational Commons

One of the success stories related to telecommunications is the development of indigenous manufacturing capacities such as switching technologies manufactured by the Centre for Development of Telematics (C-DoT), under Sam Pitroda. More than 29,000 of low-cost, rugged, indigenously manufactured telephone exchanges have been installed in Indian villages and the technology has been exported to a number of countries. However, in spite of the fact that it has played a key role in telecommunications R&D,

it has become a pawn in the telecommunication turf wars being fought over by different ministries, of whom, some support the importation of technology, including components and not its local manufacture. As the erstwhile telecommunications observer T. H. Chowdary (2003) has pointed out:

> The C-DOT did a magnificent job of bringing into being 20 switch manufacturers and scores of vendors of parts and sub-systems required for the digital switch. It was the availability of these switches with indigenous knowhow and parts that ultimately brought down the price of digital switches from Rs. 12,000 per line with imported technology to less than Rs. 4,000. These switches were deployed in rural areas and facilitated the extension of national and international dialling to the remote corners of the country.

Similarly, the development of the corDECT wireless local loop (WLL) technology at the Indian Institute of Technology (IIT), Madras, uses radio signals to connect subscribers to the public telephone network. The achievements of both these success stories have been lost in the context of the general euphoria over technological imports.

More recently, state–civil society partnerships directed towards strengthening the case for and deployments of Free and Open Source Software in the public sector have led to the establishment of the public sector software movement (see Chapter 8). The Bengaluru-based NGO, IT for Change (2010), describes public sector software as follows:

1. Public software can be defined as software developed for the public good, which is publicly owned. Public ownership also implies that it cannot be privatized or privately owned. Public software is of two kinds:
   1. Public software developed to promote public good—that helps government (public sector) to fulfil goals of government—software that supports NREGA transactions in a transparent manner
   2. Public software itself as a public good—new digital goods such as Wikipedia where the software itself performs public interest functions

2. Public Sector for the purpose of these guidelines, is defined broadly as comprising of institutions working for public interest. While this includes not only governments but also academic institutions, civil society (NGO/CBO), community media institutions etc, there is a special role for the government as the key public sector actor in promoting public software.

Public sector software in India makes infinite sense in the context of e-governance and the government's plans to create national public information grids. Inter-operability and free flows are critical to e-governance projects. Furthermore, the availability of public sector data sets to the public will result in opportunities for the communities of interest to modify the software and adapt it to generate practical solutions in local contexts. The following excerpt from the web resource *Open Source Software for the Public Sector* from the national IT and Telecom Agency in Denmark, indicates the ways in which software can become a tool that can be used in development and social change, in the context of emerging knowledge economies. These principles are applicable to all types of public sector software, irrespective of the country of origin:

Principles for application of open source

Competition

Efficient competition is a prerequisite for an effective and varied software market. Open source support that software can be maintained and developed by multiple vendors. Software vendors must be able to offer their services to the public sector on equal terms.

Control and self-determination

Application of open source software ensures control over the software. This allows the individual public authority to determine when and how the software should be updated, developed and if the software should be distributed.

Development and innovation

When developing software, public authorities must decide which software development model, such as the open source development and business model, best supports innovation and fast development of new products and services. As a rule software developed in the public sector should be made available with an open source license. This does not mean that old methods should be deprecated, but rather that multiple approaches can be used simultaneously and new approaches can be tested so pros and cons can be identified with regard to the Danish administration.

Maximum value for money irrespectively of the type of software

The individual public authority must be able to acquire the best and cheapest software in the context of local administrative needs, whether that is closed or open source software. The software must be chosen based on a consolidated business case.

Interoperability and flexibility

Public authorities should focus on software that is constructed of smaller software components and which support communication with other software via open standards. This allows the various software components to be replaced independently which promotes flexibility, reusability and competition in the area.

Reusing software

Application of open source software can prevent taxpayers from having to pay for the development of the same software more than once. (The National IT and Telecom Agency n.d.)

Questioning the ICTs Fix

Dreze and Sen's critique, as much as that of Patnaik's, needs to be seen in the context of the political economy of ICTs in development in India, especially the growing gaps between theory and practice. While literally, millions of dollars have been expended on ICTs projects throughout India by donor agencies, NGOs and the state—there still, are issues related to the impact of these projects, especially on whether or not their claims are backed up by evidence from the field. Technological determinism and an attendant instrumentalist logic are pervasive in IT circles in India, and this combination often negates the need for undertaking proper scoping studies to determine the state of social relations in any given area that is slated to become a location for an ICT for developmental projects. Even if such studies are carried out, the tendency is to gloss over real disparities, real differences and to not make much of the feudal constancy existing in many parts of India. Space and place in the Indian context, as elsewhere, involve interpretive communities who have a lot to gain by holding on to their privileged positions and their control over power and knowledge. The story of the digital in India simply, has to address the existing divisions that become visible only when scams, such as corruption at the Commonwealth Games and 2G licensing, reveal a story that Indians would rather forget. Such disparities are not going to be set right through a technology fix. This technology-centred mindset, interestingly enough, is not just the norm in newly globalising countries such as India, but is also, as Neil Selwyn (2010: 161) observes, alive and well in developed countries, such as the UK. Writing on digital policy in the UK, Selwyn makes an observation, stated as follows:

> The biggest shift required in policy thinking is the need to recognise that the 'Digital Divide' is not merely a technical and financial issue, but is indicative of wider problems of exclusion from society, which the provision of ICT can be little expected to alter. Indeed, there is an implicit technological determinism in the assumption that public access to ICTs will impact of people's social inclusion,

educational levels, education, and employment. It is, of course, more likely to be the case that people's socioeconomic status impacts on their opportunities and need to use ICTs.

There is, in other words, a taken-for-granted conviction in the capacity of ICTs to inaugurate a level playing field, when in reality it will take more than just infusions of technology to lead towards progressive social change. What we are really seeing in India is uneven growth, a new regime of accumulation in an enclave economy. D'Costa (2005: 7) describes it thus: 'capitalism in India must be seen for what it is a market system that is evolving in an uneven way, geographically, sectorally and socially.'

When the belief in the IT fix has global cache and is backed up by billions of dollars worth of investments, the critique of this one-dimensional thinking is, for the most part, generated by certain sections of the civil society involved in IT and Internet-based initiatives. The absence of real debate in the Indian public sphere, on many blind spots of current ICT for development policy and practice, is illustrative of this lack of critique. Instead, what is highlighted in the copious literature available on ICTs projects and projections in India is, for the most part, uncritical adulation and celebration. As is unfortunately the case in donor-driven development, stories that are manufactured for global consumption take on a life of their own and are endlessly recycled, resulting in myths becoming reality. The UN and other global agencies endlessly repeat these stories—the Kothmale Community Radio project in Sri Lanka which actually is run by the state and whose impact is limited and ICT for development projects in India, including that of the Gyandoot project and those associated with the M. S. Swaminathan Research Foundation (MSSRF), especially the celebrated stories of access for fishing-folks and rural people in Puducherry. Since spot visits are not favoured in research, it is often the case that research on ICTs for development is carried out in conditions that militate against the conducting of critical research. I have, in the context of carrying out research on ICTs in India, scoured the literature for critical material, only to find a handful, predictably in journals such as the *Economic and Political Weekly* and *Information Technologies and International Development*.

To be fair, there have been, of late, some interesting publications on ICTs in India, including a co-edited volume by Carol Upadhya and A. R. Vasavi (2008) on work and workers in the IT industry in India and Govindan Parayil's edited volume (2006) on the political economy of information capitalism in India. Sreekumar's (2006: 70) critique of the involvement of the MSSRF in ICTs for development, in a chapter incorporated in a chapter in the volume edited by Parayil, highlights the persistence of feudal relationships in rural India and its impact on

IT projects in India. He observes, 'the MSSRF itself had been forced to close down some of its kiosks where Dalits were not able to enter.... The village headman and temple trustees have an upper management in the management of kiosks.' Such examples clearly suggest that the digital divide is an aspect of the larger divisions in society. Rather unfortunately, there are few studies that provide a realistic account of the social consequences of IT deployments in development throughout India. As Kennith Keniston (2002) has rather cogently observed, despite growing investments in this sector, there are few empirically grounded assessments of the social impact of ICTs in development.

> Unfortunately, the hopes so widely expressed are built almost entirely on an empirical vacuum. We know almost nothing about the factors that make for effectiveness or ineffectiveness of grassroots ICT projects in developing nations. Thus, critics can point out that the cost of creating a working Internet connection in a developing nation like India is the same as that of providing immunization against six fatal childhood diseases to thousands of children. Others have argued that the introduction of ICT into communities otherwise unchanged will merely heighten existing inequalities. But instead of comparative research to counter or address such claims, we have *stories*—to be sure, largely true stories of successes—from which trustworthy generalizations are impossible. At least fifty grassroots projects are currently using modern ICT for development in India. Surprisingly, these projects have rarely been studied. No comparisons have been made between them. They are seldom in touch with each other. Lessons learned in one project are not transmitted to others. Appropriate technologies are rarely evaluated. Central questions of financial sustainability, scalability and cost recovery are hardly ever addressed. So, opportunities to learn from the diverse, creative Indian experience so far remain almost entirely wasted.

From such observations, it is clear that there is the need for independent evaluations of the impact of Information and Communication Technologies for Development (ICT4D) projects in India.

The Politics of Governance

The public sector, despite 'disinvestments', continues to play a key role in establishing the policy framework for the digital in India. One of the significant issues in this regard, is 'governance'—meaning, stake-holder engagement in policy-making processes, which in the case of the IT sector, has been dominated by the state and the private sector. The software trade body NASSCOM, for example, is closely linked to the government and is involved in IT governance.

NASSCOM acts as the advisory, consultative and co-ordination body for the IT software and services industry. NASSCOM has representatives in various committees of the Government of India including the Ministry of Information Technology, Ministry of Commerce and Industry, Ministry of Finance, Ministry of External Affairs, Department of Telecommunications and Ministry of Human Resources Development. (NASSCOM website n.d.)

NASSCOM is involved with the government in the making of IT policy and is also represented on the National Taskforce on Information Technology and Software Development that is involved in making a long term IT policy for the country. The representatives of NASSCOM and Manufacturing Association of IT Industry (MAIT) are also present on the National Informatics' Centre's apex body linked to E-governance Standards. While the role of NASSCOM as an industry lobby and apex body has paid dividends for this sector, it is arguable as to whether or not their lobbying serves the broader public interest. A good example of such lobbying is in the adoption of technological standards for e-governance in India. While the FOSS community in India has lobbied for open and royalty free standards, industry lobbies such as NASSCOM and MAIT have pushed for multiple and royalty-based standards. One issue for FOSS enthusiasts is that the Department of Information Technology (DIT) that is involved in creating a draft policy veers towards industry. Deepa Kurup (2009: 92), writing in the Indian magazine *Frontline*, highlights the nature of this contestation over governance and policy.

The DIT, which made public the first draft of the policy in June 2008, has not placed subsequent drafts for public review. Fosscomm has protested against the 'unparticipatory nature' of this policymaking process, which has considerable public-interest implications, not to mention an outlay of over Rs. 5,000 crore for 27 national e-governance projects. The FOSS community believes that for a standard to be truly open, its specifications must be unconditionally accessible and royalty-free in perpetuity. This includes associated patents and extensions. NASSCOM, on the other hand, has sought standards that are open but tied to royalties, on what in policy parlance is called RAND (reasonable and non-discriminatory) licensing terms. However, RAND standards are inextricably linked to intellectual property right (IPR) regimes. The government may have to pay royalties to patent holders throughout the lifetime of the standards.

What this example also reveals, is the absence of civil policy participation in the making of IT policy—this despite the fact that NGOs such as Bengaluru-based IT for Change and the Centre for Internet and Society are involved in the ongoing discussions related to public sector software and the shaping of the Internet. The issue at stake is not just involvement, but the levels of involvement. While the state does involve civil society at a workshop level—it is less open to their involvement at a policy level.

However, the fact that the civil society lobbying on matters related to open standards could lead to a policy on open standards is, by itself, a positive sign. As it is to be expected, this new policy may well accommodate 'exceptions' and the interests of the major proprietary software industries and their lobbies. The state cannot afford to alienate big business, given that they do contribute to investments in this sector. However, the fact that the government has chosen to privilege open standards, is an important victory for the FOSS movement in India. Aranda Mukherjee (2010a), writing in *Outlook*, makes the following observation:

> The government will soon announce a policy that will make it mandatory to have an open and royalty-free standard for all technologies and software used for e-governance operations and applications across the country. In other words, there will soon be one uniform thread for all government work so that all documents or databases will be accessible through any technology platform. The policy has been cleared by the Department of Information Technology and the National Informatics Centre and is likely to be made official soon. This effectively means the technology used in all government departments and offices would have to shift to an open standard. With rough estimates putting the e-governance market at around $10 billion, the new system—at the interface and data-archival levels—will shake up big companies hitherto operating in these segments through their proprietary (read paid-for) standards.

Governance, particularly the role of the civil society in media/ information governance, has been a difficult 'negotiation issue'. Equally problematic issues are being faced by those involved in the community radio movement in India. While the government today is a lot more open to community radio advocates playing a role in training, workshops and even the screening of licences in this sector, community radio advocates from the civil society are not involved in a substantive manner in policy-making processes (see Thomas 2011). In the case of community radio, the lack of a clear policy is advantageous to the government as it is not answerable to anyone but itself and can, therefore, create policy in an ad hoc manner. Despite the existence of the Community Radio Forum, the lack of a clear policy has led to non-transparent decision-making processes at the Ministry of Broadcasting. I had heard recently from a senior civil servant in the afore-mentioned ministry that in the light of the perceived inability of community radio licensees to provide content for 24-hour schedules, it plans to open up Community Radio (CR) licences to government-based Panchayati Raj (local development) institutions. If this were to happen, it would lead to more licences being given to state-based organisations rather than to those in civil society. The fact that the CR activists based in the civil society are not consulted on such issues, remains a major concern. While the input of the Community Radio Forum in India is sought by the government and the members belonging to this forum are involved in the licence screening process and are regularly invited to take part in meetings organised by the Ministry of Information and Broadcasting, their input into the making of policy is limited. Whether a situation is characterised by policy or lack of policy does not, in any way, seem to impact on governance in a context in which the private sector has become a favourite of the government (see Thomas 2011 for an assessment of the community radio movement in India).

In an era characterised by 'liquid modernity', networking possibilities and information-flows, there ought to be an increasing reliance on governance rather than government in the planning, implementation and evaluation of policy such as in the area of e-governance. Governance is not as much 'soft government' as it is a validation of the worth of knowledge generation in the context of multi-stakeholder engage-ments in the planning and operationalisation of significant public policies. It is clear that the civil society in India, be it those involved in community radio or FOSS, have substantive knowledge covering theory and practice related to these sectors. In fact, it is arguably the case that there is a lot more knowledge in this sector than in government on issues related to community radio and FOSS. This engagement with the civil society in matters of governance is clearly seen in the roles played by social activists such as Aruna Roy, Nikhil Dey and others, with the government in the planning and operationalisation of the RTI as policy and process.

Chapter Outline

The chapters in this volume are divided into four sections. The first section *Information Technology in a Liberalised Economy* includes chapters on the software and mobile phone revolutions in India. The second section *Government 1.0 and Information Technology* includes two chapters on the challenges faced by Government 1.0 that is caught between delivering on its public sector promises on information access and supporting the IT market within a liberalised economy. Telecommunications is the archetypical example of Government 1.0, although it is clear that the mobile phone revolution has, to some extent, made inroads into the government's hold over this sector. The third section *Government 2.0 and Information Technology* includes three chapters that highlight a more proactive approach taken by the government on its IT commitments in the public sector. Government 2.0 is in a better position to initiate dialogue with the civil society and take a stance on issues such as public sector software. However, Government 1.0 and Government 2.0 are one and the same and remain reflections of the multiple tendencies of a Janus-faced government that is involved in an elaborate dance, directed towards satisfying its partners and their competing interests. This is certainly the case with respect to the government's response to software patenting. The fourth section *Contested Information Technology* includes the chapter on cultural piracy. Cultural piracy involves people who are defining access on their own terms, irrespective of the plans and policies of Government 1.0 and/or Government 2.0. I have tried to make these chapters as textured as possible and each is a dialogue between theory and practice.

Conclusion

I would like to conclude this introductory chapter with a few observations on the digital moment in India. First, the digital exists in myriad forms, as product and process and is the common language for multiple projects across numerous productive sectors—in education as much as in agriculture and manufacturing. This complexity is difficult to account for and what I have tried to do in this volume is merely highlight key moments and issues in the unfolding story of the digital in India. What it does is offer insights into some of the highs and lows of the digital moment in India and the gaps between principle and practice. Second, it offers a corrective to some of the overly optimistic and uncritical readings of ICTs as a panacea and makes a case for more robust interrogations of the digital grounded in political economy and in cultures of use. And third, it provides a window to assess the ambivalent role of the state in India—the enemy of the masses in India, but also rather ironically, the hope for India's many poor through projects such as the RTI, the Mahatma Gandhi National Rural Employment Guarantee Act (MGNREGA) public sector software and other projects. This complexity points to the fact that the State in India cannot be conceived as a monolithic entity but requires to be seen as a reflection of society in India, constantly shaped by multiple pressures, trends, claims and counter-claims. The digital moment in India is being shaped, as I write, by multiple forces. The chapters in this volume contribute to a making sense of some of these 'shapings'.

References

Baghwati, J. N. and C. Calomiris. 2008. *Sustaining India's Growth Miracle.* New York: Colombia University Press, Kindle Edition.

CAG Report. 2010. 'Performance Audit Report on the Issue of Licenses and Allocation of 2G Spectrum' (CAG Report), Available at: http://www.thehindu.com/news/article889943.ece (accessed on 17 November 2010).

Castells, M. 1989. *The Informational City: The Space of Flows.* Basil Blackwell, Oxford/Cambridge: Mass.

———. 1996. *The Rise of the Network Society.* Malden, Oxford, Carleton: Blackwell Publishing.

———. 1997. *The Power of Identity.* Malden, Oxford. Carleton: Blackwell Publishing.

———. 1998. *End of Millennium.* Malden, Oxford, Carleton: Blackwell Publishing.

Chandrasekhar, C. P. 2010. 'How Significant Is IT in India?' *The Hindu*, 31 May. Available at: http://www.thehindu.com/opinion/columns/Chandrasekhar/article442421.ece (accessed on 31 October 2010).

Chowdary, T. H. 2003. 'C-DOT Merits Fresh Lease of Life', *The Hindu Online*, February 10. Available at: http://www.hindu.com/thehindu/biz/2003/02/10/stories/2003021000140200.htm (accessed on 17 October 2010).

Cybermedia News. 2009. 'Telecom Sector Contributes 1.5 p.c. to India's Economy', CIOL, *Cybermedia News*, 6 August. Available at: http://www.ciol.com/news/news-reports/telecom-sector-contributes-15-pc-to-indias-gdp/6809123286/0/ (accessed on 31 October 2010).

Dasgupta, B. 2005. *Globalisation: India's Adjustment Experience.* New Delhi: SAGE Publications.

D'Costa, A. P. 2005. *The Long March to Capitalism: Embourgeoisment, Industrialisation and Industrial Transformation in India.* Basingstoke/New York: Palgrave Macmillan.

De Certeau, M. 1984. *The Practice of Everyday Life.* Berkeley, Los Angeles, London: University of California Press.

Dreze, J. and A. Sen. 2002. *India: Development and Participation.* Oxford: Oxford University Press.

Eichengreen, B., P. Gupta, R. Kumar. 2010. *Emerging Giants: China and India in the World Economy.* New York: Oxford University Press.

Friedman, T. 1999. *The Lexus and the Olive Tree: Understanding Globalisation.* New York: Farrar, Strauss and Giroux.

———. 2005. *The World is Flat: A Brief History of the 21st Century.* New York: Farrar, Strauss and Giroux.

Guha, R. 2009. 'Two Indias', *The National Interest*, July/August: 31–42.

IT for Change. 2010. 'Software Principles for the Public Sector with Focus on Public Education', Guiding Principles for Public Software, Benguluru. Available at: http://www.public-software-centre.org/documents/Guiding_Principles_for_Public_Software.pdf (accessed on 18 April 2011).

Jacob, J. 2011. 'The House That Raja Built', *Tehelka*, 1 January: 30–36.

Jenkins, H. 2006. *Convergence Culture: Where Old and New Media Collide*. New York: New York University Press.

Keniston, K. 2002. 'Grassroots ICTs Projects in India: Some Preliminary Hypothesis', *ASCI Journal of Management*, 31:1–2. Available at: http://web.mit.edu/~kken/Public/PAPERS/ASCI_Journal_Intro__ASCI_version_.html (accessed on 17 October 2010).

Kurup, D. 2009. 'Governance: Open Debate', *Frontline*, 26, 23: 91–93. Also available at: http://www.hinduonnet.com/fline/fl2623/stories/20091120262309100.htm (accessed on 4 October 2010).

Luce, E. 2006. 'One Land, Two Planets' (23–25), *New Statesman*, 30 January, Blackfriars, UK.

McCartney, M. 2009. *Political Economy, Growth and Liberalisation in India, 1991–2008*. New York: Routledge.

Mukherjee, A. 2010a. 'Open Sesame', *Outlook*, 13 September. Available at: http://www.outlookindia.com/article.aspx?266988 (accessed on 16 October 2010).

———. 2010b. 'A Spectrum Fade-Out', *Outlook*, 31 May. Available at: http://www.outlookindia.com/article.aspx?265487 (accessed on 16 October 2010).

NASSCOM. n.d. 'NASSCOM, Partnership with Government'. Available at: http://www.nasscom.in/Nasscom/templates/NormalPage.aspx?id=5353 (accessed on 4 October, 2010).

Parayil, G. (ed.). 2006. *Political Economy and Information Capitalism in India*. Basingstoke and N.Y.: Palgrave Macmillan.

Patnaik, P. 2000. 'The Performance of the Indian Economy in the 1990s', *South Asia: Journal of South Asian Studies*, 23 (1): 193–205.

Radhakrishnan, R. K. 2010. 'Its Institutional Aberration That Needs Intervention', Interview with ex-CandIT Minister A. Raja, The Hindu, 13 November. Available at: http://www.thehindu.com/news/resources/article884339.ece (accessed on 14 November 2010).

Rangasamy N. and S. Nair. 2010. 'The Mobile Phone Store Ecology in a Mumbai Slum Community: Hybrid Networks for Enterprise', *Information Technologies and International Development*, 6 (3): 51–65.

Richter, F. J. and P. Banerjee (eds). 2003. *The Knowledge Economy in India*. Basingstoke: Palgrave Macmillan.

Sainath, P. 2010. 'Media Myths of the Ruralscape', *Himal Asia*, October. Available at: http://www.himalmag.com/Media-myths-of-the-ruralscape_nw4745.html (accessed on 28 October 2010).

Sandywell, B. 2003. 'Metacritique of Information: On Scott Lash's Critique of Information', *Theory, Culture and Society*, 20 (1): 109–122.

Selwyn, N. 2010. 'People's (Non) Engagement with Public ICT Sites', in G. Murdock and P. Golding (eds), *Digital Dynamics: Engagement and Disconnections*, pp. 147–163. Cresskill, NJ: Hampton Press, Inc.

Sinha, N. 1996. 'The Political Economy of India's Telecommunications Reforms', *Telecommunications Policy*, 20 (1): 23–38.

Sjerps, M. (ed.). 2002. *Economic Liberalisation in India: Views of Dutch and Indian Journalists*. Amsterdam: Amsterdam University Press.

Sreekumar, T. T. 2006. 'ICTs for the Rural Poor: Civil Society and Cyber-Libertarian Developmentalism in India', in G. Parayil (ed.), *Political Economy and Information Capitalism in India*, pp. 61–87. Basingstoke and New York: Palgrave Macmillan.

Sundaram, R. 2009. *Pirate Modernity: Delhi's Media Urbanism.* London and New York: Routledge.

Upadhya, C. and A. R. Vasavi (eds). 2008. *In an Outpost of the Global Economy: Work and Workers in India's Information Technology Industry.* Abingdon: Routledge.

Thakur, S. 2011. *Telecom Industry in India.* Available at: http://industrytracker. wordpress.com/2011/02/25/telecom-industry-in-india/ (accessed on 5 October 2011).

The National IT and Telecom Agency. n.d. 'Open Source Software and the Public Sector'. Available at: http://thinktankeu.olliancegroup.com/business_cases/ Danish_Open_Source_software_and_the_public_sector.pdf (accessed on 18 April 2011).

Thomas, P. N. 2011. *Negotiating Communication Rights: Case Studies from India.* Los Angeles, London, New Delhi, Singapore, Washington D.C.: SAGE Publications.

Section 1
Information Technology in a Liberalised Economy

The two chapters in this section provide an introduction to what arguably are among the most successful examples of the IT revolution in India—the software revolution and mobile telephony. While the chapter on software deals with its growth in a context characterised by uneven development, the chapter on mobile phones makes a case for a more nuanced approach towards understanding the theory and practice of mobile telephony. India's software success story is now a part of the global imaginary. While that story has been repeated ad infinitum, there is very little information available on how this industry has contributed to the reinforcement of the divides best characterised by gleaming software palaces on lands once owned by ordinary people. The chapter on mobile telephony deals with its potential and also highlights the danger of it being celebrated as a silo solution in development.

2

The Software Industry in India

The beginnings of India's software industry can be traced back to the 1960s, although the accentuated growth in this sector is of recent vintage that has occurred during the last three decades. It is said that the exit of IBM during the tenure of the Janata government in the late 1970s led to the ex-employees of IBM establishing their own firms, thus, creating the 'prior experience' that was necessary and that become the basis for software growth from the late 1980s onwards. In this regard, Upadhya (2004: 5141) has pointed out that:

> The exit of IBM from India discouraged other multinationals from investing in the sector, but in the long run, it had positive outcomes in promoting the growth of an indigenous industry. For instance, some ex-IBM employees started small software companies … and several of the major Indian software service companies, such as HCL and Infosys, emerged during this time.

The government's embrace of liberalisation articulated via its New Economic Policy led to its relinquishing core areas of growth hitherto assigned to the public sector and its opening up of computing, software and telecommunications to private companies and Foreign Direct Investment (FDI). The setting-up of Software Technology Parks in the 1990s, the IT Bill, 2000, state-based legislations such as the IT promotion policy established by the Government of Karnataka in 1997, along with an IT policy formulated by the Government of Andhra Pradesh in 1999, followed by an ITes policy in 2002 played important roles in strengthening the environment for IT and IT services in the country. A number of measures to strengthen the electronics industry in India were adopted during the 1980s, including the policy on software exports, development and training.

While this predominantly export-led industry earned revenues totalling US$22 million in 1984, it was worth US$76 billion in 2011—making it one of the world's largest sources for software and IT-enabled services. In 2008, this sector employed close to 1.5 million people, up from 160,000 in 1996. Of more than 2,500 software exporters, the top five—Tata Consultancy Services, Infosys, Wipro, Satyam and HCL—accounted for more than 35 per cent of the exports in early 2000. In 2003–2004, TCS, Wipro and Infosys each exported to the value of US$1 billion. While all the major global software companies have set up subsidiaries in India, Indian software companies have in turn established subsidiaries in the major metropolises that are currently, the hubs in the informational economy. This includes the US where there are 266 software companies of Indian origin and Europe where there are 122. The major destination for exports is the US that accounts for more than 60 per cent, followed by the EU that accounts for 25 per cent. Taken as a whole, software companies from India offer a range of services—from the making of software products to the provision of IT-enabled services, including consultancies, BPO, turnkey and customised solutions, e-commerce, along with business services, chip design along with a range of other options. With a predominant share of total export revenues and increasing share of the GDP, this sector seems to have achieved in less than three decades what other sectors such as manufacturing and agriculture have failed to achieve in over 60 years. In 2004, for example, software export revenues accounted for 16.3 per cent of total export revenues and the IT industry contributed to 2.87 per cent of the GDP. The software industry has been credited with making the Indian economy global and competitive. This exponential growth has, of course, become staple fare for both national and global media who have consistently feted this industry. Growth in this sector has also been enabled by quality certification for its exports. Out of the 23 Software Engineering Institute—Capability Maturity Model Level 5 certified companies from around the world, 15 are from India. With the exception of the scandal at Satyam Computers in early 2009 that took some shine off from this industry, it can still boast of being in possession of an unsullied reputation, a source for professional work and management practices and also, devising ways of doing business that were unlike the norm in India. The Satyam episode seems to have already been forgotten by the media and today, the story is once again upbeat.

This chapter will deal with the software industry in India, but within a critical understanding of the larger political economy of software in India. While one can argue that both the success of this sector and the knock-on effects this has had on other sectors need to be celebrated—particularly, its impact on improving what used to be derisorily termed as the 'Hindu rate of growth', it can also be argued that this sector is becoming a victim of its own success. Bill Gates is reputed to have said that, 'One cannot eat computers'. In other words, the value of sectoral growth as opposed to multi-sectoral growth is a critical issue in India where vast sections of the working classes rely on agriculture. The fact that the government seems to be placing all its eggs in the IT basket is problematic, given that growth in this sector is far outstripping growth in all other sectors, thus, resulting in a lopsidedness which may be detrimental to the overall development of the nation. Salim Lakha's (1990: 49) observations on the setting-up of a software park in Pune, highlights the preferential terms given to what already had been touted as a sunrise industry.

> In line with the general government policy, the Pune park will offer a variety of benefits in addition to the advantage of direct satellite links. These include the waiving of import license for equipment imported into the technology park; no duties on imports and no requirements for custom bonding of the premises in the park.

Today, there are 51 Software Technology Parks housing 8,000 units spread throughout the country, along with numerous Special Economic Zones (SEZs) and Export Oriented Units that continue to benefit from a variety of incentives, including a 100 per cent exemption from income tax of export profits that has been extended until 31 March 2011, along with exemptions of service tax, excise duty and other taxes. Moreover, this sector is supported by government and quasi-government units, including the Software Technology Parks of India established under the Department of Information Technology and the Electronic and Computer Software Export Promotion Council. Kumar (2001: 4290), departing from the normal tendency to eulogise this sector, poses some pertinent questions related to this perpetual tax holiday.

> Software exporters receive an income tax holiday for profits from software export. There is a need to rethink the relevance of these tax incentives. In an industry where India enjoys a natural comparative advantage (on account of low cost manpower), where exports have been growing at more than 50 per cent per annum, where profit margins are around 22 per cent of revenue (much higher than any industry in the country) there seems to be little relevance of these tax breaks on a sustained basis. Furthermore, given the opportunity cost of software development for the domestic market, the bias created by tax breaks in favour of exports is not desirable. Our back-of-the-envelope calculations suggests that the revenue loss on account of these tax breaks to the exchequer on account of these tax incentives to the industry could be in the order of Rs 20 billion (Rs 200 crores).

It has been argued that it is precisely such preferential treatment which has strengthened the comparative advantage that India has over other countries with respect to its software and IT-enabled sectors. These advantages include a widespread availability of an English-speaking workforce, a tiered network of educational institutions specialising in software engineering, networking and management—from the premier

IITs, the Regional Engineering Colleges to the National Institutes of Technology (NITs) and other institutions and comparatively low costs, especially in salaries when compared with counterparts in the US and Europe. Indian academies graduate more than 60,000 qualified IT and software engineers each year, making it one of the largest pools of IT labour in the world. A number of these graduates opt to work abroad, especially in the US and Europe, thus, becoming part of the global IT labour circuit. In this regard, Xiang (2006: 175) makes the following observation:

> India has become the major source of migrant IT labour worldwide, with Indians having accounted for 63 per cent of all foreign IT professionals entering the United Kingdom in 2000.... In the US, of all the computer systems analysts and programmers on H-1B visas, a visa type created in the late 1990s specifically for high-tech personnel, 74 per cent had been born in India.

It has been estimated that the US companies save up to 80 per cent of costs when they set up subsidiaries in India, given the per hour salary costs in the US/India that work out to US$35/₹18 (see Chandrasekhar 2006). This comparative cost advantage, however, cannot remain a constant 'given' that it is natural for a globalised industry to relocate to countries where the wages are even lower. It is also the case that progressively, high-end salaries in the software sector in India have become closer to the salaries in the West, resulting in a closing of the salary gaps, while salary divides within India—between those working in this sector and other sectors have become greater. The search for even lower salary costs is also being played out within India, as is indicated by the announcement that inmates at the Cherlapally Central Jail in Hyderabad will be involved in BPO activities for about ₹100–140 per day, costs that are much lower than average daily BPO wages (see Blakely 2010).

This emphasis on knowledge production and knowledge economy is part of a dominant, even hegemonic, ideology that is widespread among the major governments, inter-governmental and lending agencies such as the World Bank and the IMF. While knowledge certainly can be used to strengthen existing economies, the need for a balanced approach to productivity across sectors, seems to have been sidelined in the quest to become a knowledge superpower. This technocratic attitude is illustrated in a book on the knowledge economy in India, written by Carl Dahlman and Anuja Utz (2005: xvii), for the World Bank.

> In India, great potential exists for increasing productivity by shifting labour from low productivity and subsistence activities in agriculture, informal industry, and informal service activities to more productive modern sectors, as well as to new knowledge-based activities—and in so doing, to reduce poverty and touch every member of society.

Given that more than 70 per cent of the current work force in India is involved in agriculture and agriculture-related activities—while hardly one per cent is involved in the information economy, a change in the ratios is not imminent. However, the logic behind this need to change the present work ratio is flawed, precisely because the Indian economy is diverse, and it is this diversity that undergirds the nation's economy. One can, in this context, argue that food sovereignty for small and marginal farmers is of much greater priority than for them to be turned into knowledge producers for the global market. Similarly, the informal economy in India offers services to vast numbers of people who otherwise, would not have had access to essential goods and services. This monolithic, myopic approach taken by the World Bank and other pro-market institutions is, however, attractive, because the software industry in India characterises a resurgent India—India Inc. is key to the country's identity as a global power-house. So, if all of India were to embrace this technology, the thinking goes that it would be the answer to India's myriad problems. This technologically determinist way of thinking can be considered hegemonic, precisely because it is part of a ruling ideology in India, shared by technocrats, policy-makers, politicians and their counterparts in supranational agencies and the Bretton Woods institutions. Joseph Femia (1981: 39), on Gramsci's notion of hegemony, observes that it embodies 'a hypothesis that within a stable social order, there must be a substratum of agreement so powerful that it can counteract the division and disruptive forces arising from conflicting interests. And this agreement must be in relation to specific objects—persons, beliefs, values, institutions'. In India, the information industry is sacrosanct. This is best illustrated by the fact that the premier apex body for software and ITes in India, the NASSCOM, is more than just a trade lobby. The statistics on the software industry in India that the government puts out is largely based on the information generated by this trade body. Needless to say, NASSCOM has not been equally proactive with respect to dealing with problematic trade and labour practices within this sector from cooking the books, as was the case at Satyam and the continuing issue with the procurement of H1-B visas that enables Indian engineers to work in the US.

In my way of thinking, state support can be assessed in terms of two phases—(*a*) the pre-New Computer Policy (NCP) of 1984—during which period, this was seen as a low priority sector and (*b*) the post-NCP period, where there has been a complete turnaround, reflected in both central and state government's policies that are supportive of this sector, indeed to the extent as some have argued, of being detrimental to other sectors, such as agriculture. During the heydays of Indian socialism in the 1960s and 1970s, Multinational Corporations (MNCs) were only grudgingly welcomed and that too, only if they abided by Foreign Exchange Regulation Act

(FERA), Monopolies and Restrictive Trade Practices (MRTP) and other laws designed to restrict monopolies and support the growth of domestic industries. Rafiq Dossani (n.d.: 14–15) from Stanford University, describes the pre-NCP days as follows:

> Since software development could not come to India, Indian programmers were sent to developed countries. It began in 1974 with the mainframe manufacturer, Burroughs, asking its India sales agent, Tata Consultancy Services, to export programmers for installing system software for a U.S. client.... Other firms followed, including foreign IT firms that formed FERA-1973 compatible joint ventures. Initially, the exported programmers worked for global IT firms. Later in the decade, as IBM grew in market share, end-users such as banks used Indian firms to convert existing applications software into IBM-compatible versions. By 1980, there were 21 firms with annual exports of \$4m. The state remained hostile to the software industry through the 1970s. Import tariffs were high (135% on hardware and 100% on software) and software was not considered an 'industry', so that exporters were ineligible for bank finance. These protectionist policies favored established firms with conglomerate interests and access to finance over small firms.

However, today, there are few, if any, import tariffs although there are policies related to intellectual property that are supportive of software patenting, anti-piracy, semi-conductor policy, the opening up to venture capital, the creation of special export zones and software parks, etc., do indicate changed circumstances and attitude.

Arora and Gambardella (2005: 25) argue that the IT industry in India has made a difference despite an indifferent government.

> The Indian case shows that a weak and inefficient bureaucratic structure works best when it attempts not to do too much. It also shows the virtues of decentralization. Competition among Indian states to develop software has obviously kept political excesses in check and has focused government policy on addressing issues such as physical infrastructure instead of attempting to channel the industry into high-tech and high-value-added directions, or attempting to regulate entry and entrepreneurship. This situation is also an instance of the political economy of success: the success of the software industry has provided celebrity status for Indian software entrepreneurs and political clout for the industry, which the industry has used to push for sensible tax and capital market policies.

In the case of India, the turnaround from the embrace of import substitution and endogenous industrialisation to export-oriented industrialisation (EOI) has been predicated on the assumption that a trade-based integration of the country into a global market will result in overall growth and development. In the case of India, software and ITes are the sectors that enjoy a comparative advantage and therefore, growth in these specialised sectors, it is hoped, will have a spillover effect, leading to a strengthening of the overall domestic and export economies. Stough et al. (2005: 23) explain the assumptions behind an EOI orientation, in the following words:

> The main arguments for the implementation of EOI lie in its capacity to create spillovers. That is, exports create a dynamic effect on overall economic growth. According to EOI trade allows countries to allocate resources more efficiently (according to their comparative advantage), has access to foreign capital (for example, foreign direct investment [FDI]), and enables the learning of new techniques and processes. Furthermore, it increases familiarity and access to new production technologies and new goods invented abroad.... As a result, a country that seeks an outward orientation should be bale to benefit from technological spillovers generated by trade and better participate in the international flow of goods and technologies.

Whether or not there have been spillover effects in India, is contested, although it is clear that the relative immaturity of the domestic market is a cause for concern. Whether or not India's EOI strategy has been beneficial to the strengthening of the domestic market, will be dealt with in a separate section in this chapter.

Manuel Castells (1989), in *The Informational City*, was one of the first theorists to explore the various ramifications of the 'informational mode of production' and its implications for the development of cities linked together by the logic of networks. Castells' insights can be usefully applied to an understanding of the spatial logic of the information industries in India—and the ways in which SEZs, investments in communication infrastructure by the state, preferential policies and the remaking of a state's identity in line with these industries, have become the aspirational logic of post-modern India. The visit by Bill Gates to Amethi, Uttar Pradesh, which is Rahul Gandhi's electorate, in May 2010, reflects this aspirational logic. His visit to Uttar Pradesh, the most populous but also backward state in India, is akin to a visit by a software Houdini whose very presence has the potential to kick-start what is, as of now, a moribund economy and leap-frog Uttar Pradesh to a post-modern age. Castells (1989: 13–14) describes the foundational basis for this new mode of production—a vision that perhaps sits uneasily with the existing modes of production in Uttar Pradesh, which are animated by different expectations and intermeshing of labour and capital.

> The new technological paradigm is characterised by two fundamental features. First, the core new technologies are focussed *on information processing*. This is the primary distinguishing feature of the emerging technological paradigm ... what differentiates the current process of technological change is that *its raw material*

itself is information, and so its outcome ... the output of the new technologies is also information. Their embodiment in goods and services, in decisions, in procedures, is the result of the application of their information output, not the output itself.... The Second major characteristic of the new technologies is in fact common to all major technological revolutions. The main effects of their innovations are on *processes*, rather than on *products*. (Author's emphasis.)

This then, is the basis for the knowledge economy that is reflected in the increasingly major role played by industries, products and services associated with the manipulation of the digital to national and global economies. The copyleft activist Roberto Verzola (2004: 48–49), in the book *Towards a Political Economy of Information*, describes the gradual shift from white collar workers to blue collar workers in the US.

In 1956, for the first time, white-collar workers outnumbered blue-collar workers in the United States. In 1967, the information sector accounted for 46 % of the U.S. GNP and 53 % of the income earned. In the 70s only 10% of new U.S. jobs were produced by the goods-producing sector. By 1983, only 12% of the U.S. population was directly engaged in manufacturing activities.

The Indian economy, however, is very different from the US and includes larger sectors that are dependent on subsistence agriculture. Economic globalisation, best illustrated by the global flows of finances, skills and labour and flexible production, was to a large extent, accentuated by the new, convergent technologies, such as telecommunications, computing and the Internet.

The Theory of Uneven Growth and Software in India

There is an unfortunate tendency in the analysis of the software and IT-enabled related industries in India, to begin and end with the story of a largely internal dynamic—the shift from a mixed economy to a liberalised model—as the basis for India's newfound growth. That however, is only a part of the story. It is critical to locate the story of software in India within a larger context of global capitalism, characterised by 'uneven and combined development'. First employed by Leon Trotsky to understand the nature of development in Tsarist Russia, it was reflected in the later-day Marxian theories of development and underdevelopment associated with the dependency school, which in turn, was linked with Andre Gundar Frank and others, along with Immanuel Wallerstein's World System's Theory. World System's Theory, in particular, had posited a measure of independent growth for nations in the South, within a global capitalist economy. The theory of uneven and combined growth suggests that such growth is inherent to the logic of capitalism. Global capitalism's ceaseless quest for markets inevitably results in different gradations of intermeshing between the local and the global and this, in turn, results in different levels of separateness of for that matter coexistence between different modes of production at local levels—which, in the case of India, is based on agriculture, manufacturing and information processing. Uneven development is a reality in India, best illustrated by the visibility of IT enclaves in a handful of key cities, that are almost always surrounded by more traditional economies based on earlier modes of production as well as by a great variety of informal economies that are increasingly, the basis for employment and livelihood, be it in Chennai or Mumbai.

David Harvey's (2006: 112–113) observations on the impact processes of uneven development is worth reiterating.

> If competition between territorial units (such as states or cities) drives the capitalist dynamic ever onwards, for example, then the rise of particular regions as successful and highly competitive centres of capital accumulation affects the global situation. If the Pearl River Delta, for example, becomes one of the most dynamic and successful centres of capital accumulation through manufacturing in the whole world than this sets base-line standards everywhere with respect to labour costs, acceptable conditions of work, technological mixes, union organising, and the like. The de-industrialisation of the rest of the world (even in low wage countries like Mexico and Brazil) occurs as the China powerhouse takes over.

What is true of manufacturing is also true of the information industries—for not all countries and not all cities are in a position to compete within the informational economy. The bulk of software exports in India in 2008–2009 were from six states—Andhra Pradesh, Haryana, Tamil Nadu, Maharashtra, Karnataka and Uttar Pradesh. While there are numerous 'aspirational' cites in India that are keen to get on the software and ITes bandwagon, their destiny will be no more than a location for low-end IT-enabled services. The location of the key software industries in Karnataka, Tamil Nadu, Andhra Pradesh and Maharashtra reflects the competitive edge that these states share, for example, in the matters related to the quality of training and access to certified engineering colleges and tertiary education (see Arora and Athreye 2002). This is by no means, universal in India. The 'key sources of competitive advantage were: ever-improving advanced skills, rivalry, clustering and government vision/policy' (Heeks 2007: 30). In the context of India, the result of uneven development is immediately apparent in media stories of mergers and alliances, new innovations and opportunities in the software and BPO sectors on the one hand and all the real struggles in civil society and outside of it, by armed groups, such as the Maoists, to force a dialogue on the limits of predatory forms of capitalism and to find support for a more humane approaches to local development, on the other. One of the critical scholars on the information industries in India, D'Costa (2003: 221) has described the stark geography that results from combined development.

> Combined development is suggestive of the immense gaps that have arisen between the software industry and other sectors of the economy. The list is long but some of the key gaps can be found in the areas of organisational and technological capability, skill levels, incomes and wages, and education levels. For example, rural India is characterised by debt bondage, social servitude, excessive poverty, illiteracy and limited opportunities for social and economic mobility.

The privileging of some sectors, at the expense of others, can result in lopsided growth. It is clear that in India, the government has placed an enormous emphasis on information technology as the means to leapfrog development and to remake the country into a developed nation. While the three decades of experience clearly shows the potential of this industry to contribute towards the development of the nation, that experience also suggests that the technology fix cannot, by its own means, result in equitable social change. Structural obstacles, from caste and gender discrimination to the lack of employment opportunities, need proactive policies and the required political will. In the context of deep, structural divides, tele-centres on their own, simply cannot make a difference. Krishnan (2005) in a vision document, *Karnataka Vision 2025*, describes the reality of uneven development in a state whose capital city, Bengaluru, is the IT capital of India and the fourth largest IT hub in the world.

> A ... careful study of the state shows that there are huge regional imbalances in the state—north Karnataka has two-thirds of the most backward talukas in the state. These arid, less-irrigated, drought-prone talukas have development indicators that are comparable to some of the underdeveloped regions of India and pull down the state averages resulting in the moderate ranks of the state. Further economic growth in the state is centered around the metropolitan city of Bengaluru which accounts for one-fourth of the state's economic activity. Bangalore is struggling to cope with the influx of people, and consequent increase in traffic, and demand for urban infrastructure.

Growth in the IT sector has not been complemented by growth in any of the other sectors. Not only is Karnataka experiencing an agrarian crisis, but there has been an increase in farmer-related suicides in the context of rising input costs and a drought that has particularly hit Northern Karnataka. There has also been a growth in urban poverty in Bangalore.

In this context, Sivaraman (2005) makes a pertinent observation of the scenario in Bangalore.

> More than a third of the city's 60-lakh plus population lives in slums; but, as on 31 March 2001, there were only 1,390,079 ration card holders in the city. Large numbers of slum-dwellers, especially migrant labourers, have no ration cards. Poverty in Karnataka acquires a larger urban face. A study by the Planning Department of Karnataka reveals that—contrary to popular belief—the incidence of poverty in Karnataka is more acute in urban than rural areas. It reveals that though the urban population is 31% of the state's population, the urban poor make up 39% of the state's poor people. The Karnataka government doesn't have a single low-cost housing scheme for workers and the urban poor but is planning to acquire 3,000 acres around Bangalore to give it gratis to the industries.

Software, Land Grabs and SEZs

Land allotments to the IT sector has not been without controversy. A report on the impact of SEZs, compiled by the Centre for Education and Documentation (2009), is critical of Infosys and other companies.

> Case studies in Hyderabad–Secunderabad have shown how the villages and local people have been displaced due to hi-tech spaces which are characterized by social and spatial segregation. These enclaves—for example, the Infosys campus or the Indian School of Business, that are major points of contention—enjoy very high levels of amenities whereas there are 17 villages in Cyberabad area, where civic amenities such as water and education are just not available. A special mention needs to be made of the Dalit ('untouchable') colony that existed next to Infosys for nearly 25–30 years. They had proper ration cards and all that they needed was a right to their few square yards of land whereas Infosys wanted this land for the second phase of its expansion. They were shifted to a place almost 15–18 kms away, with absolutely no facilities. Their entire livelihoods have been ruined because they do not get any work there. They have to travel all the way using two-three modes of transportation back to these hi-tech areas to get some work engaging in either construction work or domestic labour.

Issues related to the real estate and the IT was graphically illustrated by the rise and fall of an iconic software company—Satyam computers, in late 2008. Its owners, the Raju brothers, were deeply involved in real estate and infrastructure projects. The tens of thousands of acres owned by the Rajus, the owners of Satyam computers via their real estate business, Maytas Properties, is currently being investigated by the Government of India—a direct consequence of the revenue scam that affected Satyam Computers in early 2009. As Venkateshwarlu (2009) has observed:

> It remains a mystery how Raju managed to acquire 6,800 acres of land, with preliminary reports suggesting *benami* (assumed names) purchases or the floating of a number of companies to circumvent laws ... revenue officials are looking at reports that he had bought up large chunks of lands originally assigned by the government to the Scheduled Castes and Scheduled Tribes, some in connivance with a local Congress leader in Ranga Reddy district neighbouring Hyderabad.

A key issue in India is the state-sponsored evictions of poor farmers from agricultural land and the conversion of these lands into free trade zones, IT hubs and media centres. In Goa, for example, the RTI applications led to the scrapping of licences for the SEZs that were hastily signed off by a single minister. Nikhil Dey, one of the architects of the RTI in India, in a personal interview, described the episode as 'a David and Goliath battle— the RTI applications led to the exposure that the permit for seven of Goa's SEZs were signed, in the same handwriting, by the same person within three days.' The Indian activist-lawyer Lawrence Liang, following a visit to the Infosys headquarters in Bangalore describes it thus:

> The demands for land by the IT sector are huge, given the requirements of large campus-like spaces. These spaces are built like large US college campuses with in-house malls, mini golf courses, swimming pools, gyms, air conditioned work spaces and well landscaped gardens to provide a comfortable work and play environment for the software engineers, the vast labour pool of the information city. The best example of this is of course the pride and joy of Bangalore, Infosys.... While there do walk around the picture postcard lawns, and if you do have a chance to chat with the *malis* (gardeners) who take care of the lawns, you may be a little surprised to find that these gardeners are often the farmers whose lands had been acquired for the IT city. The founder of Infosys had guaranteed all of them employment in exchange for their land, but unfortunately unlike the other employees at Infosys, these upgraded employees do not benefit from the wealth generating Employee Stock Options Scheme. (Personal interview with Nikhil Dey, Bengaluru, 27 January 2010)

The CEO of Infosys, the largest software exporter in India, Narayan Murthy, has been involved in acquiring more than 1,500 acres in Mysore, Mangalore and Bangalore for Infosys projects, including staff accommodation during the tenure of the Congress Chief Minister S.M. Krishna in Karnataka. Srinivasaraju (2005: 51), writing in the magazine *Outlook*, points out one example of such favouritism:

> The opposition put up in 2002 by Bellandur villagers, outside Bangalore, where Infosys tried to set up a campus on 100 acres of farm land, is well known.

The farmers alleged that the land was undervalued—land costing between Rs 45 lakhs and a crore per acre was being sold by the Karnataka Industrial Areas Development Board (KIADB) at Rs 9 lakh per acre.

There is a need for more studies on the links between politics, power and the software industry in India. Oftentimes, the land acquired for SEZs are directly appropriated from poor and marginal farmers, who do not have the political clout to stand up to the power of the government. As Mody (2010) has stated, the Land Acquisition Act, 1894, is most often used to purchase land that is allocated to SEZs.

> In the main, land for SEZs has been acquired using the Land Acquisition Act 1894 (LAA).This law permits the government (central and state) to acquire land for a 'public purpose' or 'a company'. Over the years state industrial corporations have also used this provision of the LAA to acquire land for industrial estates, industrial townships and even single company projects. Under The Land Acquisition Act 1894 land can be compulsorily purchased, at prices set by the district administration in consonance with prevailing market prices. A landowner whose land is notified for acquisition under the act does not have any choice but to sell. The act does not acknowledge customary rights or the rights of those who have settled on or are cultivating revenue land. Political protests against this form of land acquisition have forced a degree of re-thinking. A draft Land Acquisition Amendment Bill that addresses some issues of concern was introduced in parliament in February 2009.

The political economist of communications, Graham Murdock's (1990: 3) observations on the relationship between power and control in the media can equally be applied to making sense of the software industry in India.

> The potential it bestows over production does not arise solely from specific exercises of power within the corporations directly owned or influenced. It is also a function of pre-existing and enduring asymmetries in the structure of particular markets or sectors, which deliver cumulative advantages to the leading corporations and enables them to get the terms on which competitors or suppliers relate to them.

Conclusions

While the software and the BPO industries in India have benefited from consistent growth for over two decades and have played an important role in earning export revenues, much of this growth is tied to a single market—the US. A downturn in the US market, therefore, can have an adverse impact on the Indian software and BPO industries. A key issue facing the software industry in India is the need for it to diversify its market through an emphasis on local R&D, the creation of high-end software services and a complementary emphasis along with its export orientation on strengthening the domestic market. The BPO market, while certainly lucrative, is the archetypical example of flexible production in a globalised world. Unlike high-end services that require skilled labour, ITes generally involves data entry skills. The relatively low educational requirements to become a BPO worker means that such services can be sourced from the cheapest markets. If that market is India today, it can be Myanmar tomorrow.

References

Arora, A. and A. Gambardella. 2005. 'The Globalisation of the Software Industry: Perspectives and Opportunities for Developed and Developing Nations', in A. B. Jaffe, J. Lerner and S. Scott (eds), *Innovation Policy and the Economy*, Volume 5: 1–32. Massachusetts: The MIT Press.

Arora, A. and S. Athreye. 2002. 'The Software Industry and India's Economic Development', *Information Economics and Policy*, 14: 253–273.

Blakely, R. 2010. 'Inside Job Gives Call Centres a Pool of Cheap Labour', *The Times Online*, May 13. Available at: http://www.theaustralian.com.au/business/news/inside-job-gives-call-centres-a-pool-of-cheap-labour/story-e6frg90o-1225865832459 (accessed on 15 May 2010).

Castells, M. 1989. *The Informational City: The Space of Flows*. Oxford/Cambridge, Mass: Basil Blackwell.

Centre for Education and Documentation. 2009. 'The Impact of Special Economic Zones on Small Farmers in India'. Available at: http://base.d-p-h.info/en/fiches/dph/fiche-dph-7976.html (accessed on 15 May 2010).

Chandrasekhar, C. P. 2006. 'The Political Economy of IT-Driven Outsourcing', in G. Parayil (ed.), *Political Economy and Informational Capitalism in India: Digital Divide, Development and Equity*, pp. 35–60. Basingstoke/New York: Palgrave Macmillan.

D'Costa, A. 2003. 'Uneven and Combined Development: Understanding India's Software Exports', *World Development*, 31 (1): 211–226.

Dahlman, C. and A. Utz. 2005. *India and the Knowledge Economy: Leveraging Strengths and Opportunities*. Washington D.C.: World Bank Institute.

Dossani, R. n.d. *Origins and Growth of the Software Industry in India*, pp. 1–33. Asia-Pacific Research Centre, Stanford University. Available at: http://iis-db.stanford.edu/pubs/20973/Dossani_India_IT_2005.pdf (accessed on 18 May 2010).

Femia, J. V. 1981. *Gramsci's Political Thought: Hegemony, Consciousness and Revolutionary Process*. Oxford: Clarendon Press.

Harvey, D. 2006. *Spaces of Global Capitalism: Towards A Theory of Uneven Geographical Development*. London/New York: Verso.

Heeks, R. 2007. 'Using Competitive Advantage Theory to Analyse IT Sectors in Development Countries: A Software Industry Case Study Analysis', *Information Technologies and International Development*, 3 (3): 5–34.

Krishnan, R. T. 2005. 'Karnataka Vision 2025', Indian Institute of Management, Bangalore. Available at: http://www.indiaat75.in/vision-statewise-pdf%27s/KARNATAKA.pdf (accessed on 15 May 2010).

Kumar, N. 2001. 'Indian Software Industry Development: International and National Perspective', *Economic and Political Weekly*, 36 (45): 4278–4290.

Lakha, S. 1990. 'Growth of Computer Software Industry in India', *Economic and Political Weekly*, 25 (1): 49–56.

Liang, L. n.d. 'The Other Information City'. Available at: http://www.t0.or.at/wio/downloads/india/liang.pdf (accessed on 12 November 2008).

Mody, A. 2010. 'The Politics of India's Special Economic Zones', Book Preparation Workshop, Centre for Policy Research, New Delhi, January 10–12. Available at: http://indiasezpolitics.com/nopubdocs/Anjali%20Mody%20Briefing%20Note%201_6_10.pdf (accessed on 15 May 2010).

Murdock, G. 1990. 'Redrawing the Map of the Communications Industries: Concentration and Ownership in the Era of Privatisation', in M. Ferguson (ed.), *Public Communications: The New Imperatives—Future Directions for Media Research*, pp. 1–15. London, Newbury Park, New Delhi: SAGE Publications.

Sivaraman, B. 2005. 'Bangalore's IT Boom and the Grim Reality of Globalisation in Karnataka'. Available at: http://www.cpiml.org/liberation/year_2005/january/globalisation_in_karnataka.htm (accessed on 15 May 2010).

Srinivasaraju, S. 2005. 'Is It All for Land', *Outlook*, pp. 50–53, 7 November.

Stough, R. R., K. E. Haynes and M. E. Salazar. 2005. 'Economic Development Theory and Practice: The Indian Development Experience', in T. Thatchenkery and R. R. Stough (eds), *Information Communication Technology and Economic Development: Learning From the Indian experience*, pp. 11–28. Cheltenham, UK/Northampton, Massachusetts, USA: Edward Elgar.

Venkateshwarlu, K. 2009. 'Maytas Twins', *Frontline*, 26 (3): 31 January–13 February. Available at: http://www.frontlineonnet.com/stories/20090213260301000.htm (accessed on 21 April 2011).

Verzola, R. 2004. *Towards a Political Economy of Information: Studies on the Information Economy*. Quezon City: Foundation for Nationalist Studies, Inc.

Upadhya, C. 2004. 'A New Transnational Capitalist Class? Capital Flows, Business Networks and Entrepreneurs in the Indian Software Industry', *Economic and Political Weekly*, 39 (48): 5141–5143, 5145–5151.

Xiang, B. 2006. 'Working with Uncertainty in the IT Industry', in G. Parayil (ed.), *Political Economy and Information Capitalism in India: Digital Divide, Development and Equity*, pp. 174–195. Basingstoke/New York: Palgrave Macmillan.

3

Mobile Phones in India: Issues Related to Access and Use

The extraordinary growth of mobile phones in India has earned a number of column inches in the popular and business press. In this regard, Rajendran (2010) makes a very pertinent observation, stated as follows:

> In 1995, when private operators launched their services, the number of mobile subscribers in India was 77,000. In 2000, that count stood at 3.6 million—a 116 per cent CAGR (compound annual growth rate). Since then, thanks largely to competition and increasing affordability among consumers, the sector has grown manifold. According to data released by Telecom Regulatory Authority of India (TRAI), at the end of June 2010, India had 653 million mobile connections, with 10–15 million subscribers being added every month. On an average, developed countries added 3–4 million subscribers, Latin America added about 5–7 million, Africa added 1–1.5 million and Asia added 8–10 million.

Falling tariffs and increasing competition have resulted in the availability of all types of handsets and 'plans' that cater to the needs of a variety of audience segments—from fisher-folk to the affluent. The fact that in 2008, fixed density penetration ratios, after more than four decades of investment, was 3:100, while mobile densities, in less than a decade, was already 27:100, reveal the extent of this growth. While there is certainly much to cheer about in terms of greater 'access', there is a sense in which the discourse that has accompanied these developments, veers towards a technological determinism based on correlational models which are strong on causal links, but weak on evidence beyond what is available on the basis of econometric modelling. This is illustrated in the following quotation from a Vodafone-sponsored study:

> There is a *causal* relationship within the same country between higher mobile penetration (mobile subscriptions/population) in a region and higher economic growth. Indian states with high mobile penetration can be expected to grow faster than those states with lower mobile penetration rates, by 1.2% points a year more on average for every 10% increase in the penetration rate. (Kumar 2009)

This way of thinking was rather infamously suggested in a piece in the *Economist* (2005) that has been widely circulated:

> The digital divide that really matters ... is between those with access to a mobile network and those without.... Instead of messing around with telecentres and infrastructure projects of dubious merit, the best things that governments can do in the developing world is to liberalise their telecoms markets, doing away with lumbering state monopolies and encouraging competition.

This advice has been taken to absurd lengths in India. Raja Murthy (2010), writing in *Asia Times Online* on issues related to food security, refers to a case in India where the government distributed mobile phones to starving villagers.

> More evidence of peculiar economic logic appeared with the central government doling out free cell phones to 1,000 poverty-stricken families in Phagi village in Rajasthan. CNN-IBN news channel, reporting the strange event on September 10, quoted baffled recipient Gyarasi Devi asking, 'We could have done with some grain or a job. What will we do with these mobiles?'
> Her fellow villager, Govind, replied: 'Mobiles will actually add to our expenses. The food grains in the godowns are rotting. Why can't the government distribute food grain?'

Such industry-led models have been complemented by an approach towards research that primarily focuses on an exploration of the penetration and use of mobile phones—an approach that largely emanates from the tradition of uses and gratification and on a lesser scale, from studies which explore the mutual shaping role between technologies and users. Jonathan Donner (2008), in a comprehensive review of research into the use of mobile in the developing world, makes the case for more research on the integration between ICT4D and non-ICT4D studies, mobile-sharing and use between richer and poorer communities and for studies that explore the complexity of the artefact itself and differential uses by different communities (p. 151). His point is clearly stated in the following quote:

> Mobiles do not exist in a telecommunications vacuum, even in places where landlines are scarce. In many developing-world contexts, there is a different ecosystem of communication options, of cybercafés and public phone booths, of face-to-face encounters and the ubiquitous television...it would be helpful to understand mobile use as part of this distinctive and changing overall communication dynamic ... PCs, landlines, and mobiles (not to mention TVs) are likely to interact and coexist with each other for a long time.... Further research should capture the nuanced interplay of these devices across various contexts in (the) developing world. (p. 152)

While there is a certain merit in exploring what different segments of a population use their mobile phones for and comparative, cross-country case studies that illustrate mobile phone use (see Katz and Aakhus 2002), the findings, for the most part, are of an obvious nature—such as that youth in India use mobile phones to keep in touch with their families and friends. As Matanhelia (2010: 234) explains in his findings from a study that looked at mobile phone use among young people in Mumbai and Kanpur: 'The communication needs for which the participants used cell phones were: to connect with family and friends, contact family and friends during an emergency, to inform family of their whereabouts.' There is also a tradition of research that is strongly influenced by 'pro-sumerism'—the independent, autonomous, producer consumer, who is using mobile phones to engage with culture and the social on his/her terms. Henry Jenkins (2006: 18), who is one of the better-known supporters of this view, explains that convergence is driven by both industry and by 'pro-sumers'.

> Media companies are learning how to accelerate the flow of media content across delivery channels to expand revenue opportunities, broaden markets, and reinforce viewer commitments. Consumers are learning how to use these different media technologies to bring the flow of media more fully under their control and to interact with other consumers.

There are, it would seem, few if any, intervening variables in this relationship. It is extraordinary that studies on the political economy of mobile telephony, of structures, politics and policies are less forthcoming.

One of the most interesting theoretical traditions that can be used to understand mobile phone use is Bruno Latour's 'actor-network theory' (alluded to in other chapters of this volume), according to which, cultures develop in the confluence of the individual user of mobile technology and the technology itself. In other words, any technology, including mobile phones, are always becoming, being made and remade in context and as a response to specific situations that individual users find themselves in. There is, in his approach, an emphasis on an 'agency of things' that is based on a deliberate de-positioning of the Enlightenment man as the only bearer of agency (see Law 2007). Latour's is a Constructivist approach to theory-building, which in this specific case, could be used to understand how mobile phone cultures are formed and reformed. Katz and Aakhus (2002: 11) use the neologism 'Apparatgeist' (literally 'machine spirit') to capture the 'intersections of these two domains, namely the social person and mobile machine'. What is, of course, undeniable is that the everyday uses of mobile phones are extraordinarily varied and use is, in many ways, influenced by the 'distinctions' and markers of class, caste, gender and other identity positions. Van Beck's (2009) study, for example, on the traditional healer and his phone in Cameroon, reveals the use of the mobile phone in long-distance treatment in which, the phone is an aid in the privatisation of medicine and the maintenance of secrecy related to the traditional medicinal knowledge. 'The phone plays straight into these mechanisms of secrecy: by using a phone, separating the product from its use is made easier. The plants bear little information as to their use and by sending them and phoning afterwards, this separation is enhanced.' This is just one example of everyday uses of the mobile phone. Goggin (2006: 2) describes this phenomenon in the following words:

> A bewildering and proliferating range of cultural activities revolve around cell phone: staying in constant contact, text messaging, fashion, identity-construction, music, mundane daily work routines, remote parenting, interacting with television programs, watching video, surfing the Internet, meeting new people, dating, flirting, loving, bullying, mobile commerce, and locating people. Cell phones have come to be associated with qualities of mobility, portability, and customisation. They fit into new ways of being oneself (or constructing identity and belonging to a group); new ways of organising and conducting one's life; new ways of keeping in touch with friends, romantic intimates, and family; new ways of conducting business; new ways of accessing services of education.

A Short History of Mobile Phone Policy in India

Without a doubt, the frenetically changing, convergent, mobile phone environments in India are home to many cultures of mobile phone practices. However, these environments are by themselves, merely one aspect of the larger global–local environments in the making, which are powered, in the main, by economic liberalisation. In this larger context, the story of the mobile phone is as much the story of what people and technologies jointly create as it is about the mobile phone industry itself and the larger policy context of mobile telephony in India. The story of the mobile phone in India is congenitally linked to the liberalisation of telecommunications in India, which began in the early 1990s and gathered speed during the rest of that decade. One can begin the story with the liberalisation of telecommunications, encapsulated in the Telecoms Policy 1994 that supported the deregulation of this sector, thereby heralding the possibility for future competition and privatisation and, also, opened up a number of services to both the private and public sectors. A major policy plank was the opening up of telecommunications to foreign investment. The creation of TRAI in 1997, to govern this sector, was a radical departure from the norm that included many earlier failed attempts at regulating another related sector—broadcasting—a process that continues (in perpetuity?) with no outcomes in sight. The New Telecoms Policy (NTP), 1999, furthered the policy of deregulation and more importantly 'shifted the fee structure for licenses for both fixed line and cellular services from a fixed license fee (set by auctions), to a plan where a percentage of revenues would be passed to the government for use of the spectrum' (McDowell and Lee 2003: 374). Spectrum is, of course, critical to the effective utilisation of a number of services, including mobile services. A key issue in the literature is its availability as a 'common good' (see Prasad and Sridhar 2009), although in the light of its limited availability and the fact that spectrum in broadcasting and other services in India are mainly available to those who have been able to bid the most for licenses, it would perhaps, be best not to use the term 'common good', but substitute it with 'finite good'. The move to explore an NTP was based on the fact that the high entry fees were an obstacle towards the roll out of services and its commercialisation. This paved the way for what eventually came to be a national roll-out of mobile services. The auctioning of spectrum for both basic and cellular services began in 1991, through a process by which the country was divided into 20 circles, categorised by revenue potential into A, B and C sectors. There were separate bids for licenses in the four major metros in India—Kolkata, Mumbai, Chennai and New Delhi. The first of these spectrum auctions were for Groupe Spécial Mobile (Global System for Mobile Communications) (GSM) services. A number of contingent factors, from high auction fees to slow license clearance rates, inability to own licences in contiguous areas and corruption in the awarding of these licenses led to a number of court cases against the DoT. Jain (2001: 677), in one of the better articles on spectrum allocations in India describes it as follows:

> The 'circle' approach limited the participating bidders to large corporate entities, due to the high investments required…and net worth conditions set out in the pre-qualification round. The high bid amounts that successful bidders paid resulted in the licensees covering the more commercial and revenue yielding cities and towns, leaving the semiurban and rural areas virtually uncovered in the early years.

In 2001, the Basic Service Operators were also allowed to offer Wireless Local Loop (WLL) services and this placed them on a collision-course with the GSM providers, who had paid large amounts of money for their licenses. This resulted in protracted litigations and in response, TRAI issued a consultation paper on Unified Access Services Licensing (UASL) on 16 July 2003 following which, the government endorsed this plan that enabled providers to offer mobile services based on any mix of technologies. This move was also a response to the reality of convergence and the blurring of distinctions between previously separate technologies. By 2001, there was further liberalisation of this sector, particularly, in fixed and in national long distance and international services. However, the scarcity of spectrum continued to prevent the entry of, but a small group of players. In 2005, spectrum allocation was reviewed by TRAI, following which the Defence forces vacated spectrum, and with this availability of spectrum, caps on ownership were removed. The reasoning behind removing caps was that, in a competitive world, mergers were a reality and subject to the condition that at least, three operators were to provide services, a merger of licenses across five licensing sectors could be allowed. These five sectors were:

(i) Cellular Licence with Cellular Licence; (ii) Basic Service Licence with Basic Service Licence; (iii) Unified Access Services Licence (UASL) with Unified Access Services Licence; (iv) Basic Service Licence with Unified Access Services Licence; (v) Cellular Service Licence with Unified Access Services Licence. (TRAI 2007:114)

Mobile Phone Concentrations

By early 2008 and as a result of both mergers and market expansion, three services, inclusive of Bharti Airtel, Reliance Communications and Tata Teleservices, accounted for over 50 per cent of the 31.58 million new mobile customers in the first quarter of that year. Rajendran (2008), writing in the *Business World*, highlights another aspect of the scenario.

Such is the intensity of the battle in the high-stakes telecom game, numerous powerful people appear to have applied for licences to operate mobile phone companies in a benami manner. The media is still busy trying to unravel the mysterious owners of companies such as Loop Telecom, Swan Telecom and Bycell. The names of various senior politicians are doing the rounds, and while sources in the telecom ministry identify the owners privately, they are unwilling to do so publicly.

By 2008, some of the major cities, including Chennai and Mumbai, had reached near-saturation point with respect to mobile coverage. By 2010, almost all of the 23 circles were serviced by an average of 14 providers and the competition has led to one of the lowest per call tariffs in the world— ₹1 per call. The auction of 3G licences in April 2010, had, by Day 8, already earned the government nearly US$2 billion and by the end of the licencing process, had earned the government US$14.4 billion. There were three pan-Indian 3G licences available for US$3.6 billion each, which were not sold. However, six top mobile companies in India, including DOCOMO, Airtel, Reliance, Aircel, Bharti and Vodafone were awarded 3G licences. In this connection, telecoms watcher and blogger, Mohit Agrawal (2010) has the following observation:

> [I]t is clear that most of the operators have tried to bid for their stronghold circles except for Reliance and Tata. Airtel's largest circles are Delhi, Karnataka, Andhra Pradesh, Bihar and Rajasthan where it has won the 3G licenses as well. Similarly, Idea has got 3G licenses for its strong circles like Maharashtra, Kerala, Haryana and Andhra Pradesh. Airtel and Vodafone have tried to ensure that their bid amounts for their key circles remain below the annual revenues, e.g. in Karnataka, Airtel has to pay $351 million which is just 49 per cent of the income generated there. On the other hand, Bharti dropped out of the race in Maharashtra and Gujarat where the bid amount had crossed the company's annual revenue numbers. Clearly, the aim of the operators was to protect their current strongholds and current revenues.

The very next auction for Broadband Wireless Access spectrum, held in June 2010, earned the government US$5.5 billion.

Mobile Freedoms and Their Obverse

How to deal with the political economy of mobile telephony in the context of the seeming 'abundance of access' is an issue that is worth exploring. On the one hand, it is clear that competition and the various economies of scale achieved through mobile penetration, has led to the availability of services in most parts of India, to the lowering of the price of handsets, to the lowering of tariffs, even free person to person calls in the same network and also, to a variety of 'plans' for segmented audiences. On the other hand, a handful of national and global mobile phone companies with deep pockets have cornered the prime market share. The issue here is not market share in one sector, but across multiple license sectors, cross media ownership and cross-business ownership that effectively reveal the corporate power of a small, but influential and extraordinarily wealthy group of business interests. And as importantly it highlights their power to construct and market a narrative of an object of desire—that is by no means a stand-alone product but is intimately tied to other consumer technologies, the globalisation of multiple desires and cultures. In other words, one of the issues worth exploring in the context of mobile phones, is to ascertain whether or not the real power to define the possibilities of the 'material-semiotic', over and beyond what people do with the mobile phone as 'pro-sumers', lies with these companies? The icon of this avalanche of modernity that people are currently experiencing in India is the mobile phone and its ability to tap into new freedoms of everyday use. And, while such uses have certainly enhanced freedoms, one can argue that its everyday use connects each user to a complex informational grid that has both structural and cultural impacts.

From a theoretical perspective, the possibilities of both freedom and control in the context of the digital offer a fertile ground to explore digital policy and practice. The mobile revolution is not just about the market and audiences, but also the state that has played a major role in facilitating and controlling 'competitive' environment. A good example of such control is the attempts made by the Indian government in forcing Blackberry to allow governmental access to their networks for reasons of national security. While it is clear that the majority of studies related to the use of mobile phone tend to veer towards a celebration of the 'digital sublime', to use the title of a book by the political economist Vincent Mosco and are validations of the various types of access and use, it is also necessary to undertake studies that offer both correctives and macro understandings of the nature of digital transactions, interactivity as well as larger understandings on the actual beneficiaries of the digital world. In other words, while we certainly need to read the offerings made by digital futurists such as Derrick de Kerckhove (1997) and Bruce Mazlish (1993), there is also a need to read and understand problematisations of digital capitalism by a range of scholars, including Dan Schiller (2000), Mark Andrejevic (2007) and Nicholas Carah (2010) among others. It is worth our while to spend a few moments dealing with these opposing understandings—particularly because devices, such as the mobile phone in India, have become integral to the newly mobile Indian, whose destiny is integrally tied to the story of India as an emerging economic power-house and global power base.

In real-life contexts in India, it is clear that cultural industries have harnessed the power of interactive audiences, but also, in that process, redefined interactivity primarily as a means to enhance visual interfaces and audience loyalties. A good example of the former is the marketing speak of Barco, an organisation that has built the 'interactive backdrop solution' for CNN-IBN, a company that is 'stimulating realtime interactions with its viewers'. In the words of their operational manager, explaining the need for this change: 'We permanently strive to deliver sustainable value to our viewers by providing them with an exceptional viewing experience.'

The manager speaks further, as quoted below, on the coverage during the Mumbai terrorist attack:

> With the new Barco wall, we were perfectly able to capture the news as it happened. In the past, the viewing was limited and screens could capture only one image at a time. Today, the Barco solution allows us to display three different views of the event, with outstanding picture quality, vibrant colors and high contrast. (CNN-IBN 2010)

The advent of wall-to-wall satellite and cable television in India that coincided with the growth of mobile telephony, has certainly led to synergies and to what Nalin Mehta (2008: 255–256) argues is the development of 'argumentative television'. Mehta's analysis suggests that one form of interactivity is a corporate means to maintain audience loyalties in what is a highly competitive, 24-hour news environment.

> The rise of private telephony and mobile phones has coincided with the rise of the Indian satellite television industry.... The people who own mobile phones are often those who also watch satellite television and television channels use mobile technology as a means for building linkages with their subscribers. This is done through SMS technology.... This is mostly done through SMS polls of viewers that are economically beneficial to channels as well as to telecom companies. News channels conduct opinion polls on a daily basis.

In what is a frantic bid for corporations to be more interactive than their rivals, mobile phone companies have adopted interactivity as their symbol of customer friendliness. Airtel, one of India's largest mobile services, announced its latest project in the following words:

> Bharti Airtel, India's leading integrated telecom services provider, today announced it has entered into an innovation and technology partnership with Infosys Technologies Limited (Infosys), to deliver superior customer experience to the customers of Airtel digital TV, its Direct To Home (DTH) TV service. As part of its Digital Convergence Platform, Infosys will provide a suite of products including devices, application servers and interactive applications that will focus on providing an enhanced digital lifestyle to Airtel digital TV customers. (http://www.airtel.in/wps/wcm/connect/About%20Bharti%20Airtel/bharti+airtel/media+centre/bharti+airtel+news/dth/pg_airtel_launches_next-gen, accessed on 12 March 2012)

Similarly, a start-up firm extols the virtues of yet another interactive 'revolution', in the following words:

> SMS2.0 is a next generation technology innovation in the mobile media space. It is bringing a paradigm shift in mobile user interactivity. Users are experiencing enhanced messaging services, search and access to relevant content,

and promotions of interest in a personalized and non-intrusive way. (http://www.affle.co.uk/news/press-coverage/sms2.0-is-bringing-a-paradigm-shift-in-mobile-user-interactivity.html, accessed on 2 September 2010)

In the book *Connected Intelligence* (1997: 31), de Kerckhove, who is often described as the 'Marshall McLuhan' of the 21st century, describes interactivity in the following words:

> The electronic extensions of the human body allow rapid crossover back and forth between hardware and software, between thought, flesh, electricity, and the outside environment.... We have shared our minds with TV for four decades.... With the interactive systems, our psychotechnological development is taking us one step further. The video screen is often becoming a necessary intermediary not only for our imagination, but also for our thinking processes... We are about to recognise the fact that we wish to enjoy the same freedom of mental action on our screens that we can experience in our brains.

While de Kerkhove, as a futurologist, sees technology as a 'second skin', he views the relentless developments of the digital as an evolutionary given, a process whereby man and machine are involved together in creating the 'digital sublime'. Interactivity, in this way of thinking, is the basis for a newer and higher intelligence. There are certainly many stories from laboratories around the world, of new and improved versions of artificial intelligence, although the laboratory context is wholly different from the real contexts where politics and economics as much as culture and the social play their roles through which any given technology becomes the norm.

Mobile Phone Use among Fishing Communities as Actor Networks

There are others ways of discussing 'interactivity', not as an evolutionary given that is realised in these new confluences of man and machine, but as processes that are materially instituted and culturally signified. In this way of thinking, mobile phone interactivity cannot be divorced from the environment of possibilities offered by any given phone. The mobile phone specially designed for fishermen and marketed by the MSS Swaminathan Biocentre in Puducherry, certainly helps the fishermen in accessing information on weather and fish stock and in the setting of prices, although it also locks him into a particular vendor, whose major objective in designing such phones, is to get the maximum numbers of fishermen to use this device and to get market share. An article in the

Wall Street Journal (2009), entitled 'Dial M for Mackerel', extols the role played by Nokia and others, in making available customised handsets for specific sectors in India, including farmers and fisherman, leading to their 'empowerment'.

> Following a nationwide launch this summer of Nokia Life Tools (NLT), India's farmers can use their mobile phones to access tailored information to help them grow, harvest and sell their crops and manage their livestock.... As for Nokia and others in the mobile phone industry, it's no surprise why they're attracted to an emerging economy such as India.... And like other mobile phone companies, Nokia says much of the growth in India is coming from outside the major urban centers. India already is the number-two market for the Finnish company, thanks in large part to the strong distribution, market share and mindshare in rural and small town markets.... Much of the service's development has happened through partnerships that Nokia has forged locally. This includes a content-sharing agreement with Reuters Market Light (RML), a mobile phone-based information service owned by Thomson Reuters of the U.S. and the UK. Since RML's launch in Maharashtra in 2007, it has sold more than 250,000 quarterly subscriptions to some 100,000 farmers in over 12,000 villages.

'Empowerment' as Krishna Kumar (2010) points out, is not only a much-abused term in India, but also, in his terms, a 'footloose linguistic device' that 'camouflages the sharply unequal distribution of power in society by promising that those without power will gain it without some else losing it'. While there is certain evidence of the fact that mobile telephony is having a positive impact on the lives of farmers and fisher-folk (see Abraham 2007; Mittal et al. 2010), it is not clear whether the efficiencies and securities, that are a consequence of access to information and its uses, are outweighed by real social and economic constraints that affect the translation of information into sustainable economic security. Mittal et al. (2010: 30) do highlight some of the constraints facing poor farmers, including 'shortcomings in physical infrastructure affecting access to markets, storage and irrigation', the lack of availability of access to 'critical products and services including seeds, fertilisers, medicines and credit' and the need for enabling policies. It would seem from the available evidence that the unanticipated effects of mobile phones, such as its role in strengthening the 'security' of fishermen in a potentially hazardous occupation, is equally as important as its 'anticipated' effects.

Nevertheless, literature on mobile use among fisherman in Kerala does seem to indicate that mobile phone use is changeable and that at any given time it can be used to strengthen individual and/or collective modes of operation, cooperation and/or competition. Robert Jensen's (2007: 919) five-year study (3 September 1996–29 May 2001) of mobile phone use, based on surveys among fishing communities in Kasargod, Kannur and Kozhikode in northern Kerala and conducted during the early years of mobile phone adoption in India, found that 'the addition of mobile phones reduced price dispersion and waste and increased fishermen's profits and consumer welfare'. The 'results demonstrate the importance of information for the functioning of markets and the value of well-functioning markets; information makes markets work and markets improve welfare'. Reuben Abraham's (2007) study among the fishermen in south-western Kerala, indicates that one of the more important effects of mobile phone use among fishermen is 'one of reduced risk and uncertainty' (p. 13) although and rather paradoxically, the evidence also indicates that 'neither the risk nor the reduced losses seemed to translate into increased incomes' (p. 13). He is of the opinion that while there is proof that information-flows enhance overall productivity, the fishermen themselves have no illusions in respect of this technology. In a survey on technological improvements that made the most difference in their lives, they listed the mobile phone 'third to mechanisation and improved roads and transportation'. Sreekumar's (2011: 178) findings from interviews and surveys conducted among fishermen in Kerala, is an interesting departure from the norm. Instead of exploring how mobile phone use has enhanced market efficiencies, his study reveals something different, as quoted below:

> [T]he community's collective logic and cooperative spirits, developed over centuries of struggle for survival, found new expression in the mobile-enabled environment. In particular, it may be noted that information sharing about the availability of fish in specific locations, which was found to be absent in the initial phase of the adoption of the phone, has now become a new cooperation norm. In the context, the mobile phone thus emerges as a 'collectivist machine', in contrast to the individuality-enhancing device generally discussed in the literature.

Customised Consumerism

However, it is important to also point out that it is in the nature of this digital product to maximise the advantages of convergence and to facilitate applications that result in the micro-management of any given consumer's daily routines. An article in the *Economist* (2010) refers to one such activity:

> Instead of waking up in the morning to a jarring beep from his alarm clock, his cell phone can sing a melodious aarti (prayer) that stimulates his senses at dawn.

To experience this divine start to his day, he pays 30 rupees ($0.63) a month. Depending upon his religion, he can subscribe to daily quotes from his God which are fed to him, like medicine, three times a day at regular intervals. For this service he can either pay seven rupees for a 'weekly pack', or 28 rupees for a 'monthly pack', which includes a free screensaver. To accommodate variations in the popularity of local deities, the operators have customised their services for different regions. There are more Krishna followers in Gujarat (West India), whereas Kolkata (East India) is known for worshipping Durga.

While one can argue that this certainly is a service, it can equally be argued that interactivity is largely a controlled activity in which the user interacts within the possibilities offered by any given mobile phone vendor.

The customisation of mobile phones is, of course, a means by which the promise and reality of interactivity is operationalised. However interactivity, as Mark Andrejevic (2007) notes, is located within 'digital enclosures' and is the perfect means for both the state and private companies for the surveillance of users for security reasons and from a market perspective. The furore over access to the codes to Blackberry messaging in India in the year 2010 indicates that the government is keenly involved in the surveillance of mobile data flows. Andrejevic (p. 98) further makes note of the following:

> There is a price to be paid for convenience and customisation – and we will likely end up paying it not just by sacrificing and privacy, but by engaging in the work of being watched: participating in the creation of demographic information to be traded by commercial entities for commercial gain and subcontracted forms of policing and surveillance.

The current focus on accessorising the mobile phone, customising its design, colour and features in line with young teenage girl cultures, is just one rather obvious example of mobile consumerism. Such marketing of mobile products however, feed into larger strategies of marketing whereby, the promise of interactivity is the means of participating in a variety of 'participatory' cultures. In other words, the power of the 'pro-sumer' is harnessed in the marketing of goods and services. A potent example of such strategies is captured in Carah's (2010) book on pop brands, based on fieldwork in Australia that explores the ways in which large corporations, such as Virgin and Coke, engage with existing 'interactive' youth cultures in the context of music festivals to create environments of consumption. Mobile phones as well as social networking in festival time and outside of it have become an integral aspect of the manner in which individuals define and construct their experiences online and offline and thus help in the 'branding' process. A fascinating aspect of this approach to branding is that the individual and collective experiences of meaning-making are couched in the language of pleasure, fun and good times, dipped in a bit of responsibility. Carah describes this scenario through his observation, as quoted below:

> The audience are empowered to use devices, capture content and actively participate in the performance. The avid enjoyment and participation in the event create shared meanings and emotions attached to the brand. This participation also creates a valuable surplus in the media commodities generated and distributed as content to corporate spaces like the festival screens, websites and content-sharing sites such like MySpace, Facebook and Flickr.... The live performance is deployed as a reservoir of authenticity, a quilting point that brings together the audience's participation with the technical apparatus of the brandscape. The live performance is a catalyst for the production of information commodities. This apparatus both extracts surplus value and constructs notions of authentic music culture valuable to the brand. (p. 56, see also Chesher 2008)

In Zambia, the distributors of Coca Cola make payments via text messaging, while the Coke Cool Summer Contest in 2002 generated 4 million SMS messages in 34 days (see Castells et al. 2007: 108). In the case of globalising India, key occasions for heightened 'interactivity' is before and during religious festivals and during the New Year sales. One site (Free Press Release 2010) puts it in a very succinct manner.

> As the four months of celebrations and festivals progress, India is certain to see a large burst of activity and color in the online and mobile world. You can count on seeing websites with more vibrancies and festival themes. There will also be a lot of activity on the social media platforms to announce and greet communities during the festivals. The virtual world is looking ever so exciting and this year should bring in new trends in activity, design and communication.

I think it is important that we recognise the complexity of mobile phones, in particular, the many possibilities as well as limitations of its use. As an everyday item, it has become an extraordinarily ubiquitous medium that has indeed, taken a life of its own, as users adapt to it and companies explore infinitely creative ways to profit from its many applications. A cynic would probably argue that mobile phone applications are bound to grow massively in the light of the need for these companies to recoup the huge amounts that they spent on acquiring 3G and 4G licences! However and while that certainly might be the case, farmers and fishermen, migrants and those with disabilities, women and minorities, small businessmen and petty traders, the urban poor, indigenous people and Dalits along with civil society, social movements, the middle classes, teenagers, business sectors and governments are contributing, in their own capacities, to the evolving story of mobile India and, therefore, towards extending the global network society. With information becoming a premier commodity in our world today, there is a great rush to enclose subscribers and mine the generated information. However, this too is not a straightforward process given that in India, the mobile economy includes more than just the established players. Assa Doron (2010), writing on mobile telephony in the sacred city of Varanasi, Uttar Pradesh, makes the point that the grey economy in mobile telephony is also playing a role a leading role in innovation and applications.

> The mobile *axis mundi* of Varanasi is the bustling Muslim market of *dal mandi*. This busy market mainly offers illegal sets and various mobile accessories. On display is a variety of mobiles for very reasonable prices, including the ePhone—a rip-off of the iPhone. Colloquially, these sets are known as 'China mobiles,' and while everyone knows that China mobiles have 'no guarantee, no warranty,' it is these phones that are setting the standard for other more reputable brands. The most notable example of this competitive environment is the emergence of cheap mobiles that can use two and three SIM cards simultaneously, responding to the fact that people want to take advantage of the variable rates that different cards offer. Samsung and other Indian brands have recently taken up this innovation, and Nokia is likely to follow—a remarkable example of the lower classes driving the market.

The mapping of the political economy in these circuits of mobile telephony and its everyday uses, has yet to be made in India and is yet another strand in the evolving story of mobile telephony in India. Nimmi Rangaswamy's (2009) ongoing work on ICTs in a mesh-economy highlights the role played by the grey market in mobiles in everyday business practices in a slum in Mumbai.

> The mesh-economy relies on street level activities and daily transactions among individuals with shifting impermanent addresses, who still are reliable clients and business partners. The mobile phone services are the backbone of mesh economies and explain its huge adoption rates. It allows for the individual/shared user with no fixed or permanent geographic identity to have one capable of translating communication into transactions. The mobile phone is a clear connector of spaces and creator of social networks across socio-geographic boundaries. Armed with a mobile phone, small scale entrepreneurship and street level economic activities begin to acquire the status to merge with mainstream commerce and transform existing capacities to transact.... ICT usages through their dissociation from a purely spatial and stationary communication channels liberate the marginalized and uprooted trader, especially in a magnetic megapolis like Mumbai, to transact and migrate towards more stability in business.

Conclusions

There is a sense in which the mobile revolution in India is the moment that millions of Indians have experienced as their first introduction to the digital. That this introduction is potentially a two-edged sword has been alluded to in this text. Nevertheless, the freedom to connect should not be dismissed lightly, given that it has provided the hitherto silent sectors, with possibilities to 'talk', to bypass dominant cultural codes of conduct, to experience new forms of sociality and consequentially, strengthen agency (see Tenhunen 2008). It is possible that such uses are strengthening the public sphere and feeding into social change that is impacting on the local political economy. Dominant meanings are being contested at a variety of levels as multiple uses of the mobile phone come to light. However, it would also be important that we are not carried away by the mono-technological stories of social change, but locate such everyday uses of mobile technologies in the context of policy changes that are can broadly be described as democratic. The RTI movement in India and allied projects, such as the Right to Food movement offer larger opportunities for the mainstreaming of democratic values and entitlements. And in such contexts, mobile phones can be used for social mobilisation, networking and enhancing movement dynamics. Value-added solutions that are devised are increasingly being made on the basis of how and what people do with their phones in everyday use. Such validations are, of course, the basis for economic opportunities, although they are at the same time recognition of the specificity of cultures and of use. In other words, the market is now taking people seriously and is chary of adopting one-size-fits-all solutions.

References

Abraham, R. 2007. 'Mobile Phones and Economic Development: Evidence from the Fishing Industry in India', *Information Technologies and International Development*, 4 (1): 5–17.

Agrawal, M. 2010. '3G Auctions—What Next', *Telecom Circle*. Available at: http://www.telecomcircle.com/2010/05/3g-auctions-over-what-next/ (accessed on 1 September 2010).

Andrejevic, M. 2007. *iSpy: Surveillance and Power in the Interactive Era*. Kansas: University Press of Kansas.

Carah, N. 2010. *Pop Brands: Branding, Popular Music and Young People*. New York: Peter Lang.

Castells, M., Fernandez-Ardevol, J. L. Qiu and A. Sey. 2007. *Mobile Communication and Society: A Global Society.* Cambridge, Massachusetts, London: The MIT Press.

Chesher, C. 2008. 'Becoming the Milky Way: Mobile Phones and Actor Networks at a U2 Concert' in G. Goggin (ed.), *Mobile Phone Cultures,* pp. 77–85. London and New York: Routledge.

CNN-IBN India. 2010. 'Stimulating Realtime Interactions with Its Viewers'. Available at: http://www.barco.com/projection_systems/downloads/SMD_apl_network18_l.pdf (accessed on 2 September 2010).

De Kerckhove, D. 1997. *Connected Intelligence: The Arrival of the Web Society.* Toronto: Somerville House Publishing.

Donner, J. 2008. 'Research Approaches to Mobile Use in the Developing World: A Review of the Literature', *The Information Society,* 24: 140–159.

Doron, A. 2010. 'India's Mobile Revolution: A View from Below, Inside Story: Current Affairs and Culture'. Available at: http://inside.org.au/india-mobile-revolution/ (accessed on 4 September 2010).

Free Press Release. 2010. 'Festival Season Will See Renewed Online Activity', *Free Press Release,* 1 September. Available at: http://www.free-press-release.com/news-festival-season-will-see-renewed-online-activity-1283336816.html (accessed on 3 September 2010).

Goggin, G. 2006. *Cell Phone Culture: Mobile Technology in Everyday Life.* London and New York: Routledge.

Jain, R. S. 2001. 'Spectrum Auctions in India: Lessons from Experience', *Telecommunications Policy,* 25: 671–688.

Jenkins, H. 2006. *Convergence Culture: Where Old and New Media Collide.* New York, London: New York University Press.

Jensen, R. 2007. 'The Digital Provide: Information (Technology), Market Performance and Welfare in the South Indian Fisheries Sector', *The Quarterly Journal of Economics,* 122 (3): 879–924.

Katz, J. E. and M. Aakhus (eds). 2002. *Perpetual Contact: Mobile Communication, Private Talk, Public Performance.* Cambridge: Cambridge University Press.

Kumar, R. 2009. 'India: The Impact of Mobile Phones', *The Policy Paper Series,* No. 9, January: 1–66. Available at: http://www.vodafone.com/etc/medialib/public_policy_series.Par.56572.File.dat/public_policy_series_9.pdf (accessed on 3 September 2010).

———. 2010. 'Empowerment by Verbal Chicanery', *The Hindu Online,* 31 August. Available at: http://www.thehindu.com/opinion/lead/article605995.ece?homepage=true_(accessed on 3 September 2010).

Law, J. 2007. 'Actor Network Theory and Material Semiotics'. Available at: http://heterogeneities.net/publications/Law2007ANTandMaterialSemiotics.pdf (accessed on 4 September 2010).

Matanhelia, P. 2010. 'Mobile Phone Use by Young Adults in India: A Case Study', PhD Thesis submitted to University of Maryland. Available at: http://drum.lib.umd.edu/bitstream/1903/10255/1/Matanhelia_umd_0117E_11079.pdf (accessed on 31 August 2010).

Mazlish, B. 1993. *The Fourth Discontinuity: The Co-evolution of Humans and Machines*. New Haven and London: Yale University Press.

McDowell, S. D. and J. Lee. 2003. 'India's Experiments in Mobile Licensing', *Telecommunications Policy*, 27: 371–382.

Mehta, N. 2008. *India on Television: How Satellite News Channels Have Changed the Way We Think and Act*, New Delhi: Harper Collins Publishers.

Mittal, S., S. Gandhi and G. Tripathi. 2010. 'Socio-economic Impact of Mobile Phones on Indian Agriculture', Working Paper No. 246: 1–47, Indian Council for Research on International Economic Relations.

Murthy, R. 2010. 'Manmohan Opts for the Poor to Starve', *Asia Times Online*, September 10. Available at: http://www.atimes.com/atimes/South_Asia/LI11Df02.html (accessed on 11 September 2010).

Prasad, R. and V. Sridhar. 2009. 'Allocative Efficiency of the Mobile Industry in India and its Implications for Spectrum Policy', *Telecommunications Policy*, 33: 521–533.

Rajendran, M. 2008. 'Telecom: The Great War', *Business World*, February 15. Available at: http://www.businessworld.in/index.php/Telecom/The-Great-War/Page-3.html (accessed on 1 September 2010).

———. 2010. 'Ringing in Success', *Business World*, August 14. Available at: http://www.businessworld.in/bw/2010_08_13_Ringing_In_Success.html (accessed on 1 September 2010).

Rangaswamy, N. 2009. 'ICT for Mesh-Economy: Case-study of an Urban Slum', Proceedings of the 10th International Conference on Social Implications of Computers in Developing Countries, Dubai, May. Available at: http://www.ifip.dsg.ae/Docs/FinalPDF/Work%20In%20Progress/ifip_21_nimmi%20rangaswamy.pdf (accessed on 25 October 2010).

Schiller, D. 2000. *Digital Capitalism: Networking the Global Market System*. Cambridge, Mass., London: The MIT Press.

Sreekumar, T. T. 2011. 'Mobile Phones and the Cultural Ecology of Fishing in Kerala, *The Information Society*, 27 (3): 172–180.

Tenhunen, S. 2008. 'Mobile Technology in the Village: ICTs, Culture, and Social Logistics in India', *Journal of the Royal Anthropological Institute*, 14: 515–534.

The Economist. 2005. 'The Real Digital Divide', *The Economist*, March 10. Available at: http://www.economist.com/node/3742817 (accessed on 10 October 2011).

———. 2010. 'Nearer My God to Thee', *The Economist*, 26 May. Available at: http://www.economist.com/blogs/babbage/2010/05/religion_and_mobile_phones_india (accessed on 2 September 2010).

The Wall Street Journal. 2009. 'Dial "M" for Mackerel: Can a New Mobile Phone Service in Rural India Help Promote Economic Empowerment?', *The Wall Street Journal*, 26 August. Available at: http://online.wsj.com/article/SB125126978512659859.html (accessed on 3 September 2010).

TRAI. 2007. 'TRAI Consultation Paper on Review of License Terms and Conditions and Capping of Number of Access Providers', 12 June. Available at: http://www.trai.gov.in/WriteReadData/trai/upload/ConsultationPapers/116/cpaper12june07.pdf (accessed on 1 September 2010).

van Beek, W. 2009. 'The Healer and His Phone: Medicinal Dynamics among the Kapsiki/Higi of North Cameroon', in M. de Bruijn, F. Nyamnjoh and I. Brinkman(eds), *Mobile Phones: The Talking Drums of Everyday Africa*, pp. 125–133. Bamenda/Leiden: Langaa/Africa Studies Centre.

Section 2
Government 1.0 and Information Technology

The two chapters in this section—on telecommunications and universal service obligations and the ICT for development—deal with state investments in public ICT services, explore issues around access and offer a critical perspective on the 'dominant' ICT for development projects that, for the most part, have not factored the role played by the 'context' in extending, although more often than not, limiting access. Government 1.0 is patriarchal and top-down in its style, as is clearly the case with its investments in ICT4D. And yet, these are extensive projects, supported by the only entity in India that has the capacity to include and service India's many forgotten people.

4

Telecommunications and Universal Service Obligations in India

The liberalisation of the telecommunications sector in India that began in the early 1990s and that has been accompanied by privatisation and deregulation has completely changed a staid public sector monopoly into a dynamic, market-led sector. Beginning with the opening up of competition for basic services in 1992, followed by fixed and mobile services and national and international services, progressive liberalisation has affected most, if not all, telecommunications sectors. The establishment of a strong telecommunications infrastructure provided the foundations for growth in ICTs and, therefore, can be considered as the backbone for growth in this and affiliated industries, linked to the digital. The Indian government's intent to selectively privatise this sector has helped to consolidate the interests of the state player, Bharat Sanchar Nigam Limited (BSNL), which is the seventh largest telecommunications company in the world today, with the largest subscriber base for telecommunications services (fixed and mobile) in the country. Today there are a number of domestic private firms, such as Bharti Airtel, Reliance Telecommunications and Tata Communications, who have made major inroads and between them, accounted for close to ₹70,000 billion in revenue in 2009 (*The Economic Times* 2009). The entry of FDI and foreign institutional investors (FII) has added a third layer of players now competing for fixed line and mobile revenues in one of the world's most lucrative markets. Foreign players include Vodafone, the second largest operator in India, Nokia, Ericsson, Huawei among numerous others.

In this chapter, I will explore key moments and critical issues related to this evolving sector. Rather than deal with the history of telecommunications in India that has been adequately covered by others (see Bagchi 2000; Choudhury 1998; Desai 2006; Dossani 2002), I will use select examples to illustrate some of the political contestations that have shaped this sector, including the issue of how the telecommunications industry managed to remain autonomous during a time of debt and structural adjustment and, in the spirit of the chapters in this book, deal with a key public service issue—that of the relationship between telecommunications and universal service obligations in India.

Debt, Telecommunications and Privatisation

One of the interesting questions related to telecommunications in India is that of how the country was able to avoid, being under pressure, the wholesale privatisation of this sector in the late 1980s and the early 1990s, when reform was on the agenda. A severe fiscal crisis in the mid-1980s had led the government to borrow heavily from the IMF and the World Bank in order to pay off its short term debt. As Warlekar (1989: 29) has observed, as the world's sixth largest borrower, 'India's debt service liability was US$1.5 billion in 1984 and US$3.7 billion in 1987 and is likely to be US$4.3 billion in 1990'. The reform of the telecommunications sector was a 'loan conditionality' and a key agenda item for these two lending agencies. In fact and until then, India's indigenous manufacturing capacities in telecommunications hardware and software were strictly limited and the import of both manual and automatic switching technologies had been the norm. Mani (1989: M–189), in a study of telephone switching gear, has made the point that 'very often the technology' was 'imported at a very high cost. Scant attention was paid to the sustainability of the imported equipment to the Indian conditions and its subsequent assimilation has been far from satisfactory'. Incompatibility-related problems were rife and equipment was indiscriminately sourced from a variety of foreign firms. BM (1989: 1942), writing in the *Economic and Political Weekly*, highlights issues with loan conditionalities through the specific example of a loan received from the World Bank worth US$350 million in May 1987, for the import of telecommunication products, although the telecommunications department wanted to renegotiate that loan so that it could import components instead '$150 million has already been drawn for import of cables, jelly-filled cables and certain other equipment. But these products can be manufactured indigenously' (BM 1989).

The World Bank alone had financed more than US$5 billion worth of rural telecommunications infrastructure in the developing world by 1993. In later years, the Bank shifted its focus from infrastructure support to sector reform and policy reform and arguably, this change in focus has had a massive global impact. In fact, it can be argued that the World Bank's emphasis on Structural Adjustment Policies (SAPs) as a condition for loans was the necessary foundation for economic globalisation and the global spread of ICTs. Christina Courtright (2004: 345) describes the change in the following words: 'The cornerstones of its new sector reform focus are privatisation of national telecommunications carriers, the development of an adequate regulatory and policy framework and promotion of full competition among carriers.' One can argue that tied loans connected to imports, defeated the purpose of planned development and remained an ever-present discourse in the very midst of India's avowed commitment to socialist development (see Bagchi 1984).

This accent on deregulation, privatisation and economic liberalisation was a key aspect of multilateral trade negotiations, from the General Agreement on Tariffs and Trade (GATTS) to its successor, the WTO. The progressive liberalisation of telecommunications, for instance, the Basic Telecommunications Policy, was among the first globally binding attempts to harmonise national telecommunications policies with global policies that facilitated multilateral trade.

Debt, Telecommunications and Dependent Development

A key question posed by studies in the tradition of political economy is 'who benefits' from economic growth and development. One way to attempt an answer to this question is through an exploration of the relationship between debt and communication—a largely under-theorised area. The issue here is about investments in capital-intensive projects, such as in telecommunications and the impact of this on the debt burden of the countries in the South. Telecom and IT investments have become a core part of investments in development. As high-return investments, it has attracted an array of financial investors ranging from multilateral institutions, such as the World Bank and the IMF, to private banks, investment firms and government lending institutions, such as Export–Import (EXIM) banks. The World Bank has projected a US$60 billion investment in telecommunications in the South for the period between 1995 and 1999. It has long been involved in telecom financing. However, such examples of financing reveal an agenda that was firmly committed towards privatising this sector. The World Bank for example, funded three telecom development projects in Kenya, of which the third (1987–1992) was worth US$90 million. These were not, by any stretch of the imagination, give-aways. The loans had strings attached—more precisely that Kenya Post and Telecommunications Corporation become two entities—posts and telecommunications that they establish a regulatory framework favourable to competition and that the new institutions be run on commercial lines.

Such conditions are a part of the normative framework of World Bank/ IMF largesse. This is explicitly stated in the US$400 million World Bank Project No: BDPA9557, a telecommunications project in Bangladesh, whose objectives include the 'establishing of an enabling environment for promoting private sector participation and competition in the sector, including the regulatory framework'. Altruism does not, as a rule, figure in bank-lending philosophies. And similar conditionalities are an aspect of all the major lending banks. In the case of telecom financing by the EXIM Bank of Japan, which made credit commitments of US$1,649 million for overseas telecom investments in the 1986–1991 period, loans were 'provided to the countries which Japan deem(ed) politically and economically essential' and was linked '"to such purposes as" the promotion of "direct investment from Japan"'.

While the World Bank and IMF are among the pioneers in the business of telecom investments, their role today is increasingly oriented towards creating a free trade environment in line with the WTO and smoothening the way for the entry of private investors in core areas, such as telecoms and IT. In fact, most IMF/World Bank initiatives today in these areas are jointly funded by private sector banks and equity foundations. The presence of the private sector in telecom financing is most evident in the Internet. A cursory browse through the Yahoo search engine in the mid-1990s revealed 85, mostly US-based, websites for Telecommunication Finance, including VenGlobal Capital, RFC Capital Corporation, DynaFund Ventures, Zacson Corporation among many others. The underside of private financing of telecom ventures is high interests and stringent penalties for defaulters. Many finance firms have become specialists in market-based debt conversion programmes. An array of debt-reduction schemes are available, each more versatile than the other, in squeezing the last ounce of flesh from any given debtor country that has defaulted on payments. Debt-equity swaps, debt pay-backs, debt securitisation, debt for exports, debt for nature, debt for development, debt for arms—the list is endless. The most celebrated of the debt-equity swaps—basically, a means by which, the debtor country's external debt is traded for equity in a local firm, is that of the Argentinian phone company, La Empresa Nacional de Telecomunicaciones (ENTEL).

The words of the debt and development scholar Susan George (1992) may be quoted in this regard:

> In late 1990, Citicorp made the biggest single debt-equity deal in history buying 60 per cent of ENTEL's southern division in partnership with Telefonica de Espana for $114 million in cash and $2.7 billion in debt. Manufacturer Hanover got the northern half of the same phone company in partnership with Atlantic Bell and on roughly the same terms: $100 million in cash and $2.7 billion in debt.

Other beneficiaries of this sale included France Cable et Radio, Compania Naviara Perez, Techint and the bankers, J P Morgan. Debt-equity schemes have led to the alarming disappearance of local assets at fire sale prices. In the case of the sale of ENTEL, it has been noted that Argentina received 'the lowest price per main line of companies privatised in developing countries' at the moment of sale. It would seem that these schemes, approved by the World Bank and the IMF, merely accentuate a debtor country's further indebtedness. When restrictions to investments are lifted, ownership rules relaxed and returns guaranteed, the assets of any and every debtor nation becomes a potential target for rapacious investors. Mandeville Partners, a US-based venture capital, merchant banking and investment group involved in telecom, technology and media financing, is one such company. It seems to have made a windfall in liberalised Argentina. Their web page informs the world that in December 1996 they began acquiring 'cable companies in Argentina through a joint venture with Hicks, Muse, Tate and Furst' and that by September 1997, they had 'acquired 64 different companies and negotiated the sale of the company to Citicorp Equity Investments' for a cool profit in excess of US$100 million, 'a return of more than 120%' (Mandeville Partners 2003). At this rate, will there be anything left to cry for in Argentina? There is also an indirect relationship between debt and communication. The establishment of free trade zones, technology parks, the *Maquiladora* Program in Mexico., etc., is related to exports production, to the creation of foreign currency earnings, a portion of which will, in turn, be expended in the servicing of the country's external debt (also see Thomas and Nain 2004).

The Politics of Telecoms Reform

The Indian government had come under pressure from the United States Trade Representative (USTR) and key telecommunication firms in the US and had, as a result, agreed to a partial opening up of this sector as per its commitments to the WTO's Basic Telecommunications Agreement, the first global trade-related commitment to the liberalisation of this sector (see Venugopal 2003). However, the liberalisation of this sector was a fraught process and the Indian government had to manage both external pressures that were pro-reform and internal pressures that were anti-reform. The anti-reform movement gained in strength in the aftermath of policy directives on telecommunications reform, including the report of the Athreya Commission that recommended the restructuring of the DoT. The Commission's recommendations were contested by

IT bureaucrats and the 450,000 strong telecommunications labour force that belonged to the three key telecommunications unions, who were against privatisation—the National Federation of Telecom Employees (NFTE), the Federation of National Telecom Organisations (FNTO) and Bharatiya Telecom Employees Federation (BTEF). The moves to allow the entry of foreign firms as service providers and equipment manufacturers, such as Siemens and AT&T, was also 'fiercely resisted by the Telecom Equipment Manufacturers' Association (TEMA), which called for severe restrictions on the entry of foreign players' (Sinha 1996: 35). The relentless privatisation of this sector has pitched the major telecommunications unions against the state. The moves in 2010, to make 100,000 employees redundant at BSNL, have met with union resistance from a Joint Action Committee. 'Workers' support for the strike expressed deep concerns over the government's plans to sell off 30 per cent of the company's shares, shed 100,000 jobs through a so-called voluntary redundancy scheme (VRS) and outsource work to private contractors' (Kumar and Dev 2010). If the current fixation to maximise revenues from licensing and spectrum auctions are any indication—the government made US$14.6 billion from 3G licencing auctions that were completed in May 2010—then Anupama Dokeniya's assertion (1999: 114) that India introduced competition primarily to raise revenues and not because it inherently believed in the value of competition for raising efficiencies is a credible reason.

> In India, the introduction of competition was adopted not as a regulatory tool to introduce efficiency in the functioning of the incumbent monopoly or to provide a diversified portfolio of services to a demanding corporate consumer base. Rather, it was introduced as a strategic tool to raise resources for network expansion, to overcome the funding constraints of the departmental monopoly and fulfil the burgeoning demand for basic telecom services. Competitive discipline in the market was not by itself the main policy objective.

DoT and Telecoms Reform

Not only were there major labour-related issues, but also internal struggles linked to curb the influence of the DoT that had an all-powerful hold on this sector. This internal contestation came to a head in the immediate aftermath of the establishment of TRAI in 1997—a move that was widely seen to be an attempt to professionalise the sector, but also clip the incumbent DoT's wings. One of the better accounts of the conflict between

DoT and the regulator TRAI is Desai's (2006) *India's Telecommunications Industry: History, Analysis, Diagnosis* in which he describes the bruising battles between the incumbent and the regulator and the highly politicised nature of this battle. Desai (2006: 20–21) graphically describes the early years of TRAI: 'The regulator has been defanged by the incumbent and the appellate tribunal, and while it watches helplessly, operators have erected various barriers to competition around their own systems.'

The National Telecommunications Policy (1994), followed by the NTP 1999 articulated the objectives of liberalisation and deregulation. However this task was given to the incumbent DoT that had the most to lose from reform and restructuring. Choudhury (1999: 220) describes it thus:

> The implementation of NTP 94 was entrusted to the DOT. And therein lies the tragedy. The DOT is the ministry; is the telecom authority and therefore the licenser; it is the policy maker; it is the regulator; it is the arbitrator (… over disputes between subscribers and itself and between licensed companies and itself) and the incumbent operator, as a government department.

More than a decade later, turf wars between the various IT ministries and TRAI continue to reverberate and impact on the story of telecommunications in India (see Dokeniya 1999; TRAI 1999). While the DoT's powers have been clipped, it continues to oversee four public sector companies—the BSNL that is the largest landline and second largest mobile service provider is really DoT's jewel in the crown, the Mahanagar Telephone Nigam Ltd. (MTNL) that caters to telecommunications services in Mumbai and Delhi, the Telecommunications Consultants of India (TCIL) and the capital-intensive Indian Telephone Industries (ITI) that has been involved in the manufacture of indigenous telecommunications devices. Liberalisation and deregulation have impacted on these public sector companies and the ITI, in particular, has been unable to cope with the demands of functioning in a competitive and rapidly changing technological environment. A substantial part of the reason for this failure can be blamed on ITI's penchant to import technology, its inability to forecast and prepare for the mobile era and lack of support and investment in indigenously owned proprietary hardware. Dilip Subramaniam (2004: 5242), in a comprehensive assessment of ITI in the *Economic and Political Weekly*, deals with the impact of inter-ministerial politics, competition, wage costs, competition and pricing along with other factors that have contributed to the decline of ITI.

> A combination of factors, related to state policy decisions, the company's relations with DoT and technological changes, worked in unison to bring about a dramatic deterioration in the performance of ITI. Far from achieving

the government's stated objective of introducing greater efficiencies in public sector enter-prises, deregulation, as we have shown, only succeeded in weakening ITI by transforming a once-profitable firm into a chronic loss-maker.... Nor were its interests better served by the decision of neo-liberal bureaucrats to indiscriminately expose it to competition by throwing open the domestic market to foreign companies—which were often inclined to dump equipment at throwaway prices—without taking care to provide appropriate checks and balances. These policy-makers chose to consciously disregard the fact that Indian firms, irrespective of their efficiency, were in no position to compete on equal terms with transnational corporations backed by their huge research departments, tremendous marketing strengths and global reach.1 15 These serious omissions on the part of the government were compounded by indifferent attitude adopted by the DoT with respect to ITI.

These contestations from within and without have shaped telecommunications in India. Unlike in other countries, where privatisation led to a complete restructuring of the telecommunication sector, in India, privatisation has been a lengthier process and each stage has been characterised by contestations and counter-contestations. Ben Petrazzini (1996: 47) has put forward an explanation for the reason behind the Indian situation turning out to be different from that of other countries in the developing world for whom deregulation led to wholesale privatisation of the telecommunications sector.

India's electorate is well known for its entrenched distrust of private business, and in particular foreign firms. Therefore handing over the whole national telecommunications system to private interests through the full privatisation of the national carrier—as in Latin America—was never seriously considered by the government. Furthermore, India has not suffered the profound economic and fiscal troubles that Latin American countries confronted in the 1980s. The absence of such major economic crisis strengthened those in government who opposed privatisation and weakened arguments in favour of radical and draconian economic reforms. In a context of 'politics as usual', and facing deeply entrenched negative perceptions and distrust of foreign and local businesses among the Indian population, it became extremely difficult for the government to justify economic strategies that the central administration itself had attacked in past years.

The Eclipse of Fixed Lines in the Time of the Mobile

When I was growing up in India, between the 1960s and late 1970s, the telephone was a luxury item. We did not own a phone. In fact, the first phone that my parents owned in India was in 1990. As Indians who had worked abroad, they were able to avail themselves of a facility that enabled access to a fixed-line phone on payment of a hefty fee. This was the only way to get around waiting lists that were in the tens of thousands all over the country. That situation has radically changed over the last decade and a half. In June 2005, the subscription base for fixed lines was 46.85 million, although the actual usage figure was much higher, while cellular phones subscribers were in the region of 57.4 million. While the annual growth rate for fixed lines was 7.7 per cent, for mobile phone, it was 52 per cent in 2005 (TRAI 2005). In fact, in mid-2005, the monthly average of new mobile subscribers had been around 1.5 million. By April 2010, there were close to 612.2 million mobile phone subscribers in India, and an average of 12 million subscribers are being added to this network every month. It is clear that fixed line subscriptions, at around 35.9 million, will decline further in the context of competition from mobile phones and cheaper tariffs. In fact, the largest fixed line vendor in India, the public sector company, the BSNL, suffered a net loss of US$395 million in the fiscal year 2009/2010 (see Lamont 2010). Even in the more remote parts of India, such as in the North Eastern hill state, Mizoram, more than half the population of 1 million people own mobile phones (see Bhaumik 2010). These statistics are, of course, open to interpretation. It is probably the case that a good portion of the early subscribers of mobile phones were those who already had access to fixed lines—in other words, socio-economic status conditioned adoption in the early years of mobile telephony in India. However, that situation too is changing. Today, for those living in urban environments, especially for the middle-classes and to some extent, the lower-middle classes, mobile telephony and in particular, access to competitive tariffs have made landlines, a not-so-attractive option. These mobile telephony services are being used by a broad cross section of the population. Our local fish merchants in Bangalore and Chennai give my folks a call when fresh fish arrives and small entrepreneurs—from cooking oil merchants to auto rickshaw (three wheeler taxis) drivers—now use cellular phones for bookings. The mobile has become an income source for small businesses and to a large extent this is a consequence of the lowering of tariffs and the availability of mass market handsets, such as that offered by the Indian company Reliance Infocomm. So in urban environments and for at least, a third of the population—access and network externalities have led to efficiency, to business-related benefits and to economic and social development. It has become advantageous for small-scale traders to plug into this communicational grid. Studies are beginning to emerge of the relationship between mobile telephony and economic development among small businesses and service providers such as auto rickshaw drivers (see Abraham 2007; Ilavarasan and Levy 2010; Rashid and Elder

2009; Tenhunen 2008). Presumably, this reality is being replicated in most major cities in India—and in that sense, the deregulation of the state monopoly provider in 1994, along with the separation of its roles as licensor, regulator and service provider has been beneficial, given that it neither had a reputation for efficiency nor transparency (see Chapter 5 for an analysis of the mobile revolution in India).

One can, in other words, argue that the entry of the market has resulted in limited public service benefits for people belonging to specific low-income sectors in the population, hitherto ignored by the public sector. There is today a major push by mobile telephony providers to facilitate rural market access. Reliance Infocomm's forays into rural teleservices have become a part of the mythology of telecommunications access in India. 'The Monsoon Hungama scheme', launched on 1 July 2003 was an extraordinary success.

> This unprecedented scheme allowed customers to get a mobile phone for an upfront payment of just Rs 501 (US$11), bringing down the entry barrier to a bare minimum. The scheme also permitted a low monthly spend, allowing the customer to restrict the fixed monthly outgoing (postpaid) to Rs 449 (US$10), inclusive of the Rs 200 (US$4.4) paid as club membership and privilege charges. Reliance Infocomm's Monsoon Hungama offer of a phone for Rs 501 (US$11) was a runaway success. Monsoon Hungama pushed Reliance to the top of the telecom market in terms of subscribers. It was the biggest promotional success in the history of mobile telephony in India. 1 million subscribers joined Reliance Infocomm in just 10 days after the launch of the Monsoon offer. The ripples of the offer were not limited to Reliance. This offer led GSM handset prices to fall to as low as Rs 1,500 (US$33.3). In the footsteps of Reliance Infocomm, during the same period, many competitors started offering flexible pre-paid options at less than Rs 500 (US$11.1) per month for their GSM mobile services. (Verghese n.d.: 5)

As Jagadeesh (2006: 38) has observed, competition has led to declines in average revenues per user (ARPUs) in metros and to the servicing of B and C circles—small towns semi-urban and rural areas. These sectors have projected growth volumes far in excess of the metros—projections supported by growth trends. 'Over a period of nine months, from January to September 2005, the subscriber base in B and C circles grew by 44.5 per cent and 46.7 per cent respectively—more than double the 22.2 per cent growth in metros.' Given that the potential for value added services is yet to develop on account of continuing bandwidth and spectrum problems, many of the major mobile telephony companies—Samsung, Motorola, Reliance, Bharti, Nokia and Hutch have begun targeting rural areas and, in the process, rolled out inexpensive handsets (under ₹1,400 (US$31—Motorola), language-adapted handsets (seven languages—Samsung) and the distribution of pre-paid and recharge options through rural retail outlets. While this approach by no means reflects altruism on the part of the mobile phone companies and is more likely than not part of a strategy to gather a captive subscriber base, its immediate 'social' consequences, however limited, cannot be discounted. One can, however, argue that despite such roll-outs, vast sectors in rural India live lives that are unconnected to the telecommunications revolution in India.

A Brief History of Universal Service in India

Just as the notion of public service has lent itself to context-specific meanings, the concept of universal service too, has meant many things to many people. As Jayaker and Sawhney (2004: 341) have observed: 'At various times, it has meant a fully inter-connected national network; universal access for all consumers; a geographically ubiquitous service; service at "reasonable", "affordable" rates; subsidised access for disadvantaged consumers such as rural users and the disabled.' Today both notions—public service and universal service have had to reckon with and respond to the increasing pressure to redefine meanings and redraw the terms of reference in the light of dominant capital interests. Just as public broadcasting in India, both radio and television, has steadily withdrawn its commitment to the 'public' and largely opted for commercial futures, universal service is no longer a defined public commitment, but is a contested notion that is imbued with meaning in specific contexts. Today, the meaning of universal service has been expanded in the context of a strong commitment towards access to the Internet, in addition to access to telecommunications.

In India, access and affordability are the key words that define the proviso of ensuring a 'phone in each village'. However, even the 'phone in each village' slogan is comparatively new. Until the early 1990s, the telephone was considered a luxury item—and in the context of a dirigiste economy with a distinctly socialist twist, the provision of such a luxury item was not a priority. The focus up until the Fifth Five Year Plan (FYP) was ensuring a country-wide postal service. It is only during the Sixth FYP (1980–1985) that mention is made of telecommunications for rural services:

> 18.6 During the Sixth Plan, the communication services, particularly the postal and telecommunication services, will be extended to all parts of the country with a view to subserve a balanced and sustained growth in the key sectors of development. Special attention will be given to the development of communication facilities in rural areas including backward, tribal and hilly areas

in order to correct the persisting imbalances in the communications net work. For the North-Eastern region, special measures will be aimed at strengthening the postal and telecommunication facilities. (Planning Commission n.d.a)

And it is during the Sixth FYP (1980–1985) that terms such as tele-density and phone on demand are mentioned and the country's commitment to universal services unequivocally spelt out.

> 10.7.2 In addition to the availability of telephones, accessibility, connectivity and reliability will be the primary goals. Accessibility to telephones will be ensured by providing a telephone in all the Gram Panchayats by April 1, 1995 and having LD-PTs, in additional 1.5 lakh villages by 1st April, 1997 so that 3.6 lakh of the total 5.7 lakh villages in the country are covered by the facility. One Public Call Office (PCO) will be provided for every 100 households in the urban areas. Provision of highway telephones on the national highways will also be a part of this programme. (Planning Commission n.d.b)

In other words, until the 1990s, the provision of basic public services (food, shelter, employment) did not include access to a telephone. It is with India's embrace of economic liberalisation, the recognition of technological convergence and the digital as a key factor in economic production, deregulation, privatisation and multi-stakeholder involvement in telecoms provision that universal service became a public concern. The two National Telecom Policies, 1994 and 1999, specifically dealt with universal service in terms of access and the proviso Part X Universal Service Obligation Fund was inserted in the Indian Telegraph Rules, 1951 and came to effect on 24 March 2004. The change from treating telephones as a luxury item to an essential commodity was first mooted in the NTP 1999. Universal Service recognises the fact that market forces alone often, do not have the inclination, or for that matter, internal policy support to connect rural regions, given the likelihood of low returns. How to provide a minimal telecommunication service for all, at affordable prices, is the core issue in the concept of universal service. It is founded on the assumption that there are some services considered to be essential, that ought to be provided on a non-discriminatory basis.

The Funding of Universal Service Obligations (USOs) in India

In 1999, the government announced its New Telecommunications Policy, with universal service as one of its main objectives. Section 6.0 of the policy stipulated a number of Universal Service targets, many of which are yet to be met. The Universal Service Support Policy came into effect on the 1 April 2002. On 9 January 2004, the Indian Telegraph Act (1885) was amended to include the Universal Service Obligation Fund that was based on a 5 per cent of Adjusted Gross Revenue sourced from license fees paid to the government. The USO, at least on paper, is broadly progressive and not only supports access, but also on demand, data services, broadband connectivity and the progressive transformation of village public telephones (VPTs) into ICT community centres. Universal Service Objectives are met via a Combination of Initiatives, including a universal access levy funded via termination charges, access deficit charges and government funding.

There have been four methods used to finance USO in India: (*a*) mandatory service obligations for all telecommunications licensees. This approach has failed miserably in India for with the exception of the public sector BSNL, none of the other firms involved in fixed line provisions, took this obligation seriously; (*b*) cross subsidisation—for example, through the levying of higher call charges for international and national phone calls and using surplus revenues to fund the USO, (*c*) access deficit charges—basically, subsidies paid by all telecommunications operators to those involved in USO provision that in the case of India, is the BSNL; and (*d*) Universal Service Funds collected via a number of levies placed on the service providers. These funds, in turn, are allocated to specific projects, such as the shared mobile infrastructure scheme, the rural broadband scheme and the optical fibre connectivity augmentation (see Gulati 2010). The Universal Service Obligation Fund (USOF) was established in 2002, and all telecom providers pay 5 per cent of their annual revenues towards this fund.

This USO fund is used to support initiatives linked to rural connectivity, including the following:

1. Installation, Operation and Maintenance of Village Public Telephone in the revenue villages identified
2. Provision of additional rural community phones in areas after achieving the target of one Village Public Telephone in every revenue village
3. Replacement of Multi Access Radio Relay Technology Village Public Telephone installed before 1st day of April 2002.
4. Provision of household telephones (RDELs) in rural and remote areas
5. Provision of Broadband connectivity to villages in a phased manner

6. Creation of general infrastructure and induction of new technological development in rural and remote areas for development of
telecommunication facilities. (Moni 2010)

While access to USO funds was initially open to fixed line providers,
mobile services and broadband connectivity received a major boost by
the passing of an ordinance in 2006.

> An Ordinance was promulgated on 30.10.2006 as the Indian Telegraph
> (Amendment) Ordinance 2006 to amend the Indian Telegraph Act, 1885 in
> order to enable support for mobile services and broadband connectivity in
> rural and remote areas of the country. Subsequently, an Act has been passed
> on 29.12.2006 as the Indian Telegraph (Amendment) Act 2006 to amend the
> Indian Telegraph Act, 1885. The Rules for administration of the Fund under this
> Ordinance, Indian Telegraph (Amendment) Rules 2006 have been published
> on 17.11.2006 USOF rules have further been amended vide notification dated
> 18.7.2008 to enable USOF support for operational sustainability of rural wirelines
> installed prior to 1.4.02. (USOF 2010)

Issues with the Implementation of the USO

The Report of the Working Group on the Telecom Sector for the Tenth
Five Year Plan (2002–2007), Government of India, Department of
Telecommunications, Ministry of Communications, refers to some of
the obstacles related to the achievement of rural connectivity during the
Ninth FYP (1997–2002).

> Out of 6.07 lakh villages, 4.09 lakh villages have been provided with Village
> Public Telephones (VPTs) as on 31.3.2001. It has further been noted that about
> 72% population has only about 18% of the total number of phones. The rural
> tele-density is only about 1% as against 10.16% in urban areas. The progress
> has been slow in rural areas due to inadequate availability of funds, equipment
> and material and the fast changing technologies. Unreliable connectivity,
> inadequate maintenance in rural areas and irregular and lack of power supply
> also contributed to slow and tardy growth of telecom network. (p. 19) (http://
> planningcommission.nic.in/aboutus/committee/wrkgrp/wg_telecom.pdf
> (accessed on 24 February 2012)

The question as to whether there ought to be a commitment to universal
service as opposed to universal access, is a fraught one in India today.
There are both internal and external pressures towards the greater
commercialisation of services and for universal service to become a

preserve of the state-owned BSNL that is responsible for local services and domestic long-distance services in India, with the exception of the Delhi and Mumbai regions. The pressures are generated from industry within—from private sector companies involved in the provision of both fixed and cellular services and their lobbies, for instance, the Cellular Operators Association (COA) and from analysts from within, for example, T. H. Choudhury, who regularly makes an informed although arguable case for universal service to be made the preserve of the state-owned service in the weekly journal *Economic and Political Weekly* (see Choudhury 2000a, 2000b, 2002a, 2002b), analysts from outside of the country—for example, Roger Noll and Scott Wallsten (2004, 2005) and Heather Hudson (2004), the USTR's Annual Section 1377 Review of Telecommunications Trade Agreements and the progressive telecommunications liberalisation agenda of global trade bodies, such as the WTO. Private sector lobbies have lobbied hard to amend the Indian Telegraph Act, so as to enable cellular service providers to access the USO Fund (Rao 2005), while at the same time trying to restrict the entry of public service companies, such as BSNL in the provision of cellular services. Sridhar (2002: 4) for instance, has made the following observation:

> Those who have followed the fortunes of the publically-owned companies in business point out to the systematic manner in which they have been tied down even as space has been opened up to private operators. For instance, it was only in November 2001 that BSNL was allowed to enter the cellular telephony business, though it had held the license for the last five years. In effect, BSNL, the company that was logically best suited for unrolling cellular telephony, was prevented to enter a business that constituted probably the fastest growing segment in an otherwise recession-ridden economy.

This denial of access to a key public company is a reflection of a larger and systematic attempt to curb the public sector and to maximise revenues from the private sector through licensing. Not surprisingly, politicians belonging to both the incumbent Congress party and their key opposition, the Bharatiya Janata Party (BJP), have been accused of receiving large kickbacks in the process of licensing cellular operations in India.

Until 1994, the monopoly public service provider, the DoT was solely responsible for extending universal service. Rural connectivity was allocated expenditures from the Sixth FYP onwards and by 2005, numerous FYPs later, close to 80 per cent of India's 650,000 villages had been connected with a VPT by BSNL. The DoT was involved in extending a number of rural telecommunications schemes, although despite the best efforts, rural tele-density in 2002–2003, was 1.55 phones per 100 persons as opposed to urban tele-density of 20.8 in the same period. While mobile phone penetration has certainly improved rural tele-density figures and the USO now also extends to mobile phone provision, private firms have been slow to contribute towards fulfilling their USO obligations. While private firms have been involved in extending universal service, these have been half-hearted initiatives and the prospect of low tariffs and the costs associated with wireline infrastructure have resulted in firms opting to pay penalties for infringing contractual license obligations related to US rather than invest in rural connectivity. In this regard, Malik (n.d.) has made the following observation:

> Most of the rural DELs installed by Bharat Sanchar Nigam Limited (BSNL), the public sector incumbent, have been funded by the government through license fee relief. Other licensees did have contractual obligations for the installation of DELs and a certain number of public phones in the villages. However, not a single operator has met this commitment. As against their commitment of establishing public phones in about 98,000 villages, they have in fact covered only about 12,000 villages. They opted instead to pay the penalty amount of INR 530 million (USD 11.8 million) as specified in their contracts.

Malik and de Silva (2005: 37), in a pro-competition, pro-private sector paper, have argued that the USOF fund, as it is currently operationalised, is flawed, since the incumbent BSNL is, for the most part, the sole beneficiary of this fund, given that it is the only company involved in extending universal service.

> The incumbent had an edge over its competitors as it had a large amount of the static infrastructure or backbone, and it has been able to foreclose entry by making entry for the new entrants into rural markets unviable even with subsidy. It is not surprising therefore that almost 75 percent of the subsidy auctions were won by the incumbent ... rural connectivity could have been seen as an opportunity and not as an obligation, had this structurally imbalanced situation in which the incumbent had a huge volume of the essential facility on which the new entrants relied had been shared for extending access. If that had been allowed then the viability concerns for the new entrants would have been limited to the costs of technology that go into the backbone i.e. the access network costs. In the current design, the new entrant has to factor in the costs of laying the backbone while deciding its entry into the rural markets ... this was not done despite the presence of excess capacity in the backbone infrastructure. India has vast infrastructure resources lying in the ground or underwater—but the fibre has not been lit.

While their critique needs to be heeded, I think that it is disingenuous to argue that if universal service had been communicated as an opportunity rather than an obligation, it would have resulted in the private sector investing in rural connectivities. When companies opt to pay penalties rather than invest in rural connectivity and find any number of loopholes to renege on their contractual obligations related to US, it would suggest that their only interest is in making profit. It is only of late, given the saturation point reached in urban mobile diffusion, which the peri-urban and accessible rural areas have become areas of interest to private companies.

Indigenous Capacities and the USOs

A key stimulus to the growth and deployment of public service telecommunications in India was the establishment of the C-DoT in 1984 under the directorship of Sam Pitroda. If one were to specify a period that best illustrates innovations in public service telecommunications policy and provision, it was the period 1984–2000 during which C-DoT was involved in a variety of R&D initiatives that led to substantive innovations in telecommunications hardware design and provision. Pitroda, quoted in an article by Karan Thapar (1989: 77), highlights five problems that gave rise to the C-DoT.

> First, 1940s organisation to handle the 1980s technology. Second, too much borrowed technology tired to loans which means we end up using a French this, a German that and a Swedish the other. Third, not enough properly trained people to keep pace with changing technology. Fourth, not enough funds, and fifth, lack of recognition and commitment to telecom as part of tomorrow's resources.

The C-Dot's emphasis on access rather than tele-density, local manu-facturing and commitment to import substitution led to numerous innovations, notably technologies and systems that resulted in the nation- and village-wide spread of phone booths and the rural automatic exchange (RAX), phone switches that became integral to the extension of the rural telecommunications backbone in India. The scale of the innovations need to be seen against what hitherto was the norm—India's dependence on imported switching and transmission technologies—from the stowger, the common control crossbar and digital electronic switches. Not only did the C-DoT create state-of-the-art digital switches, it also contributed to the following:

> [It brought into] being 20 switch manufacturers and scores of vendors of parts and sub-systems required for the digital switch. It was the availability of these switches with indigenous knowhow and parts that ultimately brought down the price of digital switches from Rs. 12,000 per line with imported technology to less than Rs, 4,000. These switches were deployed in rural areas and facilitated the extension of national and international dialling to the remote corners of the country. (Choudhury 2003: 3)

The C-DoT did have support from the Rajiv Gandhi government, although its most favoured status was contested by the incumbent DoT and a coterie of politicians, leading to at first, its marginalisation and more recently, its rehabilitation as a centre for excellence in telecommunications R&D. In this connection, Pitroda (1997: 11) made the following observation:

> By 1987, within out three-year limit period, we had delivered a 128-line rural exchange, a 128 line private automatic branch for businesses, a small central exchange with a capacity of 512 lines, and we were ready with field trials of a 10,000 line exchange. Better yet, the components for all these exchanges were interchangeable for maximum flexibility in design, installation, and repairs, and all of it was being manufactured in India the international standard.... By 1993, DoT was installing 25 rural exchanges every day.

Conclusion

It is clear that public service telecommunications in India is in a state of what one can call 'paradoxical marginality'. In spite of the tremendous growth that has occurred in the telecommunications sector during the last decade, there is a sense in which the continuing provision of public service telecommunications by the Government of India is being constantly hedged in by a variety of internally and externally generated pressures that are aimed at restricting the scope and provision of public sector telecommunications. There is, however, a far greater threat—and that is the technological determinism that accompanies the project of the USOs. The USO simply cannot be seen in isolation from other sectoral reforms. As Archana Gulati (2010: 15) observes in easily one of the better, critical and forward looking pieces on the USO in India:

> Some may argue that for a developing country the focus should first be on universal connectivity and the rest may be tackled subsequently. In the author's opinion however, India must embark on a programme of not only rural connectivity but also its concurrent and urgent exploitation to quickly reach out and mainstream the populations of rural and remote areas. This requires multi-sectoral and cross-sectoral thinking and an unprecedented level of coordination of efforts from the Government and industry as opposed to the present tendency to plan in silos and to guard one's turf. The Department's of Information Technology, Ministries of Human Resource Development, Rural Development, Women and Child Development, Panchayati Raj, Health and Family Welfare, etc., need to work together so that maximum utility is derived from the Government's spending on developmental schemes through mutual coordination and leveraging each other's programmes. There would for example be little use of subsidised broadband for schools, health centres and panchayats

unless committed and trained computer literate teachers, health care providers and officials are able to access useful content and facilitate the use of the same by the rural population. In the author's interactions with teachers and private entities involved in education including software development for education, it was found that there is a heartening level of enthusiasm when it comes to tapping into ICT to progress rural education. However, the required capacity building and coordination amongst various government agencies is a very difficult task in India, more so in the more backward states.

There are continuing issues related to access to unutilised USO funds that is now, in the region of US$5 billion. While there is a need to make the USOF, an independent agency, thus bypassing the bureaucracy at the DoT, what the USO experience in India clearly shows is the ability of the private sector to renege on/even bypass its commitments to the USO and the inability of regulatory bodies, such as TRAI to ensure compliance. Another issue that has been highlighted is that of indigenous capacity and investments in local R&D. While there are moves to make available soft loans from the USOF to private sector firms for extending broadband connectivities in rural areas, perhaps USO funds should also be made available to those involved in the development of indigenous hardware and software, that will be used to extend connectivities in rural India.

References

Abraham, R. 2007. 'Mobile Phones and Economic Development: Evidence from the Fishing Industry in India', *Information Technologies and International Development*, 4 (1): 5–17.

Bagchi, A. 1984. 'Towards a Political Economy of Planning in India', *Contributions to Political Economy*, 3 (1): 15–38.

Bagchi, P. 2000. 'Telecommunications Reform and the State in India: The Contradiction of Private Control and Government Competition', CASI Occasional Papers #13, pp. 1–58, Centre for the Advanced Study of India, University of Pennsylvania. Available at: http://www2.ssc.upenn.edu/research/papers/Bagchi_2000.pdf (accessed on 25 October 2010).

Bhaumik, S. 2010. 'Remote State in Vanguard of Indian Mobile Phone Craze', *BBC Online*, April 23. Available at: http://news.bbc.co.uk/2/hi/8640473.stm (accessed on 19 October 2010).

BM. 1989. 'Battle for Self-Reliance in Telecommunications', *Economic and Political Weekly*, 24, 34: 1941–1943.

Choudhury, T. H. 1998. 'Politics and Economics of Telecom Liberalisation in India', *Telecommunications Policy*, 22 (1): 9–22.

———. 1999. 'Telecom Demonopolisation: Why Did India Get It So Wrong?', *Info*, 1 (3): 218–224.

Choudhury, T. H. 2000a. 'Telecoms to the Villages', *Economic and Political Weekly*, 10–16 June: 1–7.

———. 2000b. 'Telecommunications in the Tenth Plan', *Economic and Political Weekly*, 25–31 August: 1–9.

———. 2002a. 'Sense and Nonsense on Village Public Telephones', *Economic and Political Weekly*, 39, 6 April: 1–3.

———. 2002b. 'Rural and Village Public Telephones: A Sensible Solution', *Economic and Political Weekly*.

———. 2003. 'C-DoT Merits Fresh Lease of Life', *The Hindu Online*, Business Section, 10, Feb. Available at: http://www.hinduonnet.com/thehindu/biz/2003/02/10/stories/2003021000140200.htm (accessed on 23 August 2006).

Courtright, C. 2004. 'Which Lessons Are Learned: Best Practices and World Bank Rural Telecommunications Policy', *The Information Society*, 20 (5): 354–366.

Desai, A. V. 2006. *India's Telecommunications Industry: History, Analysis, Diagnosis*. New Delhi: SAGE Publications.

Dokeniya, A. 1999. 'Re-Forming the State: Telecom Liberalisation in India', *Telecommunications Policy*, 23 (2): 105–128.

Dossani, R. (ed.). 2002. *Telecommunications Reform in India*. Westport, Connecticut: Greenwood Press.

George, S. 1992. *The Debt Boomerang: How Third World Debt Harms Us All*. Transnational Institute, London/Amsterdam: Pluto Press.

Gulati, A. G. 2010. 'Universal Service Policy in India: Theory and Practice', *Social Science Research Network*, pp. 1–15. Available at: http://papers.ssrn.com/sol3/papers.cfm?abstract_id=1611745 (accessed on 23 October 2010).

Hudson, H. E. 2004. 'Telecommunications Policy under Strain: Toward Universal Access in India', *Telecommunications Management and Policy Programme*, University of San Francisco.

Ilavarasan, P. V. and M. R. Levy. 2010. 'ICTs and Urban Microenterprises: Identifying and Maximising Opportunities for Economic Development', *IDRC Report*, July, pp. 1–166. Available at: http://web.idrc.ca/uploads/user-S/12802403661ICTs_and_Urban_Microenterprises_104170-001.pdf (accessed on 7 October 2011).

Jagadeesh, N. 2006. 'Connecting with Small-Town India', *Business World*, 23 January: 38–40.

Jayaker, K. P. and H. Sawhney. 2004. 'Universal Service: Beyond Established Practice to Possibility Space', *Telecommunications Policy*, 2 (3–4): 339–357.

Kumar, R. and G. Dev. 2010. 'Indian Telecom Unions Sell Out Major Strike', *World Socialist Web Site*, 22 April. Available at: http://www.wsws.org/articles/2010/apr2010/indt-a22.shtml (accessed on 24 October 2010).

Lamont, J. 2010. 'Fixed Lines Weight Heavily on India's BSNL', *FT.com*, August 2. Available at: http://www.ft.com/cms/s/0/0253af18-9e4f-11df-a5a4-00144feab49a.html (accessed on 19 October 2010).

Malik, P. n.d. 'Chapter 9: Universal Service Obligations: To Incumbents', *IDRC*. Available at: http://www.idrc.ca/en/ev-118644-201-1-DO_TOPIC.html (accessed on 30 October 3010).

Malik, P. and H. de Silva. 2005. 'Diversifying Network Participation: Study of India's Universal Service Instruments', *WDR Dialogue Theme 3rd cycle Discussion Paper WDR0504, The World Dialogue on Regulation for Network Economies*, pp. 1–48. Available at: http://www.lirneasia.net/wp-content/uploads/2006/02/Malik%20de%20Silva%20Sept%202005%20final.pdf (accessed on 24 October 2010).

Mandeville Partners. 2003. Available at http://www.mandevillepartners.com/overview.html (accessed 6 February 2003).

Mani, S. 1989. 'Technology Acquisition and Development: The Case of Telephone Switching Equipment', *Economic and Political Weekly*, 24 (47): M–181–M–191.

Moni, V. S. 2010. 'Universal Service Obligation (USO) Funds in India', September 22. Available at: http://www.articlesbase.com/communication-articles/universal-service-obligation-uso-fund-in-india-3317604.html (accessed on 24 October 2010).

Noll, R. G. and S. J. Wallsten. 2004. 'Telecommunications Policy in India', Joint Centre: AEI-Brookings Joint Centre for Regulatory Studies.

———. 2005. 'Universal Telecommunications Service in India' (pp.1–27), Joint Centre: AEI-Brookings Joint Centre for Regulatory Studies.

Petrazzini, B. A. 1996. 'Telecommunications Policy in India: The Political Underpinnings of Reform', *Telecommunications Policy*, 20 (1): 39–51.

Pitroda, S. 1997. 'The Village Phone', *Voices*, 1 (3): 11–13.

Planning Commission. n.d.a. 'Sixth Five Year Plan. Communication, Information and Broadcasting, Chapter 18.' Available at: http://planningcommission. nic.in/plans/planrel/fiveyr/6th/6planch18.html (accessed on 24 February 2012).

———. n.d.b. 'Eighth Five Year Plan. Communication, Information and Broadcasting, Chapter 10.' Available at: http://planningcommission. nic.in/plans/planrel/fiveyr/8th/vol2/8v2ch10.htm (accessed on 24 February 2012).

Rao, E. S. 2005. 'Reform in Reverse', *Frontline*, 22 (16). Available at: www. hinduonnet.com/fline/fl2216/stories/20050812002109500.htm.

Rashid, A. T. and L. Elder. 2009. 'Mobile Phones and Development: An Analysis of IDRC Supported Projects', *The Electronic Journal on Information Systems in Developing Countries*, 36 (2): 1–16.

Sinha, N. 1996. 'The Political Economy of India's Telecommunication Reforms', *Telecommunications Policy*, 20 (1): 23–38.

Sridhar, V. 2002. 'Disinvestment: Ringing Questions', *Frontline*, 19 (14): July 06–19. Available at: http://www.flonnet.com/fl1914/19140910.htm (accessed on 23 August 2006).

Subramaniam, D. 2004. 'Impact of Deregulation on a Public Sector Firm: Case Study of ITI', *Economic and Political Weekly*, 39 (49): 5233–5245.

Tenhunen, S. 2008. 'Mobile Technology in the Village: ICTs, Culture and Social Logistics in India', *Journal of the Royal Anthropological Institute*, 14 (3): 515–534.

Thapar, K. 1989. 'Busy Lines of a Technology Czar', *South*, 109: 77–78.

The Economic Times. 2009. 'India's Leading Telecom Companies', *The Economic Times*, September 17. Available at: http://economictimes.indiatimes.com/ articleshowpics/5020647.cms (accessed on 17 October 2010).

Thomas, P. N. and Z. Nain. 2004. *Who Owns the Media: Global Trends and Local Resistances.* Southbound, London, Penang: ZED.

TRAI. 1999. 'New Telecom Policy, 1999.' Available at: http://www.trai.gov.in/ npt1999.htm.

————. 2005. 'TRAI: The Indian Telecom Services Performance Indicators April-June 2005', September. Available at: http://www.trai.gov.in (accessed 3 August 2009).

USOF. 2010. 'Universal Service Obligation Fund: What Is Universal Service?' Available at: http://usof.gov.in/usof-cms/usof_home_contd.htm (accessed on 31 October 2010).

Venugopal, K. 2003. 'Telecommunications Sector Negotiations at the WTO: Case Studies of India, Sri Lanka and Malaysia', ITU/ESCAP/WTO Regional Seminar on Telecommunications and Trade Issues, Bangkok, Thailand, 28–30 October 2003. Available at: http://www.unescap.org/tid/mtg/ituwtoesc_s51b. pdf (accessed on 30 October 2010).

Verghese, S. n.d. 'Reliance Infocomm's Strategy and Impact on the Indian Mobile Telecommunication Scenario', *Media@LSE*, pp. 1–18. Available at: http:// www.scribd.com/doc/27794982/Reliance-Infocomm%E2%80%99s-Strategy-and-Impact-on-The (accessed on 23 October 2010).

Warlekar, S. 1989. 'The Making of a Problem Debtor', *South*, February: 29.

5

A Critique of ICTs in Development

ICTs, inclusive of computing, telecommunication, mobile phones, digital radio and television, can be used to distribute, share, produce, gather, store, communicate and organise information in the context of development and social change. Typically, ICTs are networking technologies that are mutually complementary and that can be used to maximise the delivery of information and also its use in the context of intensive or extensive development. ICTs are used in a variety of ways around the world in the context of development and social change. These range from education, job training, e-governance, e-commerce, capacity-building, health care, business services, advocacy and networking, agricultural development. Increasingly, ICTs are being used to deliver a range of objectives—from behavioural change to education and advocacy. ICTs in development projects are found throughout the world, in the north and the south. These projects vary in their aims and objectives and are based on different paradigms of communication and social change. Many are motivated by the need to bridge the 'digital divide' in society. ICTs are seen as a potent means to close the knowledge gap in the societies and help them to leapfrog from a relatively un-advanced state of development to an advanced state.

So What Are Some of the Key Assumptions Related to ICT4D?

1. That these technologies can help leapfrog a country that has not had the benefit of going through the stages of growth that have characterised many of the so-called developed societies and into the knowledge economy. The accent, therefore, is on the need to build the necessary infrastructure, liberalise the economy, strengthen the intellectual property regime and to progressively computerise every sector—from government to manufacturing. This would

enable countries in the developing world to connect to the global knowledge economy.

2. That technological innovation and its applications will help bridge the digital divide. Critical scholars have pointed out that this is an example of technological determinism, the belief that the ICTs act as a sort of magic bullet, transforming everything in its path, a panacea for the world's many problems.

3. There is also a widely held view that the lack of information—information poverty is a reason for under-development. This scarcity of information, it is argued, can be plugged via the deployment of ICTs. While there is certainly a case to be made for more information, one issue is whether what is needed is more computer-mediated information or information generated through a right to information campaign.

4. ICTs strengthen productivity across multiple sectors and evidence suggests that this is what is required to transform moribund economies into dynamic ones.

5. It has been argued that one of the effects of ICT4D is what is called 'disintermediation'—the fact that it allows people to connect directly to information, thus doing away with middlemen and brokers. A good example of this effect is in the context of the Bhoomi project in India. This project, based in the southern state of Karnataka, involved the computerisation of more than 12 million land records. Small farmers in India are dependent on local village revenue officials who are the keepers of land records. Given the issues related to illiteracy and corruption, millions of farmers have been played out—and this new biometrics-based system has eased their dependence on the local revenue officer. All they have to do is to visit a Bhoomi kiosk, identify their fingerprint and for a payment of 15 rupees, get a copy of the land record. This project has worked to some extent because of political will, commitment and investment and of course most importantly, because of an environment conducive to the project and pre-existing ICT policy. However, as it has been argued later on in this chapter, 'disintermediation' in itself needs to be complemented by a host of other commitments, including political will and other investments.

These assumptions are by no means fanciful for ICTs do have the capacity to contribute to development and social change. Having said that it is important to reiterate the point that ICTs on their own cannot bring about development and social change. These technologies cannot be treated as panaceas. With the benefit of hindsight, there is ample empirical evidence that proves that such technologies make a difference when they are located in politically, socially and culturally conducive environments. Geoff Walsham's (2010) study on the literature on ICTs for development in India highlights the available literature inclusive of ICTs and development goals, ICTs to support better lives for the poor, health information systems, tele-centres, mobile phones, ICTs to support improved government services, computerised back-end administration system, e-government direct services, use of Geographic Information System (GIS), ICTs to support enhanced internal economic activity, Internet banking and e-commerce, adoption of ICTs in private sector companies, ICT in agricultural supply chains, ICTs to support improved civil society, computers records and reform and provision of broader information on civil society. However, his concluding remarks point to the deep challenges that face ICT for development projects in India.

> What problems have been encountered in trying to use ICTs to support the achievement of development goals? A first problem relates to who benefits from the technology and the answer that comes across in a consistent way from the literature is almost always not the very poor, landless farmers, lower castes or sometimes women. Initiatives such as tele-centres, e-government direct services, ICT-facilitated agricultural supply chains and computerised land reform tend to benefit those who are already in a relatively privileged position. It is also noticeable that the poorer Indian states such as Bihar and Orissa are not mentioned at all in the ICT-based literature in contrast to reported work in relatively richer states such as Kerala, Andhra Pradesh or Gujarat.

A second problem is that many of ICT initiatives are limited in scope and scaling them up to deal with whole states or the whole country involves a complex socio-political process that is very difficult indeed. For example, cases of the beneficial use of mobile phones, such as in the Keralan fisheries industry discussed earlier, are interesting but, as yet, do not demonstrate a widespread and scalable development effect across the country as a whole. Initiatives to improve health information systems in India require wholesale change across the entire health system in terms of the way in which work is carried out and recorded, people's attitudes to information and its use, and issues of hierarchy and control.

> This leads on to a third problem which can be argued to be the most fundamental for ICT-based initiatives aimed at development. Many of the studies reported in this paper emphasised the crucial need for major attitudinal and institutional change in order for an ICT-based initiative to be successful. For example, core administrative processes need to be reformed in government institutions in order for the front-end e-government services to be effective. However, it is

widely recognised that such reform of the administrative culture in government is enormously difficult to achieve. Computerised systems, such as those involved in land registration for example, do not by themselves reduce corruption if this is deeply embedded within existing attitudes and processes. (p. 16)

Part of the challenge of dealing with ICTs in development and social change is keeping up with assumptions related to development—for example, that Development 2.0 as an IT-enabled model, can impact on the reality of development in ways that are different from earlier approaches to development (see Heeks 2010), that Government 2.0 committed to e-governance will make a qualitative difference in the lives of its citizens and that the bewildering array of consumer and social networking technologies have a positive impact on the trajectories of development and social change. In other words, there is an assumption that the free flows of information and possibilities for interactivity will result in new engendering of democracy and enactments of citizenship. As is the case with such assumptions, they are based on partial truths. While SMS texting can certainly be used to mobilise the masses, as has been done in the Philippines to bring down the government of Joseph Estrada, the feudal constancy of Filipino politics remains in place with or without the interventions of mobile phone–based applications or for that matter, social networking. And, similarly—while a case can be made that CGNet-Swara, a project in Chhattisgarh, has enabled tribal communities to upload news that counts and access this news, thus validating Voice, voicelessness has deep, structural roots that lie beyond the efficacy or otherwise, of mobile phones. While a case can certainly be made for the positive impact of some ICTs for development projects in India, there is a woeful lack of critical, impact studies that provide empirical data on the operationalisation and long-term consequences of the digital in context. Kenneth Keniston (2002: 2), in a study of 50 ICTs projects in India, has made the following comment in this regard:

[The] hopes widely expressed [that] are built almost entirely on an empirical vacuum. We know almost nothing about the factors that make for effectiveness or ineffectiveness of grassroots ICTs projects in developing nations ... projects have rarely been studied. No comparisons have been made between them. They are seldom in touch with each other. Lessons learned in one project are not transmitted to others. Appropriate technologies are rarely evaluated. Central questions of financial sustainability, scalability and cost recovery are hardly ever addressed. So, opportunities to learn from the diverse, creative Indian experience so far remain entirely wasted.

While there are exceptions, such as Michael Best and Rajendra Kumar's (2008) study of sustainability failures in the Sustainable Access in Rural

India (SARI) Project and studies by Prakash and De (2007) and Benjamin, et al. (2007) on the Bhoomi project, in general, the studies available on ICT projects in India are weak on critique. Keniston's critique needs to be heeded for until we have significant data from the field on the impact of ICTs in development, we will be left with assumptions and assertions that are not backed up by any evidence whatsoever. Sreekumar (2007: 885) in an analysis of three, globally feted, tele-development projects in India, namely Gyandoot, TARA Kendras and village knowledge centres belonging to the MSSRF, points out the gaps between the claims available globally on the social inclusivities achieved by these projects and on-ground realities.

> The participation of women and the underprivileged in these projects is abysmally low and this is strikingly in contrast to the projected image of these initiatives as being overtly sensitive to issues of gender and social divisions. Nonetheless, ICT-based NGOs are often wrongly credited with social achievements that decades of social and political interventions and struggles have been striving to attain, such as reducing gender inequalities and mitigating caste oppression.

Sreekumar's critique reinforces the point I have made in some of my writings (see Thomas 2010) that the feudal constancy and institutionalised inequalities that exist in rural India, cannot be wished away nor can the existing gaps bridged through techno-fixes. On the contrary, these technologies are bound to replicate and even reinforce existing divisions in rural India. Technology needs to be one element in an integrated approach to rural change. As technology steams ahead and investments are made into solutions based on myriad technological permutations, we are faced with a woeful lack of empirical information on the social ecologies of these technologies and its contributions to inclusivity and sustainable social change.

The Limits of ICT4D Theory

It is also clear that the accent on projects has been to the detriment of theory. On reading Dorothea Kleine and Tim Unwin's (2009: 1060) article on ICT4D in the *Third World Quarterly*, I was struck by the fact that practice has outstripped theory and that the lessons learnt from their comparative study are no different from the lessons reiterated in the area of communication for social change.

First, sustainability issues must be built into any ICT4D initiative from the very beginning. Second, if activities are to be developed from which poor people are intended to derive benefit, it is crucial that they are implemented at costs that these people can afford. At present it seems likely that the most cost-effective and widespread mechanisms for so doing will revolve around mobile telephony. Third, new and innovative business models need to be developed to deliver services to the very large numbers of people who can afford little, rather than the few who can afford much.

One of the key areas in ICT4D is the need for robust, inter-disciplinary theorisation that goes beyond the *diffusion of technology* theory that is often openly and technologically determinist and that is supportive of technology transfers in development and social change. In this way of thinking, the globalisation of information, knowledge and network societies can be engineered through the right infusions of technology—from mobile phones to tele-centres within a conducive environment supportive of market-based, competitive growth. This model has been favoured by lending bodies, such as the World Bank and inter-governmental agencies, such as the UN and private firms, such as Microsoft, resulting in multi-billion dollar investments in a range of ICT4D projects. In many of these projects, an acknowledgement of contextual contingencies has almost always been an outcome of evaluation.

In contrast to this theoretical approach which undergirds the dominant model related to ICT4D, there is, as Chrisanthi Avgerou (2010: 4) describes it, the theory that explores the social embeddedness of technologies and people in dynamic and contingent local contexts.

The socially embedded innovation research approach finds the assumption of the transfer and diffusion perspective about the nature of information systems to be overly simplified and misleading. It has developed more elaborate ontologies of IS innovation as socially constructed entities. The focal point of such research is the process of innovation in situ…. They are theoretically grounded in social theory, such as actor network theory (ANT), structuration theory, and organisational institutionalism, which provides insights and vocabularies to address conceptual relationships, such as technology/society, agency/structure, and technical reasoning/institutional dynamics. The main objective of such studies has been the development of theoretical capacity for addressing questions concerning the way specific categories of technologies and social actors clusters are formed, shape each other, and lead to particular socioeconomic outcomes.

While this approach validates context, it also rather significantly accounts for institutional dynamics and takes an open approach towards understanding the mutual shapings of technologies, users and networks.

The context of ICT4D includes institutions—inter-governmental, state, private sector, NGOs and other organisations that have invested in the diffusion of technology paradigm and who are involved in extending policy frameworks supportive of such interventions. The structural analysis of these key players and an understanding of their motivations need to be a focus for research, precisely because they play a structuring role in the ICT4D arena. 'Who benefits from such interventions?' ought to be a key question for research—given that it is not always the case that the projected beneficiaries are actually in a position to take advantage of these technologies in the face of access-related issues that stem from caste, class, gender and other hierarchies. The Microsofts of this world have a major interest in investing in ICT4D, given the returns from software sales and extensions of their market. When governments and major companies collude in investments in software parks and the like in a country like India, there is always the potential possibilities of collateral damage, of people being forcibly removed from their lands, as was the case of the IT corridor close to Bangalore (see Mazzarella 2010).

Structural analysis needs to be complemented with more innovative approaches towards understanding the tryst with technologies at local levels in which people and technologies are involved in a mutual shaping. Actor Network Theory (ANT), for example, enables one to go beyond technological and social determinism. The mobile phone does shape behaviours even if one were to argue that that shaping is bounded by the technology itself and in this sense and in the context of an ICT4D project, it is useful to understand how the technology and its users shape each other. It can be used to understand how technologies are adapted in local contexts, made sense of and used and the negotiations involved in such adaptations. Andrade and Urquhart (2010: 358) explain why ANT is superior to the theory of the diffusion of innovations:

> Diffusion of innovations is largely focused on the innovation itself—ie. technology—and does not challenge its implementation; it accepts the innovation as it is and relies on certain individuals—for example—early adopters and opinion leaders, among others—for its diffusion. ANT's sociology of translation affords the reconstruction of the mobilisation of a complex network of players.... ANT is focussed on the arrangement of and the negotiation between both humans and non humans ... around the proposed innovation to adapt it in a specific context.

While there are issues with the operationalisation of ANT (see Mitev 2009), it offers researchers an opportunity to explore complexity and get out of the straitjacket of dominant theorising related to ICT4D.

ICT4D from Political Economy and
Cultural Studies Perspectives

It would seem to me that given the larger political economy of ICT4D and the involvement of hardware and software vendors, aid and funding agencies, inter-governmental agencies, NGOs and governments, the accent is squarely on connectivity and access issues and bridging the digital divide—thus the strong project orientation in this area. However, there are a number of areas that can become the focus for research from within a political economy and cultural studies trajectories and that could become the basis for theorising:

1. Policy Studies: Issues related to how, why and who make ICT for development policy and how international, regional and national policy processes are deliberated and framed. Policy provides the necessary explanations as to how resources are allocated, why they are allocated—for example, through capacity-building workshops and why certain pathways are preferred to others. A key issue that can be explored in the context of ICT policy is governance, for example, in the context of e-governance policy. There are bound to be variations in the involvement of civil society actors in e-governance policy—for example, in Kerala as opposed to Maharashtra. Policy can be studied at a variety of levels—for example, hardware and software policy, regulatory policy, mainstream versus grass-roots ICTs policy, contents policy, language policy, format policy. ICT for development is not a silo operation—in fact, it connects to subjects explored in a variety of chapters in this volume—including e-governance, public sector software, free and open source software. There is need to explore governance and regulation issues in this new economy and the organisations, instruments and regimes of intellectual property that protect digital property.

2. There is also the need to generate theory from a political economy perspective—for instance—the political economy of ICTs for development in India. There is a need to study the structures of ICT for development and the role of the state, the private sector and civil society in ICTs for development projects and initiatives in India. Of particular interest is the role played by private firms—both global organisations, such as Microsoft and local firms, such as Infosys in setting the agendas for ICT for development in India, not only via trade lobbies, such as NASSCOM and MAIT but also

through sponsorship, capacity-building and partnerships with the government and civil society. There is a critical need for studies that explore the leveraging of power that result in preferential deals for ICT vendors, the sourcing of hardware and software. There is also the necessity to understand the beneficiaries of ICTs in development. Also questions, such as 'Who invests, sponsors and why?'; 'Who gains from connectivity?'; 'What are the primary motivations that lead to connectivity?' and 'What are the conditions for access and use?' need to be answered in this context.

3. There is also the need to theorise information, from the perspective of inter-sectoral convergences and the universality of information applications across all productive sectors, including the manufacture, trade and ownership of genetic and biological information as well as 'human biological information' (1996). James Boyle refers to this as the 'homologisation of information' (n.d.: 3), the fact that it makes little sense today to distinguish between genetic and electronic information because both types of information have begun to overlap and face the same problems of regulation. When culture and nature are translated and commodified into digital information, the commercial exploitation and ownership of this information does have the potential to become a source of extraordinary power.

4. Understand and engage with some of the key public issues arising from the interfaces between technological convergences and society, not least the new dynamics of exclusion, that Scott Lash (2002) refers to as the 'new type(s) of stratification, in which social class depends on relations to intellectual property and rights of access to the lifted-out spaces of technological forms of life' (p. 24). These new forms of exclusion, the basis for what is referred to as the digital divide, are a result of the extension of property values to every conceivable aspect of culture and nature, animate and inanimate, critical to the growth of global capital.

5. There is also the need to theorise the principles and practices of 'participation' in ICT for development projects. Far too often, participation, along with other buzz words, such as interactivity, are viewed as a given. There is a need to interrogate the actual practices and levels of participation in the context of project planning and design, implementation and evaluation.

6. There is a need to theorise the access and use of ICT for development technologies—from computers to mobile phones and other technologies using ANT theory as described earlier on in this chapter. To reiterate, there is a need for studies that explore the

relationships and negotiations between people and technologies. A useful way of theorising this relationship is to use Bruno Latour's concept of 'quasi objects' itself borrowed from Michel Serres—to describe the ways in which technologies 'become' and are shaped by human use. In this regard, Harris (2005: 172) notes the following:

> This quasi-object is what determines humanity through the long history of exchanges between objects and subjects. Its role is not only historical but extant: our social relations continually revolve around quasi-objects. The description, exchange, creation and consumption of objects define our individual actions and collective transactions. Given this we can never grant sovereignty to either the subject or the object, what is important is the transaction or swapping, the role that the quasi-object plays in constructing and maintaining relations. Thus the quasi-object is to be seen as a generator of inter-subjectivity constructing the 'we' and 'I', the collective and the individual, which both emerge as the result of its exchange or 'passing'.

In other words, computer-use in a telecentre or one of Negroponte's One Lap Per Child (OLPC) computers at school, involves a social construction of use, a continuous transaction and mutual shaping between subject and object. The use of this concept to understand this mutual shaping is bound to generate insights into the myriad ways in which ICTs and human beings are enmeshed in a continuous, mutual shaping that affects experiences and behaviours. Hamid Ekbia (2009, 2565) in a study of digital artefacts as quasi objects highlights what needs to be done: 'By shifting the question of "What is a digital artefact?" to "How is an artefact collectively qualified?" this line of enquiry provides the possibility for us to tell "stories" about what these artefacts can do.'

7. There is the need to theorise the many different varieties of ICTs–based interventions in urban and rural contexts in India, especially those that are enabling new cultures of use and that are based on new delivery and circulation structures. There is, in other words, the need to theorise urban and rural technological interventions, inclusive of cultural piracy and localised interventions. There is also the need to learn from and explore the possibilities for 'translation'. Galperin and Bar's (2006) work on microtelcos in Latin America reveal that new cooperative telecom schemes are, for example, being explored at local levels between communities and municipalities in countries throughout that region. What such studies show is that in contexts where access is limited, there are now opportunities for options based on affordable access. While such options may not be feasible in some parts of India, it can certainly work in other

parts, such as in Kerala, where there is the political will to extend affordable access to all communities in the state. Galperin and Bar (p. 77) highlight the factors that contribute to low-cost applications.

A number of technological innovations are...eroding the economic advantages hitherto enjoyed by large telecom operators, enabling microtelcos to extend ICT services further out into areas unattractive to conventional operators. These technologies, share a number of advantages, among them lower costs, modularity based on open standards, less regulatory overhead, simple configuration and maintenance, scalability, and support for multiple applications.

8. The 'circuit of culture' model can be used to understand the ICT4D as a process that includes both production and consumption. Gerald Goggin (2006), for example, has used this model to understand the cell phone in terms of five aspects—production, consumption, regulation, representation and identity.

With the benefit of hindsight and based on evidence from the field, it is now clear that the success of ICTs projects is conditioned by an integrated approach to development and social change. ICTs cannot, on their own, contribute to sustainable development. ICTs need an enabling environment and a supportive infrastructure. These projects need uninterrupted supplies of electricity along with technical and logistical support, the availability of technical know-how and the computerisation of back-end services. The success of e-governance projects for example, is based on the online availability of government information on a range of issues from numerous government departments, the required online forms, adequate turnarounds of response and the availability of accessible hardware and affordable services. In other words, ICTs projects require an integrated approach, an enabling environment and the required capital expenditures. All too often, ICTs projects are stand-alone initiatives that remain at a pilot level. Because of its capital-intensive nature, replicability and scaling-up remain a major issue.

The following assessment of an ICT for development project illustrates some of the challenges faced by such projects. The Bhoomi project, which is based on the computerisation of land records, is by far, one of the more 'successful' ICT for development projects in India. It also stands out as an exception because it has been critically assessed by social scientists. One of the lessons out of the Bhoomi project that needs to be considered is the fact that even in the context of technological applications directed towards progressive causes—the factoring-in of the role played by context is absolutely critical to the success or otherwise, of the project. To put it bluntly, while technological projects, in principle, can cut out the middle man, the power of grounded bureaucracies is formidable.

Assessing the Bhoomi Project

The Bhoomi Project is a significant achievement on its own right and is an example of the way in which a ICTs project can be used in e-governance, for data processing, information production and access supportive of the RTI. Given the fact that the bulk of Indian labour is employed in the agricultural sector, the ownership of land is a critical, survival issue. For centuries, small farmers in India have been exploited by landlords, money-lenders and in the post-Independence period, by corrupt government functionaries, such as village accountants who were entrusted as the keepers of land records. Tens of thousands of small farmers have been tricked out of their land. For all those involved in subsistence agriculture in India, the computerisation of land records enabled their right to information. The computerisation of land records project was started by the Indian government during 1988–1989. Since then, a number of Indian states have embarked on a computerisation of land records projects, although to date and for a variety of reasons, the Bhoomi (land) project in Karnataka has been the most successful. Following on from a Computerisation of Land Records Scheme started by the Government of Karnataka in 1991, the state secretary for e-government, Rajeev Chawla, played an instrumental role in the completion of this project in March 2002. Supported with central government funding, resources from the Revenue Department of Karnataka and software designed by the Bangalore-based National Informatics Centre (NIC), the project's data processing achievements are quite staggering. These include the following:

- Close to ten thousand officials worked for 18 months on the computerisation of 20 million land tenure records
- These land records belonged to 6.7 million land owners in 176 sub-districts in Karnataka state in 27,000 villages
- The records are based on 47 information fields covering everything crops, yield, irrigation, soil, mortgage details to ownership
- The Record of Rights, Tenancy and Crops (RTC) form can be accessed via 176 ICT kiosks situated in sub-districts throughout Karnataka
- Access is based on finger-print based identification system based on a 'Bio-Matrix Fingerprint Device' (Bhoomi Online n.d.)

Richard Heeks (2004) refers to two important benefits related to the computerisation of land records. First, the role of ICTs in *disintermediating*, thereby cutting the role of middlemen and gatekeepers. In the context of Karnataka, like in the rest of India, land records were traditionally kept by village accountants who had the power to record, manipulate and change land records—a life and death issue for small farmers, most of whom owned less than a hectare. These 9,000 village accountants occupied a powerful position as they not only maintained land records, including registers and maps in these areas, but used their monopoly position to advance corrupt practices, such as bribes. For a hefty bribe, land records were frequently 'mutated', most often to the benefit of a large farmer. Many small farmers lost their land because of the operation of this corrupt system. One account of village accountants in Karnataka reveals the scale of the corruption: In the Bangalore division, under the manual system, the equivalent of US$25 billion worth of government land was manipulated and shown in the name of private elites. Second, Heeks refers to the processes of *automation* of public sector processes that effectively deny scope for corruption. Once the records have been computerised, checks and balances are employed to ensure that the mutation of records is inter-subjectively attested. There are other benefits as well. For example, there is the benefit of *network externalities*. As more farmers access these computerised databases, there is a possibility that demand for this service and other digital services will lead to an increase in the array of possibilities, e-commerce, e-education, e-governance, e-health. In the case of Karnataka, this promises an especially interesting prospect—bridging the urban–rural digital divide and the universalising of e-governance, a project that cuts across a range of government departments today, including education, revenue, animal husbandry, agriculture, forest, home, housing, planning and public works.

The political scientist, James Manor (2006), in an informative piece on governance reform in two states in India, quotes findings from an independent survey of Bhoomi that supports the view that this project is of a superior quality in comparison with the previous manually operated system of land record maintenance:

> 80.3% of respondents found the new system 'very simple' to use and 9.6% found it 'simple'. The total of 89.9% stands in marked contrast to 44.1% of users who had continued to obtain RTCs in the old way, by hand from village accountants. 69.2% of *Bhoomi* users required no help in obtaining their documents from kiosks—compared to only 25.4% of those using the other method. 42.4% of those using the new system spent 10 minutes or less doing so, and a further 33.9% spent between 11 and 30 minutes. Users of the old system met with far greater delays. 72.0% of those accessing the new system came away from their first visits to the kiosks with the job having been done, while a mere 5.1% of those resorting to the old system achieved results on their first visits.

However, as against these findings, there are real concerns with the impact of disintermediation, given that for poorer farmers, personal contact is important. In fact, evidence from the Bhoomi project does seem to suggest that 'disintermediation' is, at times, a temporary phenomenon and that bureaucracies often find ways to short-circuit transparency systems. Benjamin et al. (2007: 16), in a study of the Bhoomi project carried out in 2004, highlight the fact that corruption has become even more of a problem with ordinary farmers now having to negotiate corruption at a *taluk* office level rather than just the village accountant at a local level.

> Many of the more experienced respondents linked the increased corruption and time taken to the closure of village level offices and centralization of all functions to the taluk level. Their view was that while bribes had to be paid even in the pre-Bhoomi situation, it was limited to the VA and the RI. Some even justified this payment and argued that it was the VA and RI who helped them understand complex land procedures. More important, the location of the revenue office at the village level before the Bhoomi program meant that 'pressure' could be applied on the officials to act. With the shifting of the office to the taluk level, however, this is not possible as the process involves four administrative layers, or 'tables' as they termed it: the VA, the RI, the Siresdhar, and the Thasildar/Computer centre. Also, in the pre-Bhoomi situation, bribes were locally negotiated and affordable, and these were usually differentiated by large and small farmers and linked to complex obligatory relationships in the village. In the post-Bhoomi period, as we discuss later, the process is dominated by a network and system of various 'agents' who have set a 'market rate', and systematized bribing to make it all pervasive, especially in taluks experiencing rapid development. (See also Vasudevan 2007: 109–110.)

Notwithstanding the real, qualitative, tangible benefits associated with this project, there is a sense in which this and other ICTs projects are deeply, technologically determinist. It is simply quite extraordinary that those who execute such projects steadfastly refuse to acknowledge the need to address critical, non-technological issues that often play a determining role in the implementation of such projects. The words of Dan Schiller (1996: 169) may be quoted at length here:

> Regularly, consideration of such topics serve(s) to shift attention away from the continuing experience of social division, aggravated inequality, and political conflict. 'Information' immediately lifted analysis free and clear of 'culture's' rich sediment.... 'Information' likewise abstracted altogether away from social life and social process.... In shifting discussion onto what purported to be wholly new grounds, the ideologists of 'information' sought to re-establish a crucial analytical distance from lived, and conflictual, experience.

Operationalising Bhoomi

So what are some of these larger issues that the Bhoomi project has failed to recognise and address?

As a networked technology, ICTs work best when it is integrated into information-flows occurring at a variety of levels. In other words, the more integrated the project, the more possibilities for leveraging information for productive purposes. All too often though, ICT projects remain stand-alone or at best are only networked in limited ways thus falling short of maximising the potential of information-flows in development and social change. Despite support given to e-governance by the government of Karnataka, the Bhoomi project in the words of De and Sen (2004: 557) 'is a silo application. It was funded, staffed and promoted by the Revenue Department of Karnataka and other departments did not participate in its design nor do they use the data available on the system'. This lack of prior integrated planning for a project that has bearings on other government sectors—the agriculture department, commercial tax department, food and civil supplies department, rural development and Panchayati Raj (local self-government) department, is indicative of one of the structural barriers in the deployment of ICTs in development. Without cross-departmental computerisation, it would seem that the Bhoomi project will remain little more than an access point for land records. In fact, the larger intent of the Record of RTC form was for it to be used as a form of Social Identity that could be used to obtain bank loans, even to be used 'as collateral for bail'. It would seem that this larger intent is severely restricted, given that such data cannot easily be cross-referenced in other government departments. The lack of convergence, in other words, remains a key issue awaiting a solution.

There are, however, more elemental problems related to the Bhoomi project. The computerisation of these land records was not preceded by a thorough clean-up of records, many of which had been 'mutated' through corrupt dealings. In other words, the massive task of keying in data was, in one sense, a purely functional exercise, a job well done in a technical, bureaucratic sense, but one that merely transferred problem records from a 'manual' system to a computerised one. A report on the Bhoomi project states that in north Karnataka, a region where feudalism is still rampant, '32 farmer's lands had been recorded in the Village Accountant's (VA) names prior to computerisation.... The man immediately sold the lot before Bhoomi began' (Acharya 2003: 3). These types of irregularities have not been dealt with, resulting in a situation in which, those who are victims of the manual system, are not much better off now with the computerised system. Prakash and De (2007: 273) refer to this and other issues with the Bhoomi project.

> Landless farmers, some of whom have an unofficial sanction to the lands they farm, do not benefit from the enhanced transparency of the new system. These farmers own a document called a saguvali chit, and this is an official record that states their right to farm on the land. This document is not part

of the Bhoomi database and so such farmers cannot check their status on the system. The larger issues related to transparency in the land records adjustment and updation process though remains unaffected by the new Bhoomi system. Many respondents noted that their title deeds, which is their official record of ownership of land and is a unique document, had not been updated in many years, sometimes stretching back decades. The cadastral maps, maintained by the VA, had also not been updated and few knew the status of the maps. Other documents related to land ownership and transfer, such as the *khata* (land title) register, cadastral maps marking boundaries, *akarband* (details of survey numbers), *tippani* (sketch of the surveyed land), etc. remained unaffected by the Bhoomi system and also remained unavailable to the citizens for scrutiny. In the urgency to meet deadlines, the Bhoomi project designers bypassed such concerns affecting the overall quality of land records. Bhoomi has computerized only one document out of many that are used for land administration.

Their overall assessment is that the system favours large farmers. They also make the point that there is a need to rehabilitate the role of the VA to make it more transparent rather than excise the role altogether.

Furthermore, the new system, unless monitored, still offers the possibility for corruption—given that those who operate Bhoomi kiosks situated in the 177 district headquarters can and do exploit the ignorance of peasants and rural farmers. The role of the VAs, although diminished, is still in evidence given that they continue to be involved in updating information on land records that is keyed into the system. Such irregularities however, remain insignificant in the light of the fact that the 'modern' system of land tenure is incomplete in India. The lawyer-activist Lawrence Liang (2005: 7) has made the following observation on the present scenario:

> In ... Bangalore ... the urban planning authority ... provides for approximately 15–20% of housing requirements, while another 12-15% are met by private developers. The rest of the city emerges outside of planned development and is hence outside of the law. Most urban citizens have no choice but to build, buy or rent illegal dwellings since they cannot either afford the cheapest legal accommodation, or because there is not enough supply to meet the demands of a growing city, marked by high migration as a result of the new information technology dreams.

There are infrastructural bottlenecks and, in particular, issues to do with irregular supplies of electricity. This is a serious issue, particularly in the state of Karnataka which has had a notorious reputation for outages both in its capital city, Bangalore and elsewhere. The lack of electricity has led to dysfunctional Bhoomi kiosks that are unable to deliver on a key promise of computerisation—immediacy and prompt delivery of documents. In a study carried out in Gulbarga District, north Karnataka,

Ahuja and Singh (2006: 77) note a variety of factors from interrupted power supplies to the distances farmers travelled to access these kiosks as disadvantages in an otherwise reliable system:

> Farmers often have to travel long distances to obtain RTCs resulting in longer time and more money.... The taluka (district) centre is plagued by regular, almost daily power outages. Because the computer kiosk does not have a generator back-up for uninterrupted power supply, the process of obtaining RTCs often involved long delays.

Ahuja and Singh also refer to what is a structural problem—the inability of this system to unearth the evidence of 'surplus land' or produce the necessary evidence in support of land reform legislations (p. 74). In a real sense, therefore, this project of e-governance is based on an information management model, which has improved the efficiency of a public service but has not contributed towards citizens participating in a deliberate sense in social change. Olli Maenpaa (2004: 18) refers to one of the unintended consequences of e-governance—a digital divide: 'While the ICTs facilitate provision of services to citizens, the bureaucracy, on the other hand, becomes equipped with tools, which are considered as excessively sophisticated from the perspective of ordinary citizens unless the citizens have the requisite new skills and e-literacy.' She adds: 'Such tools could prove equally complicated for the representatives of the people thus limiting the opportunities to put information technology into beneficial use.' In a report on the provision of 'Simputer'-based handsets for the VA (Bhoomi-Suggi project), the gap between principles and practice is highlighted.

> There are clear measurable goals for the project: the productivity of VAs, the expedient access to data, and given the infrastructure of handhelds, connectivity, back-end, a trained end-user group (the village accountants in this case), the potential for additional services that can be provided to the village communities. However, none of these goals were part of the tendering process. Without such measurable benefits being part of the debate, the discussion about this project was sidetracked into which is the right handheld to use, and how to bring down the cost of the device so that 9000 units can be bought cheaply. The project has not scaled up beyond the pilot.

There is also the issue of ICT kiosks. The number 177 is small when compared to the access needs of small farmers who often spend a day or more travelling to a sub-district office to collect their land records. There is definitely a need for more kiosks—but kiosks with multi-functions. It would seem that a stand-alone kiosk only capable of supplying land records is a huge waste of a technology that can be used to provide a range of services, from telephony to e-commerce and extensive information related to e-governance. This points towards a larger issue—the fact that ICTs projects tend to be capital intensive, a major issue for extensive computerisation projects in the developing world.

The most serious issue is the lack of a political will to ensure the state-wide implementation of 'transparency'. The privacy of Bhoomi records is difficult for small farmers to maintain, especially for those who have not paid land taxes and who therefore, are vulnerable. De (2006: 326) makes a pertinent point, as quoted below:

> The data from Bhoomi is not used by the government to plan for and provide any sort of insurance or other protective package to farmers of Karnataka. This is a possibility that some supply-side officials have considered. Some agents, who help with buying and selling of land (also known as document writers), in the Bangalore periphery region, said that Bhoomi data, since it was not protected and anyone could have access to it, was being used by land sharks to identify properties that were vulnerable (as the farmers owning them had suffered repeated droughts and many loans had been taken against them). Directed queries in the database were used to identify those farmers in the taluk who had not paid land taxes (usually a nominal sum) and such farmers were targeted. The sharks would then manipulate and bribe taluk officials to grab control of the land. Very little data could be collected as to the extent of this activity but several document writers corroborated this story. This data points to the reduced security of farmers that is helped by the Bhoomi system by the facility of database queries.

While 'transparency' in the Bhoomi project has to some extent, been achieved—the corruption of 9,000 village accountants pales in comparison with the thousands of government functionaries who stand to lose by the universalisation of 'transparency' and 'accountability' measures. In this sense, it is yet to be seen whether the Bhoomi project is the beginning of a state-wide clean-up of the development process or whether it will be allowed to exist in splendid isolation from the development mainstream.

The lessons also suggest that an efficient land information–management system cannot be solely based on a potentially 'disruptive technology'. For the disruption to occur, there has to be a prior commitment to social change.

The IT Fix and Issues with E-waste

One looming issue related to ICT4D is that of e-waste. At the core of e-waste are products associated with the information and knowledge economy and digitally networked, convergent technologies. While there are certainly benefits related to connectivities, what is to be done with the mountains of discarded electronic technologies is a major environmental and health issue in India, as it is the case elsewhere. India produces 330,000 metric tonnes of e-waste annually and is also a bulk recipient of e-waste from other countries, particularly from the USA and the EU. Skinner et al. (2010: 9) make the point that estimation of e-waste in India is an inexact science, given the poor record-keeping of domestic e-waste and inadequate monitoring of imported e-waste. The government's E-Waste (Management and Handling) Rule of 2011 that will come into effect in 2012, has mandated that electronics manufacturers and government departments contribute to the establishment of collection centres and are involved in environmentally friendly e-waste management (Morden 2011).

The EU's Waste Electrical and Electronic Equipment Directive (WEEE Directive) that became law in 2003 highlights the responsibilities of manufacturers in the collection, disposal and recycling of e-waste. This legislation was a response to the need to annually recycle 6.4 million tonnes of e-waste in the EU. The UK was one of the last of the EU countries to adopt the WEEE Directive in July 2007. While the directive is sound enough, there are issues with its operationalisation, in particular, the additional costs related to the recycling of e-waste that inevitably is passed on to the consumers. The establishment of large e-waste recycling plants in Europe is definitely a step in the right direction, although the sheer volume of global e-waste is bound to result in contraventions of the Basel Convention. Canada, a country that is a signatory to the Basel Convention and that has implemented 'E-Waste Product Stewardship' in most of its provinces/territories, with the exception of Newfoundland and Labrador, the Northwest Territories, Nunavut, Prince Edward Island and Yukon, has been involved in the dumping of e-waste in some countries, including India. In 2006, federal agencies seized fifty containers of e-waste in the Port of Vancouver bound for China—merely the tip of the iceberg. 27 companies settled out of court and paid up to C$2,000 apiece (see Lachance n.d.).

E-waste is simply not an issue of out-of-date IT products and its disposal, but is also linked to the state, the exercise of state power and the extension of neo-colonial relationships in a context characterised by a generally low priority given to e-waste recycling and its exports, irrespective of whether or not countries are party to electronic waste–recycling laws. E-waste, in other words, is yet to become a global priority and is enveloped by grey areas of policy and practice. In the US, the Environmental Protection Agency that is supposed to monitor exports of the only 'officially' recognised hazardous e-waste in that country—Cathode Ray Tubes (CRTs) has done very little to enforce this rule. In an interesting Government Accountability Office (GAO) testimony on electronic waste, John Stephenson (2008: 2) reports on the findings from an undercover operation:

> Posing as fictitious buyers from Hong Kong, India, Pakistan, Singapore and Vietnam, among other countries, we found 43 electronics recyclers in the United States who were willing to export to us broken, untested, or nonworking CRTs under conditions that would violate the CRT rule.

The testimony goes on to add that some of these companies were actively involved in Earth Day 2008 recycling events, and that most 'used electronics can be legally exported from the United States with no restrictions' (p. 10). States in the developed world, whether a party or not, to such laws, continue to find ways to export their e-waste to the developed world. And most countries in the developing world are not in a position to obstruct e-waste overtures from the developed world. Praveen Dalal (n.d.) gives an example to explain this situation:

> The two largest nations exporting their e-wastes are the United States and Britain. According to a British Environmental Protection Agency Report, Britain shipped out 25,000 tons of e-waste to South Asia…in 2005 the US recycled about $2 billion worth of electronic equipment, which may be just 20 per cent of the e-waste it generated, much of which found its way to India, China, Southeast Asia and Africa.

It is clear that there is a global political economy of e-waste that involves states, manufacturers, exporters, importers, recycling and re-sale units, involved in a trade that is worth millions of dollars.

The recycling of e-waste in Indian cities is carried out by those who have been pushed out of agriculture and onto the urban fringes. Violet Pinto (2008), in an article on e-waste in India, refers to the fact that over one million people are involved in e-waste recycling:

> Of the total e-waste generated in the country, western India accounts for the largest population at 35%, while the southern, northern and eastern regions account for 30, 21 and 14%, respectively. The top states in order of highest contribution to waste electrical and electronic equipment (WEEE) include Maharashtra, Andhra Pradesh, Tamil Nadu, Uttar Pradesh, West Bengal, Delhi, Karnataka, Gujarat, Madhya Pradesh and Punjab. The city-wise ranking of the largest WEEE generators is Mumbai, Delhi, Bangalore, Chennai, Kolkatta, Ahmedabad, Hyderabad, Pune, Surat and Nagpur.

While there is a thriving refurbishment and resale market, there are issues related to the health of recyclers, the majority of whom work in the informal sectors along with the management of e-waste that currently finds its way into landfills and waterways.

In response to growing international pressure from non-government agencies, such as Greenpeace, the Indo–German–Swiss e-waste initiative and local groups, such as Toxiclink, the Government of India, has announced the finalising 'of the world's strictest set of rules on disposing of electronic waste' that also includes a 'complete ban on import of any kind of electronic and electrical equipment for dismantling, recycling and disposal purposes' (*The Economic Times* 2009). This new rule will also place responsibility on the manufacturers to recycle e-waste and encourages the setting-up of official e-waste recycling plants. However, if the Greenpeace report (2008) entitled 'Take Back Blues: An Assessment of E-Waste Takeback in India' is anything to go by, it would seem that the implementation of these rules will be fraught. The study found that with the exception of one foreign company—Acer—and two Indian companies—WIPRO and HCL—the major foreign vendors, including Apple, Microsoft, Panasonic, PCS Technology, Philips, Sharp, Sony, Sony Ericsson and Toshiba did not offer take back services (p. 10). The report also reveals that of those that did offer these services, that of Dell, HP, Lenovo and Zenith did not function (p. 2) and that none of the major vendors were involved in educating the public on this service (p. 12).

E-waste is an issue that requires serious attention by the government of India. While manufacturers and vendors certainly need to invest in e-waste management, it is also necessary for the government to recognise and support those involved in e-waste recycling in the informal sectors through the provision of policies and environments conducive to safe recycling of e-waste.

Conclusion

There is a need for balanced assessments of ICTs projects for development in India. While governments, non-government agencies such as the World Bank and the Food and Agricultural Organization (UNO), the private sector and civil society continue to invest in ICTs projects, there is also a vital need for comparative studies and assessments of the impact of ICTs projects and their contribution to development and social change. This is essential for without adequate benchmarks, learnings, knowledge of successes and failures, the potential of ICTs projects would remain a mystery. An enabling environment must, therefore, include opportunities for women and marginalised sectors of society to effectively use ICTs for their development. Their involvement in the planning and delivery of ICTs projects along with other stakeholders, is a strategic choice that needs to be made by organisations involved in supporting ICTs for development and social change.

The information technology scholar, Robin Mansell has, for example, argued that there is a need for investment in 'learning and social networking innovation' and not just innovations in technical systems. She has also argued that learning should precede ICT applications, that there ought to be significant public sector investments in achieving these goals and that ICTs need to be configured and embedded in local contexts for it to make a difference. Prof. Mansell's views are pertinent to this discussion since it can be argued that in the majority of ICT4D applications, technological criteria take precedence over an adequate grappling with social context.

Professor Mansell's observations indirectly deal with the issue of sustainability—economic sustainability, social sustainability and institutional sustainability and the need for long-term investments—financial, physical, social capital along with content capital. ICTs are complex technologies and that the best results come from it being efficiently networked. An e-governance project for instance, requires efficient two-way flows, access to information that is regularly updated, access to and affordable use of ICTs, clients who have the required training to access and process information and of course, the political will to sustain the enterprise.

An equally problematic issue is the inability to factor in social context. If a telecentre is located in a village where divisions exist—caste, class and gender—it would be more likely that not that access to and use of the tele-centre will be conditioned by these social divisions. The question is, of course, whether investors take sufficient interest in dealing with such pre-existing issues as part of their project. One can argue that the sustainability of a project will be based on the extent to which such issues are factored in. Another equally important issue is whether projects are based on the prior ascertainment of needs and whether or not all stakeholders are involved in the p'anning and implementation of the project. Again, evidence from the field would suggest that the quality of participation varies from project to project. While the Grameen mobile phone project for women in rural Bangladesh, which was based on a micro-credit initiative, certainly helped these women to earn a better income—participation in multi-stakeholder projects, such as tele-centres have been of variable quality. Needs assessment is critical to such projects, although it is not always done. In the context of poverty, unemployment and lack of opportunities, people need to be convinced that ICT projects contribute to food security, employment security and to greater opportunities for social and economic advancement. Finally, there is the need for a proactive policy related to e-waste, given the very serious health and environmental consequences of recycling, dumping and overlooking of electronic wastelands.

References

Acharya, K. 2003. 'Flaws in Boomi, India's Model E-governance Project, Infochange Technology'. Available at: http://infochangeindia.org/technology/features/flaws-in-bhoomi-india-s-model-e-governance-project.html (accessed on 24 February 2012).

Ahuja, M. and A. P. Singh. 2006. 'Evaluation of Computerisation of Land Records in Karnataka: Evidence from Gulbarga District', *Economic and Political Weekly*, 41 (1): 69–77.

Andrade, A. D. and C. Urquhart. 2010. 'The Affordances of Actor Network Theory in ICT for Development Research', *Information Technology and People*, 23 (4): 352–374.

Avgerou, C. 2010. 'Discourses on ICT and Development', *Information Technologies and International Development*, 6 (3): 1–18.

Benjamin, S., R. Bhuvaneswari, P. Rajan and Manjunatha 2007. 'Bhoomi: 'E-Governance', or, an Anti-Politics Machine Necessary to Globalise Bangalore', pp. 1–53, A CASUM-M Working Paper. Available at: http://casumm.files.wordpress.com/2008/09/bhoomi-e-governance.pdf (accessed on 27 October 2010).

Best, M. and R. Kumar. 2008. 'Sustainability Failures of Rural Telecentres: Challenges from the Sustainable Access in Rural India (SARI) Project', *Information Technologies and International Development*, 4 (4): 31–45.

Bhoomi Online. n.d. 'See Freedom in the Fields: Bhoomi Online Delivery of Land Records in Karnataka'. Available at: http://unpan1.un.org/intradoc/groups/public/documents/UN/UNPAN023395.pdf (accessed 25 February 2012).

Boyle, J. n.d. *A Politics of Intellectual Property: Environmentalism for the Net*, (pp.1–23) available at: http://www.wcl.american.edu/pub/faculty/boyle (accessed 5 June 2007).

Dalal, P. 'E-Waste in India'. n.d. Available at: http://unpan1.un.org/intradoc/groups/public/documents/APCITY/UNPAN029841.pdf (accessed 11 July 2010).

De, R. 2006. 'Evaluation of E-Government Systems: Project Assessment vs Development Assessment', *Electronic Government*, 4084: 317–328.

De, Rahul and C. Sen. 2004. 'The Complex Nature of E-Government Projects: A Case Study of Bhoomi, an Initiative in Karnataka, India', *Lecture Notes in Computer Science*, 3183: 556–557.

Ekbia, H. R. 2009. 'Digital Artifacts as Quasi-Objects: Qualification, Mediation, and Materiality', *Journal of the American Society for Information Science and Technology*, 60 (12): 2554–2566.

Galperin, H. and F. Bar. 2006. 'The Microtelco Opportunity: Evidence from Latin America', *Information Technologies and International Development,* 3 (2): 73–86.

Goggin, G. 2006. *Cell Phone Culture: Mobile Technology in Everyday Life.* New York: Routledge.

Greenpeace. 2008. 'Take Back Blues: An Assessment of E-Waste Take Back in India', *Greenpeace,* Bangalore, August, pp. 1–28. Available at: http://www.greenpeace.org/raw/content/india/press/reports/take-back-blues.pdf (accessed on 10 August 2010).

Harris, J. 2005. 'The Ordering of Things: Organisation in Bruno Latour', *The Sociological Review,* 53 (1): 163–177.

Heeks, R. 2004. 'Building Transparency, Fighting Corruption with ICTs', *Information Technology in Developing Countries,* 14 (3), December: 2–3.

———. 2010. 'Do Information and Communication Technologies (ICTs) Contribute to Development?', *Journal of International Development,* 22 (5): 625–640.

Keniston, K. 2002. 'Grassroots ICT Projects in India', *Social Implications of Computers in Developing Countries,* 11 (3): 1–7.

Kleine, D. and T. Unwin. 2009. 'Technological Revolution, Evolution and New Dependencies: What's New about ICT4D?', *Third World Quarterly,* 30 (5): 1045–1067.

Lachance, I. n.d. 'Vancouver Computer Recycler Says Illegal Canadian E-Waste Dumping "No surprise"', *Free Geek.* Available at: http://freegeekvancouver.org/en/canadian_ewaste_dumping (accessed on 8 July 2009).

Lash, S. 2002. Critique of Information. London, Thousand Oaks, New Delhi: SAGE Publications.

Liang, L. 2005. 'Porous Legalities and Avenues of Participation', *Sarai Reader 2005: Bare Acts,* pp. 6–17.

Maenpaa, O. 2004. 'E-Governance: Effects on Civil Society, Transparency and Democracy', Paper presented at the E-governance: Challenges and Opportunities for Democracy, Administration and Law Conference, IIAS-IISA, Seoul, 14–18 July.

Manor, J. 2006. 'Successful Governance Reform in Two Indian States: Karnataka and Andhra Pradesh', IDS Discussion Paper 385 [Online]. Available at: http://www1.worldbank.org/publicsector/PoliticalEconomy/GovernancereformsIndia.rtf (accessed on May 2010).

Mansell, Robin. 1998. *Knowledge Societies: Information Technology for Sustainable Development.* New York: Oxford University Press.

Mazzarella, W. 2010. 'Beautiful Balloon: The Digital Divide and the Charisma of New Media in India', *American Ethnologist,* 37 (4): 783–804.

Mitev, N. 2009. 'In and Out of Actor Network Theory: A Necessary but Insufficient Journey', *Information Technology and People,* 22 (1): 9–25.

Morden, J. 2011. 'India Passes Law vs E-Waste', *Asia-Pacific Future Gov,* 24 June. Available at: http://www.futuregov.asia/articles/2011/jun/24/india-passes-law-vs-e-waste/ (accessed on 9 October 2011).

Pinto, V. N. 2008. 'E-Waste Hazard: The Impending Challenge', *The Indian Journal of Occupational and Environmental Medicine,* 12 (2): 65–70. Available at: http://www.ncbi.nlm.nih.gov/pmc/articles/PMC2796756/ (accessed on 9 October 2011).

Prakash, A. and R. De. 2007. 'Importance of Development Context in ICT4D Projects: A Study of Computerisation of Land Records', *Information Technology and People*, 20 (3): 262–281.

Schiller, D. 1996. *Theorizing Communication: A History*. New York: Oxford University Press.

Skinner, A., Y. Dinter, A. Lloyd and P. Strothman, P. 2010. The Challenges of E-waste Management in India: Can India Draw Lessons from the EU and USA?, *Asien*, 117: 7–26.

Sreekumar, T. T. 2007. 'Cyber Kiosks and Dilemmas of Social Inclusion in Rural India', *Media, Culture and Society*, 29 (6): 869–889.

Stephenson, J. B. 2008. 'Electronic Waste. Harmful U.S. Exports Flow Virtually Unrestricted Because of Minimal EPA Enforcement and Narrow Regulation', Testimony before the Subcommittee on Asia, the Pacific, and the Global Environment Committee on Foreign Affairs, House of Representatives, United States Government Accountability Office, 17 September.

The Economic Times. 2009. 'India Prepares Strictest Rules on Disposing E-Waste', *The Economic Times*, 18 August. Available at: http://m.economictimes.com/PDAET/articleshow/4906529.cms (accessed on 23 June 2010).

Thomas, P. N. 2010. *Political Economy of Communications in India: The Good, the Bad and the Ugly*. Los Angeles, London, New Delhi, Singapore, Washington D.C.: SAGE Publications.

Vasudevan, R. 2007. 'Changed Governance or Computerised Governance? Computerised Property Transfer Processes in Tamil Nadu, India', *Information Technologies and International Development*, 4 (1): 101–122.

Walsham, G. 2010. 'ICTs for the Broader Development of India: An Analysis of the Literature', *The Electronic Journal on Information Systems in Developing Countries*, 41 (4): 1–20.

Section 3

Government 2.0 and Information Technology

The three chapters in this section—e-governance, software patenting and public sector software—deal with the challenges and opportunities for a government faced with transforming itself into a transparent and accountable Government 2.0 that is supportive of public interests. However, as the chapters indicate, this is no easy task as the government is involved in balancing out competing interests—its own interests, against that of the private sector and civil society. The chapter on e-governance explores the gaps between principle and practice and asks if 'governmentality' is the main intent of such investments. The chapter on software patenting reveals a government that is unsure of where to draw the line, given competing interests and the power of the software industry and its local supporters. Investments in public sector software are, however, indicative of the fact that the state is playing a role in contesting, even changing, the rules of the game in the matter of software deployments in e-government.

6

E-Government, E-Governance and Governmentality

India's growth as a significant software and IT hub has not only improved the country's export revenues but also led to a widespread belief that the country's embrace of the informational mode of production will provide the required momentum needed to usher India into the 21st century. There is also a concurrent belief that new information processes can likewise be deployed to create efficiencies and cut down bureaucratic red-tapism that is rife in India's gargantuan public administration network encompassing close to 18 million employees across the central, state, local and quasi-governmental sectors. Hence, the government's enthusiastic support for e-government, best illustrated by the National e-Governance Plan (NeGP) and 27 Mission Mode projects, any number of derivative policies, millions of rupees spent on the creation of infrastructure and investments on making the country e-friendly and the literally, hundreds of e-government projects spread throughout the country. The aim as described in the NeGP is to 'make all Government services accessible to the common man in his locality, through common service delivery outlets and ensure efficiency, transparency and reliability of such services at affordable costs to realise the basic needs of the common man'. The 27 Mission Mode projects include eight integrated projects, inclusive of the setting-up of 87, 419 common service centres in 17 states, e-courts, eight central projects inclusive of income tax, insurance, central excise, pensions and banking and 11 state projects inclusive of agriculture, land records, property registration and the establishment of e-Districts (see DIT: http://www.mit.gov.in/content/national-e-governance-plan, accessed on 24 February 2012). The outlay for the NeGP in the 2006–2011 period is in the region of US$5.47 billion or ₹230 billion (Prasad 2008). One key issue is the need to localise e-government and make it available in the language that people speak. While there are 22 constitutionally recognised languages in India, there are an infinite number of mother tongues and languages. There are also issues with inter-operability and standardisation. The fact that there isn't a single agency that currently enforces nation-wide standards related to e-government is also a major concern.

There are however a number of issues that the government faces in its implementation of e-government. Prominent among these are two issues highlighted by Mayer-Schonberger and Lazer (2007: 3):

> First...a prerequisite to its success is that citizens have the equipment and skills and feel comfortable and safe transacting online. General ease of use, but also security, integrity, privacy of transactional and personal data have to be maintained, as well as the authenticity of the transactional partners.... Successful implementation may therefore require significant engineering, marketing, and education efforts. Secondly, the online provision of public services requires governments to address equity questions between the digital haves and have-nots in a way that is not true of private actors.

While the government certainly has spent crores of rupees through multiple projects—Akashganga, E-Choupal, Drishtee, Gyandoot, RASI, Jagriti E-Sewa, Lokmitra to name a few, spread throughout the country—it can be argued that the mere presence of such projects and resources does not automatically signify its use, especially by the most deprived sections of the population. Perhaps one can argue that precisely due to the fact that the most deprived face a daily set of challenges linked to their very survival, that e-government options really are not a priority. When government, however, describes such options as priority, and as essential tools in its poverty alleviation campaigns—there is a need to assess whether in fact such projects make a real difference in the lives of the poor in India.

Dan Schiller (2000: 205), in his book *Digital Capitalism*, has described a scenario in the USA:

> A couple of thousand giant companies—as employers of workers labouring on networked production chains, as advertisers and, increasingly, as educators—today preside, not only over the economy but also over a large web of institutions involved in social reproduction: business, of course, but also formal education, politics and culture.

While the scale of that influence is smaller in India, there is a sense in which the spread of the network logic is inexorable, continuous and colonising. India's turn towards a neo-liberal market-led model of growth has led to what can be best described as the nationalisation of the concepts of 'efficiency, marketisation, accountability and decentralisation' (see Rajalekshmi 2007: 20). Perhaps the best contemporary example of the corporate–government nexus in India is the role played by the chairman of India's best known software exporter Infosys, Nandan Nilekani in steering the development of the National Unique Identity Project via the Unique Identification Authority of India (UIDAI) that was set up in November 2008 (see Mukherjee 2010). The private–public nexus in the context of e-government in India is worth exploring because it provides us with an opportunity to explore the extent to which the private sector is now poised to reap the benefits of India's embrace of the e-economy. While the Government of India continues to invest in public development expenditures, it is, in this post-liberalisation period, also open to the need for private sector investments in the financing, operation and management of e-government projects. There a number of different contract models of private public sector partnerships, although among the more common in India are the Build-Own-Operate (BOO) and Build-Operate-Transfer (BOT) models. While in some models, such as BOT, projects are designed, constructed and managed for a finite period after which assets are returned to the government, in the BOO model, the private firm operates the project on an indefinite basis. There is a major emphasis on the 'efficiency' coefficient in such partnerships—a belief that private sector expertise and skills will lead to a changing of attitudes of public administrators leading to a change in their delivery of services. The uptake of such models need to be seen in the context of public sector disinvestments in India and the emphasis on reduced costs, efficiency and transfers of technologies. While the private sector makes money through payment for transactions, the Indian government has given many of these firms a variety of tax incentives from import duty exemptions to subsidised land and other incentives. Typically for example, ICT kiosks and associated front-end activities are financed by firms while back end operations, such as telecommunications connections, etc. are supported by the government.

Issues with Public–private Partnerships (PPP) in E-Government

In line with the general tenor of this book though, one of the more interesting developments in India is the increasingly critical role played by some of the key private IT players in e-government, and moves by the civil society along with some actors in the government to restrict that role in the interest of the public. Microsoft, for example, has established more than 1,500 ICT kiosks in India and currently works with a number of state governments in the provision of multiple e-government services. Close to 150 e-governance applications in the country run on the Windows platform. Not only are companies like Microsoft involved in sponsoring national e-government summits, but they have also established their own awards for excellence in e-government as this press release (*Press Release* 2006) reveals:

> Microsoft India today announced the winners of its first 'Microsoft E-governance awards'. The first of the annual awards set up to recognize the most impactful E-governance applications in the country received over 300 nominations and the winners include 20 E-governance applications implemented across the country.... The projects nominated include those developed by the National Informatics Centre (NIC), State IT Departments, and Department of Information Technology, Government of India in partnership with Microsoft.

It is of course, interesting that all the awardees are state–sector institutions. Apart from Microsoft, Sun, IBM, TCS, HCL Infosystems among many other software firms are involved in PPPs in India. An example of such a project is the Bangalore-1 project that is a partnership between Karnataka state, CMS Computers Ltd. and Ram Informatics that involves the setting-up of ICT kiosks that facilitate Government–Business and Government–Citizens services. Nortel, Adobe, Cisco, Alcatel and Symantec sponsor the e-government trade show and are involved in setting-up platforms for e-government in India (see *Iways: Digest of Electronic Government Policy and Regulation* 2006). The Microsoft India website states:

> Microsoft is committed to work on transforming education, foster local innovation, and enable jobs and opportunities to sustain a continuous cycle of social and economic growth. Some of the initiatives towards this are, Partners in Learning (Project Shiksha), Project Bhasha, Project Jyoti, Project Vikas, Shared Access and Mobile Solutions. (Microsoft n.d.)

From a civil society and public sector perspective, the issue with the involvement of firms, such as Microsoft, in e-government is not as much with their partnerships that are arguably necessary, but the impact that this has on the larger political economy of informationalisation in India. A key area of concern is with the use and licensing of proprietorial software in e-government projects and its impact on the setting of open standards and support for software patents that is a subject for debate in India. Microsoft's battle with the Bureau of Indian Standards over its support for the Open Document Format against Microsoft's OXML standard is just one example of the moves by this company to extend its proprietorship over software and standards in India. There is a strong movement backed by civil society and concerned civil society that is aimed at ensuring that e-government in India is based on F/OSS.

The belief in the role played by the information mode of production in the shaping of the 'new' government is shared by a number of technocrat-politicians, most notably by the ex-chief minister of the southern Indian state of Andhra Pradesh, Chandra Babu Naidu, who become a national icon through his efforts to informationalise the public administration system in his state. Bin Yahya (2009: 382) describes Naidu's motivation:

> The chief minister's emphasis on IT was based on his belief that it could not only provide new jobs but 'SMART' governance. He was convinced that IT could transform governance and development in the state. eager to disperse the benefits of IT, Naidu provided internet connections to 22,000 *panchayats* (village councils) so that they could interact with the government and plug into a range of e-governance projects such as SmartGov, eSeva, APOnline, Online Transaction Processing (OLTP) System, Integrated Financial Information System (IFIS), e-procurement, data centre and others designed to reduce bureaucracy and expedite transactions.

While one can certainly argue against the limitations in Naidu's resolutely technocratic vision in a state that does have significant issues with poverty and Maoism, the information-fix as a way to redeem India's corrupt bureaucracy and provide services, is certainly an issue that many Indians sympathise with. A recent global report by the Hong Kong-based Political and Economic Risk Consultancy named India's bureaucracy as the most stifling. The country was given a score of 9.41 on a scale in which 10 was the worst possible score (see Morris 2010).

The New Informational Administration Model

The turn towards e-government is in a real sense, an indication of a move towards a new form of public administration, smart government, based on a qualitatively different approach to the delivery of services. The Weberian bureaucratic model is largely posited to have resulted in the creation of silos, inert empires that have presided over multiple inefficiencies in the planning and more importantly, delivery of services. As Bekkers (2007: 105) describes it, this change has multi-sectoral ramifications and is based on the adoption of new ICTs-based innovations.

- Product or service innovation, focused on the creation of new public services or products.
- Technological innovations that emerge through the creation and use of new technologies, such as the use of mobile devices and cell broadcasting to warn citizens in the case of an emergency;
- Process innovations, focused on the improvement of the quality and efficiency of the internal and external business processes, like the digital assessment of taxes;

- Organizational innovations, focused on the creation of new organizational forms, the introduction of new management methods and techniques, and new working methods. Examples are the creation of shared service centres or the use of quality systems;
- Conceptual innovations. These innovations occur in relation to the introduction of new concepts, frames of reference or even new paradigms, like the concept of New Public Management or the notion of governance; and
- Institutional innovations, which refer to fundamental transformations in the institutional relations between organizations, institutions, and other actors in the public sector. An example is the introduction of elements of direct democracy, through referenda in a representative democracy.

The adoption of such innovations is potentially revolutionary and it is therefore, not surprising that there are very few examples of governments around the world who have embraced wholeheartedly, new models of governance based on the deployment of conceptual and institutional innovations. One of the meanings of 'government' in Swahili is 'fierce secret' (see Article 19 1999), an apt descriptor of governments throughout the world, that are unsure of how to respond to new expectations from their publics, that are hinged on transparency and openness. The global spread of Freedom of Information and more potently, Right to Know–based RTI legislations, have presented governments with intractable problems mainly linked to the implementation of accountability and transparency. So, it is not altogether surprising that governments, more likely than not, have embraced product, technological, process and organisational innovations—that have resulted in a more efficient delivery of services through decentralised means, such as websites, e-government, rather than e-governance that is widely seen as the one basis for citizen's exercise of substantive democracy.

E-Government

Kunstelj and Vintar (2004: 133) describe e-government in terms of four stages:

1. Web presence—publishing basic information;
2. Interaction—more information, search engines, saving and printing of forms, communicating with employees via e-mail, links to other websites;
3. Transaction—offering transactions ranging from the triggering of processes (which correspond to particular service – using electronic forms to full electronic implementation of services and corresponding

> processes, including the case handling, receipt of the final product, and electronic signatures and payment if required;

4. Transformation—the long-term objective of e-government, allowing integrated services to be offered on the 'one-stop' principles, many processes occurring without customers having to be involved, making administrative operations more transparent and improving customer satisfaction.

They also point out that e-government in the context of the EU countries for the most part, consists of web presence and interaction but very little transaction and transformation. Such studies seem to suggest that e-government, to be fully functional, simply is conditioned by massive investments in networking, training and the computerisation of front-end and back-end services.

Thomas and Streib (2003: 98), in an article on citizen's access of e-government services in the state of Georgia, USA, report that 'those survey respondents who reported using government Web sites have been mostly seeking information rather than attempting to communicate information to government. This pattern no doubt reflects in part that government has been slow to adapt the Web to facilitate communication *from* citizens' (author's emphasis). Findings from another study, also in the USA, indicate that while individuals are largely satisfied with the services provided on government websites, they recognise that their government has 'not sufficiently addressed interactivity expectations' (Welch et al. 2004: 387). This gap signifies the vastly different approaches and expectations related to e-government as opposed to e-governance.

On the Notion of 'Governmentality'

E-government, one can argue, enhances what Foucault (1991:102–103) has described as 'governmentality'—that is essentially about administering and managing a territorially bound population. In Foucault's words:

1. The ensembles formed by the institutions, procedures, analyses and reflections, the calculations and tactics that allow the exercise of this very specific albeit complex form of power, which has as its target population, as its principal form of knowledge political economy, and as its essential technical means apparatuses of security.
2. The tendency which, over a long period and throughout the West, has steadily led towards the pre-eminence over all other forms (sovereignty, discipline, etc.) of this type of power which may be permed government, resulting, on the one hand, in the formation of a whole series of specific

governmental apparatuses, and on the other, in the development of a whole complex of *savoirs*.

3. The process, or rather the result of the process through which the state of justice of the Middle Ages, transformed into the administrative state during the fifteenth and sixteenth centuries, gradually becomes 'governmentalised'.

To Foucault, government was a body involved in shaping the very 'conduct of conduct', the shaping of relationships between the self and self, and the self and a plethora of institutions. Lemke (2001: 201–202) has argued that the turn towards governmentality needs to be seen in the context of the march of neo-liberalism and the consequent retreat of the welfare state in Europe.

> By means of the notion of governmentality the neo-liberal agenda for the 'withdrawal of the state' can be deciphered as a technique for government. The crisis of Keynesianism and the education in forms of welfare-state intervention therefore lead less to the state losing powers of regulation and control (in the sense of a zero-sum game) and can instead be construed as a reorganisation or restructuring of government techniques, shifting the regulatory competence if the state onto 'responsible' and 'rational' individuals. Neo-liberalism encourages individuals to give their lives a specific entrepreneurial form. It responds to stronger 'demand' for individual scope for self-determination and desired autonomy by 'supplying' individuals and collectives with the possibility of actively participating in the solution of specific matters and problems which had hitherto been the domain of state agencies specifically empowered to undertake such tasks. This participation has a 'price-tag': the individuals themselves have to assume responsibility for these activities and the possible failure thereof.

While Lemke's explanation may not hold entirely true for the situation in India, there is certainly a sense in which e-government has placed the onus on citizens to take responsibility, but in that process, led to the government becoming a disembodied entity, existing in virtual mode in cyberspace.

However, there are key issues in need of clarification as the scholarly focus on e-government becomes a growth industry. One issue of key importance is what to focus on—the ubiquity of informationalisation or the transformation of bureaucracy by these new technologies. As O'Loughlin (2007: 184) observes in a review of a book by Sandra Braman:

> No process is without an informational aspect and information is increasingly embedded in surfaces and bodies, then the informationality of things and events may not be our primary concern in political and social analysis. In fact, questions of bureaucratisation and other 'old' issues become more urgent and require re-thinking in today's 'informational' conditions.

This is a fair point, given that it would be wrong to surmise that an introduction of an innovation—in this case, new technologies—will automatically result in a radical overhaul of processes and of ways things are done. The deep-rooted bureaucracy linked to public administration is resilient to change and in the context of countries, such as India, the mere computerisation of courts—as for instance, e-courts—will not automatically result in the speedy clearance of the literally millions of cases that have not been resolved in courts throughout the length and breadth of India. In other words, the deployment of technologies simply has to be accompanied by a political will to train the Indian bureaucracy for 21st century tasks mediated by new technologies. One can, in other words argue, that e-government efficiencies are best witnessed in contexts characterised by the more or less complete disintermediation of middle-men, as for example, in the context of the Bhoomi project in Karnataka, but not in contexts, such as courts that exist and thrive because of a hierarchy that is deeply, synergised and based on finely graded flows of power and influence.

E-Government and E-Governance

Before we deal with whether or not the Indian government's embrace of new technologies in governance is, in fact, a strategy directed towards strengthening its control over its many and varied populations, it is best that we deal with the meanings attached to government and governance, e-government and e-governance. While government refers to that ensemble of public institutions that have authority, enforce obligations and connect to a diverse range of private people, institutions and processes, governance refers to

> the processes and institutions, both formal and informal, that guide and restrain the collective activities of a group. Government is the subset that acts with authority and creates formal obligations. Governance need not necessarily be conducted exclusively by governments. Private firms, associations of firms, nongovernmental organizations (NGOs), and associations of NGOs all engage in it, often in association with governmental bodies, to create governance; sometimes without governmental authority. (Saxena 2005: 2)

Saxena (2005: 3) also points out that e-government 'commonly refers to the processes and structures pertinent to the electronic delivery of government services to the public' while 'e-governance is the commitment to utilize appropriate technologies to enhance governmental relationships, both internal and external, in order to advance democratic expression, human dignity and autonomy, support economic development and encourage the fair and efficient delivery of services'. For the most part though, the two terms—e-government and e-governance—are used interchangeably in spite of the fact that they are related to different lineages—on the one hand to that tradition of governmentality and on the other to a multi-stakeholder and shall we say, mature vision of democracy which is conditioned by its shaping by citizens as well as by the government and other actors. A typical example of such usage is the following: 'E-governance can be defined as delivery of government services and information to the public using electronic means' (Paul 2007: 176). At the heart of public administration, there is a belief that its marriage with new technologies was long overdue, precisely because the core business of public administration is about information-gathering and its use in the allocation of resources. As Lenk (2007: 210) describes it, the core functions of public administration include 'gathering information about society in order to monitor it and to intervene when necessary, and intervening into the social fabric, chiefly by making decisions which allocate positions or resources to members of society'.

The accent on governance itself is relatively new and is, in a sense, both a recognition that citizens indeed want to participate in the making of the 'public', and is also a pragmatic response to a general fatigue with dominant politics and the evidence of massive gaps between policy and practice. To some extent, the accent on governance is led by the development industry who is keen to create a new framework for development expenditures based on multi-stakeholder processes in the many 'failed states' that exist in many regions of the world. While governance might have emerged in the context of reshaping governments in the developing world, its ramifications are just as problematic for developed world governments. While there is a general belief in the value of governance models that are inclusive, there is a contra-view that is hinged on the argument that the government is the most 'representative' of all institutions in any given country and therefore, should remain more than just 'first among equals'. Peters and Pierre (2006: 212) are critical of multi-stakeholder governance models because of the possibility of sectoral and other interests taking precedence over goal-based development. According to them: 'While this model of governance might be said to be sufficiently in touch with society to make good choices, those choice (sic) will not reflect the collective preferences of the polity but rather those of a very small segment of society.' New technological platforms, such as the Internet, offer the governments an opportunity to redeem its image as a caring and responsive entity and also offer its citizens a chance to be involved in conversations that enhance the public sphere. It offers a fresh opportunity to reinvent the practices and processes of public administration—from its moorings in what can be described as a colonial approach and attitude to its subjects characterised by a grudging reluctance to the sharing of information to one characterised by seamless, constant, top-down information-flows. While new technologies certainly do have the capacities to increase genuine interactivity, there is little evidence that the deployment of such technologies in the contexts of e-government in India have enhanced multi-way flows. While the Internet, in theory, does have the scope for such possibilities, in the context of e-government, its architectures are designed and weighted towards one-way flows from the government to its citizens. The rosy projections of e-government ushering in a promised land of communications, therefore, remains far-fetched and one can argue that what we do have in India are accentuated investments in e-government.

The key benefit of e-government is the opportunity to create one-stop windows—such as websites that allow for flows of information from the government to its citizens, leading to the strengthening of stronger governmentality. In other words, while e-government definitely extends efficiency, it also offers greater possibilities for the government to exert control through surveillance and centralised data gathering on citizens. In this sense, the Unique Identity Card project that is on the anvil will provide reliable information to the Government in India on each of its citizens, including significant and extraordinary data sets of information, resulting in a virtual memory bank of all Indian citizens. The fact that there is a huge market in personal information makes such captures of data potentially lucrative, with or without the benefit of privacy laws that have in any case been compromised in the context of the intrusive role of the state in the combating of terrorism. A lot, therefore, will depend on how governments decide to use this data. Given the potential for anti-minority politics in India, data sets on minorities and individuals can be used and abused by political parties and this remains a matter of concern. However, at the very same time, e-government can also result in people's access to information unmediated by middleman and third parties. The fact that, at least in theory, ordinary middle-class people in India no longer have to trudge to different government offices to fill in forms, wait interminable hours for service, bribe government functionaries to chase files, etc., does suggest towards the accruing of an incalculable benefit, although one can argue that the majority of ordinary people in India do not have access to the Internet and are, therefore, still reliant on the vagaries of government functionaries and their ways of functioning. The simplification of procedures and the management of records offer mutual benefits to both governments and to citizens.

In the context of India, the significance of e-government has been strengthened by the RTI movement. The citizen's right to know, to access, to deliberate, to converse and to communicate offers possibilities to enhance the exercise of substantive democracy. The mainstreaming of *jan sunwais* (public hearings) and social audits has contributed to transforming information from an abstract entity into a life-affirming force capable of change for the better in people's lives. The complementary growth of e-government and the RTI was probably unexpected and entirely fortuitous, although the synergies between these two movements can certainly make a difference. However, and in spite of possible synergies, we need to keep in mind that the two movements are based on very different conceptions of information—in the case of e-government, from the top-down and in the case of the RTI, from the bottom-up.

The Practice of E-Government in India: An Example from Tamil Nadu

There are, at any given time, literally hundreds of e-government initiatives in India. These include state-government–run websites that offer information on services, and one-stop sites for accessing application forms related to state and central government services. The Government of Tamil Nadu's website, for example, offers a number of online services, a separate section for downloading a variety of forms including birth/death certificates, nativity certificate, application for water connection, encumbrance certificate, ration card, driving license along with numerous other application forms. One can also access RTI-related material, and it also contains information on grievance procedures. On closer scrutiny, it is clear that the site does contain a lot of relevant information that can be useful for the public. However, the accent is on 'access'—not the submission of these forms. There is little or no information available on where these forms ought to be submitted. In this sense, all the website does is to facilitate access, although not enable online submissions. This is a critical oversight for it is the submission process that is riddled with malfeasance and corruption and this system will ensure that that continues. In other words, these various forms cannot be filled in and submitted online, but must be submitted at the relevant department. In other words, submission will involve travel and encounters with the bureaucracy. The Web Page Online Services of the Revenue Department includes services related to land records—a critical issue in a country in which such records are notoriously porous and open to alteration by third parties normally associated with public administration employees at Revenue, *taluk* and ·panchayat levels. While the viewing of such records is an important service, it does not allow for the printing of records. This again will require trudging to the relevant revenue office and negotiations with the bureaucracy. There is another more protracted problem related to the computerisation of land records—for if these records have not been cleaned prior to its computerisation, any verification or change will require extensive negotiations with what is the most notorious of all the bureaucracies in India. While the report on Land Reforms and Computerisation of Land Records issued by the Government of Tamil Nadu (http://www.tn.gov.in/ appforms/default.html, accessed on 9 June 2010) indicates that kiosks will be set up to access these records, the objectives of the Tamil-Nilam project, irrespective of the existence of these kiosks are, to say the least, ambitious.

> The objective of the TAMIL NILAM project is to ensure that land record data is fully computerized so that it could be used both for issue of copies of record of rights as well as for various other purposes, which are summarized as follows:
>
> * Faster processing and modification of existing data
> * Tamper proofing land data to reduce land disputes
> * Portability and easy accessibility of data
> * Quicker delivery of copies to land owners
> * Development of Cadastral based land Information System
> * To provide database for agricultural census
> * Integration of data with GIS and other administration purposes
> * Build a good decision support system and to facilitate queries on land data
> * Reduce corruption
> * Transparency & better public inter-face (Revenue Department 2012)

Whether or not the stated aims of this project are achievable, remains an issue, not only in Tamil Nadu, but also in other states, such as Goa and Karnataka that are well advanced with respect to the computerisation of land records. It is clear from this example that disintermediation remains partial and that there is ample scope for third parties to play a leading role in for example, any moves to 'modify' an existing land record. Deshpande (2007: 7) in a report on the computerisation of land records in India refers to some of the issues encountered in a central government-based Computerisation of Land Records Scheme.

> The scheme, however, is making slow progress. Some of the operational problems are: delayed transfer of funds to the implementing authority; delay in development of need-based software; poor computer training facilities for the field revenue staff; nonavailability of private contractors for data entry; and lack of administrative focus. Computerization only involves entering the available

land records (without any effort to correct them) and enabling their printout. More than computerization of land records guaranteeing the title to land should have received priority. It is a common observation in the villages that persons in whose name the land is recorded are either deceased or do not possess that land.

This project has been superseded by National Land Records Modernisation Programme (NLRMP) that is being implemented by India's NIC whose mandate includes the conceptualisation, development and implementation of e-government projects at state and central levels. While the objective of the NLRMP is to make the whole process a lot more transparent, it is still unclear as to how its objectives will be implemented.

> The main objective of the NLRMP is to develop a modern, comprehensive and transparent land records management system in the country with the aim to implement the conclusive land-titling system with title guarantee, which will be based on four basic principles, i.e., (i) a single window to handle land records (including the maintenance and updating of textual records, maps, survey and settlement operations and registration of immovable property), (ii) the mirror principle, which refers to the fact that cadastral records mirror the ground reality, (iii) the curtain principle which indicates that the record of title is a true depiction of the ownership status, mutation is automated and automatic following registration and the reference to past records is not necessary, and (iv) title insurance, which guarantees the title for its correctness and indemnifies the title holder against loss arising on account of any defect therein. (National Land Records Modernisation Program n.d.)

Table 6.1 illustrates some of the issues related to e-government in India.

Table 6.1: ICT Application and Impact: E-Governance in India

ICT Application and Development Goal	Achieved Impact	Further Implications
Computerised back-end administrative systems: more efficient services to citizens	• Relatively marginal impact due to difficulty of changing administrative culture and complex governance structures • Focus shifting to front-end systems	• Culture needs to shift to working more efficiently and creatively but very hard to achieve • Need to consider link between front-end and back-end government systems
E-government direct services: visible direct services	• Some success stories but beneficiaries are mainly the better-off • Computerised systems do not necessarily reduce corruption • Core (back end) administrative processes may remain untouched	• Pro-poor systems need to have this as a criterion for success rather than financial viability • Corruption and administrative inefficiency need to be addressed in conjunction with technology

ICT Application and Development Goal	Achieved Impact	Further Implications
Use of GIS: better planning and implementation of infrastructure	• GIS may be something of a mismatch with local cultural attitudes and administrative structures • Top-down projects may fail due to failure to deliver benefits at 'lower levels'	• Need to construct knowledge alliances that integrate top-down scientific knowledge with bottom-up indigenous knowledge

Source: Walsham (2010: 8).

What is increasingly clear from the available literature on e-government in India is that critical to its levelling up as e-governance, there is the need for political will. In the context of a variety of political formations and political rule in the various states in India, the role of political will simply cannot be underestimated. Cross-party consensus on e-governance, as is largely the case in Kerala, the role played by politicians such as Chandra Babu Naidu (Andhra Pradesh) and civil servants such as Ajay Kumar (Kerala) and C. Umashankar (Tamil Nadu), among others have been critical to the implementation and mainstreaming of e-government in some regions in India.

I would like to highlight some of the issues facing e-government in India by highlighting two concrete examples—the Akshaya Project from Kerala and Gyandoot from Madhya Pradesh.

Akshaya Project, Malappuram District, Kerala

The Akshaya Project was launched in 2002 in Malappuram District by the Kerala State IT Mission (KSITM). A key objective was to make this district the first one in India with a 100 per cent e-literacy. It is based on PPPs in which front-end operations, including computers, peripherals, etc., are set up by local entrepreneurs while the state supported e-training. These entrepreneurs were not linked to big business houses, but are people with local roots. The local self-government structure plays a key role in the selection of these entrepreneurs and in the monitoring of these centres. The kiosks provided opportunities for e-government and for a variety of fee-paying services but also opportunities for e-training and for the development of skill sets. Akshaya centres facilitate e-payment, e-filings, e-ticketing, e-*krishi* (agricultural information), e-literacy and other services. An interesting aspect of Akshaya is the use of websites to showcase specific localities with information on its history, key institutions, livelihoods, etc. As it is stated in the official Akshaya website:

> Entegramam (My Village) is an online community portal in Malayalam created and maintained by the citizens of each village. The Government facilitated setting up of the portal and allows villagers to submit articles which are edited by philanthropic editors who upload the articles on the portal. Each web portal covers detailed information of the Panchayat. Each village has its own space in the portal and the information ranges from a catalog of 'useful services' from coconut tree climbers, carpenters, and more along with their phone numbers and location where they live. You will find the history of the land, governance, information on public services, to mention a few. Locally relevant news and announcements also find its way to the portal. In the course of time the portals will be used for local transaction, enabling in it with more business features. If successful, such portals can be set up every village/panchayat of the State. This project has been implemented in nine Gram Panchayats and one Municipality in Kannur District. (Kerala State IT Mission n.d.)

Malappuram District was, in many respects, unique when compared to other districts in Kerala in the sense that it was characterised by lower literacy rates than the rest of Kerala, was mainly Muslim, had the highest emigrant population of all districts in Kerala mainly to the Middle East and consequently a large proportion of housewives who looked after the household while their husbands were away in the 'Gulf'. The objective of Akshaya was to make at least one person from every household in Malappuram District e-literate and the e-literacy program that was carried out through Akshaya resulted in the education of more than half a million people in this district. Today, the total number of people trained in e-literacy exceeds 3 million. Today, Malappuram has about 351 functional e-kendras while there are a total of 2,662 such centres throughout Kerala, out of which 87.5 per cent are in rural areas. Other districts in Kerala, including Kannur, Kollam, Kozhikode, Thrissur and Kasargode have also achieved 100 per cent e-literacy. While this was no mean achievement, the project itself faced interesting dilemmas, including a growing gender-gap in the provisioning of these centres and between the interventionist state founded on Socialist principles and the creeping neo-liberalism that has affected all states run by communist parties in India. While the architects of Akshaya had assumed that high literacy levels among women in Kerala would automatically result in their becoming Akshaya entrepreneurs, a study by Mukhopadhyay and Nandi (2007:92) of Akshaya entrepreneurs in Mallapuram, revealed women–men ratios of 78:557. Women, however, made up the largest group which was trained in e-literacy. The study found that women entrepreneurs were disadvantaged in that there was little support from the local government to help women entrepreneurs succeed in multi-skilling as homemakers and as managers of Akshaya kiosks. As a result, there were larger drop-out rates faced by women entrepreneurs as opposed to the men. As this study notes:

> The study reconfirms the view that distributional impacts of supposedly 'neutral' projects are not necessarily neutral: that the first step in countering adverse distributional impact of projects like Akshaya is to ensure project designs have built-in monitoring mechanisms to track the gender and class impact of projects, especially in situations where homogeneity of the target populations cannot be assumed. It also brings to bear the necessity of keeping in mind that sensible efforts at correcting gender imbalances on the ground need a blending of different kinds of knowledge, insights and expertise.

Another study, this time by Kuriyan et al. (2008: 101–102) explored the motivations of Akshaya entrepreneurs. While there are socially motivated, business-driven and entrepreneurs who have striven to deliver balanced goals, their study indicates a trend towards the servicing of the relatively better off in urban contexts, the active re-branding of some of these centres and a move away from its pro-poor and inclusive beginnings. This contradiction was apparent not only at the level of the project, but also at the level of local self-government and consumers. This would seem to indicate that market orientation is an emerging logic even in India's most progressive and interventionist state, Kerala. As the authors conclude:

> Our research found that the poor are not the primary customers of ICT kiosks except for a one-time, subsidised Akshaya course. The main consumers are those in the middle class, who can afford to pay for relevant applications on an ongoing basis.... Our research found that the business-driven entrepreneurs acting in their self-interest cater to middle-class customers in urban areas and that development for the poor does not factor into their business strategies. Our research also indicates that kiosks operating in urban areas with large populations of people are more financially successful than rural or even peri-urban kiosks with smaller populations.

One of the contradictions that this study clearly highlights is the state's rather impossible goal of achieving both social and financial goals via these entrepreneurs. This is difficult to achieve and the fact that there is little ongoing support from the state to achieve its social goals, has resulted in the business-driven model taking priority.

Gyandoot, Dhar District, Madhya Pradesh

Another equally commended ICT4D project is Gyandoot (Purveyor of Knowledge) that is often described as an e-governance project. Dhar is a primarily 'tribal' area represented by groups such as the Bhils, Bhilalas, the Patleiyas and others. The Gyandoot project was operationalised in January 2000 and basically consists of a district-wide Intranet that is connected to 35 cyber-kiosks (Soochanalayas [information kiosks] operated by Soochaks [kiosk operators]) in this district. While 20 of these kiosks were initially owned by the local *gram* (village) panchayat, most are now owned by private individuals, although the village panchayat continues to maintain the building and fixtures. Fifteen of these kiosks were from the very beginning owned by private entrepreneurs. An interesting feature of Gyandoot is the fact that the entire costs for this project have been borne by the local government (from untied funds available at a local level) along with some private investment with little or no support from the state or central governments. These kiosks offer a number of services, including the following: agriculture produce auction centre rates, copies of land records, online registration of a variety of applications, online public grievance redress, information regarding government grants, information on village auctions, email facilities in Hindi and e-education. While Gyandoot has been a recipient of many awards—including The Stockholm Challenge Award, 2000—its reviews have been mixed. While the survey that has been carried out by the Overseas Development Institute (Jafri et al. 2002), London, does indicate that some of its services have been beneficial, positive results have been offset by numerous, critical issues that are, in a sense, congenital to e-government projects in India.

They include the following:

1. Studies have shown that for the most part, these services benefit the better-off farmers. Women and the rural poor are infrequent users of these services. The ODI survey written by Jafri et. al. (2002: 18–18) indicates that the more educated and socio-economically better-off men are the main users of this service.

    Of the population surveyed, 90 % of the users of Gyandoot services are male. Considering the living patterns of people in Indian villages this gender ratio is not unexpected. The factor responsible for this is that in a rural set up, women are mostly confined to their homes and lack awareness about business or public affairs. Although more appropriate extension activities might be designed to promote awareness among women folk, it has to be recognised that social conditions permitting women to use the services more fully will only change over the long term.

    This finding is a critical insight into realities experienced by rural women in India, but also points to the existence of other structural factors—caste, class, poverty that impact on the use of such services in Dhar District and elsewhere in India. As Cecchini and Raina (2004: 68) have observed:

> The rural poor generally have minimal interaction with government institutions, are not aware of Gyandoot, and are not making much use of its services ... most telekiosks end up serving the middle and upper rural classes, rather than poor laborers or landless farmers.... Gender and caste are also barriers.

2. In a context characterised by a lack of political will to deal with structural obstacles, the delivery of e-government services is severely constrained. This, more than other perennial problems, such as the lack of connectivity, electricity, and in the case of Gyandoot—lack of local engineers who can maintain the CorDECT Wireless in Local Loop technology (they depend on engineers from Chennai for repairs), remains a key obstacle to e-government, let alone e-governance in India. Sreekumar's (2007: 21) direct critique of e-government and Gyandoot highlights some salient issues that cannot be wished away by the technocrats who believe that access to technology will automatically result in the withering away of feudal relations and structures in rural India.

> The idea that ICT is inherently a liberating technology and hence e-governance is a new way of transcending inept and inefficient bureaucratic systems which empowers 'end users' appears to be completely inaccurate in the rural societal setting. Moreover, despite the claims of active networking of people in rural Dhar made on behalf of Gyandoot, its ability to connect to multiple societal and economic domains was found to be extremely limited and ostensibly mediated by the social power equations that enveloped its institutional setting.

Conclusion

E-Government has come to stay in India. In fact, there is bound to be greater investments in e-government in the coming years. While one cannot really argue against access to affordable information, the issue is whether the mediation of technology will result in better governance and government. All available indicators suggest that the bureaucracy in the context of e-government will not disappear as much as reinvent itself to deal with the era of the Internet. Neither can we hope that the structural impediments to rural social change will vanish in the era of e-government. If e-government is to be successful, it is imperative that there also is a simultaneous drive to clean-up the Augean stable of deep social issues that are part of the body politic in India. While I would not go as far as to suggest that the only beneficiaries of e-government will be Big Brother and the mainstreaming of governmentality, it is clear that that project stands to remain one of the 'successes' of e-government. After all, the government is keen to collect data on its citizens and there is now the availability of a variety of technologies that will enable precisely the collection of personal data. This, after all, is the era of transactional government.

References

Article 19. 1999. 'The Public's Right to Know: Principles on Freedom of Information Legislation', *Article 19*, pp. 1–19, London. Available at: http://www.article19.org/pdfs/standards/righttoknow.pdf (accessed on 8 June 2010).

Bekkers, V. 2007. 'Modernisation, Public Innovation and Information and Communication Technologies: The emperor's new clothes?', *Information Polity*, 12: 103–107.

Bin Yahya, F. 2009. 'The Rise of India as an Information Technology (IT) Hub and Challenges to Governance', *South Asia: Journal of South Asian Studies*, 32 (3): 374–389.

Cecchini, S. and M. Raina. 2004. 'Electronic Government and the Rural Poor: The Case of Gyandoot', *Information Technologies and International Development*, 2 (2): 65–75.

Deshpande, R. S. 2007. 'Emerging Issues in Land Policy', *Policy Brief No. 16*, pp. 1–15, Asian Development Bank, New Delhi. Available at: http://www.adb.org/Documents/Papers/INRM-PolicyBriefs/inrm16.pdf (accessed on 9 June 2010).

Foucault, M. 1991. 'Governmentality', in G. Burchell, C. Gordon and P. Miller (eds), *The Foucault Effect: Studies in Governmentality*, pp. 87–104. Hemel Hempstead: The University of Chicago Press.

Iways: Digest of Electronic Government Policy and Regulation. 2006. 'Indian E-Government Kiosks Improve Citizen Access', *Iways: Digest of Electronic Government Policy and Regulation*, 29 (4): 165–172. Available at: http://iospress.metapress.com/content/66m4q87ptylmwn88/fulltext.pdf (accessed on 10 June 2010).

Jafri, A., A. Dongre, V. N. Tripathi, A. Aggrawal and S. Shrivastava. 2002. 'Information Communication Technologies and Governance: The Gyandoot Experiment in Dhar District of Madhya Pradesh, India', pp. 1–42, Working Paper 160, April, Overseas Development Institute, London. Available at: http://www.odi.org.uk/work/projects/00-03-livelihood-options/papers/wp160.pdf (accessed on 10 June 2010).

Kerala State IT Mission. n.d. 'Entegramam, Akshaya Gateway to Opportunities'. Available at: http://www.akshaya.kerala.gov.in/index.php/platform-for-services/231-ente-gramam (accessed on 11 June 2010).

Kunstelj, M. and M. Vintar. 2004. 'Evaluating the Progress of E-Government Development: A Critical Analysis', *Information Polity*, 9: 131–148.

Kuriyan, R., I. Ray and K. Toyama. 2008. 'Information and Communication Technologies for Development: The Bottom of the Pyramid Model in Practice', *The Information Society*, 24: 93–104.

Lemke, T. 2001. '"The Birth of Bio-Politics": Michel Foucault's Lecture at the College de France on Neo-Liberal Governmentality', *Economy and Society*, 30 (2): 190–207.

Lenk, K. 2007. 'Reconstructing Public Administration Theory from Below', *Information Polity*, 12: 207–212.

Mayer-Schonberger, V. and D. Lazer. 2007. 'From Electronic Government to Information Government', in V. Mayer-Schonberger and D. Lazer (eds), *Governance and Information Technology: From Electronic Government to Information Government*, pp. 1–14. Cambridge, Mass., London: The MIT Press.

Microsoft. n.d. 'Microsoft India, Our Mission'. Available at: http://www.microsoft.com/india/msindia/msindia_ourmission.aspx (accessed on 10 June 2010).

Morris, C. 2010. 'India's Bureaucracy Is "The Most Stifling in the World"', *BBC News*, 3 June. Available at: http://news.bbc.co.uk/2/hi/world/south_asia/10227680.stm (accessed on 8 June 2010).

Muhkopadhyaya, S. and R. Nandi. 2007. 'Unpacking the Assumption of Gender Neutrality: Akshaya Project of the Kerala IT Mission in India', *Gender, Technology and Development*, 11 (1): 75–95.

Mukherjee, A. K. 2010. 'Providing Unique Identification (UID) to One Billion Unique Residents', *Journal of E-Governance*, 33: 71.

National Land Records Modernisation Program. n.d. Available at: http://nlrmp.nic.in/ (accessed on 24 February 2012).

O'Loughlin, B. 2007. 'Book Review of Sandra Braman's *Change of State: Information, Policy, and Power* (2006)', *Information Polity*, 12: 183–185. Cambridge, MA and London: The MIT Press.

Paul, S. 2007. 'A Case Study of E-governance Initiatives in India', *The International Information and Library Review*, 39: 176–184.

Peters, B. G. and J. Pierre. 2006. 'Governance, Government and the State', in C. Hay, M. Lister and D. Marsh (eds), *The State: Theories and Issues*, pp. 209–222. Basingstoke/New York: Palgrave Macmillan.

Prasad, S. 2008. "'Corruption' Slowing India's E-Growth', *ZDNet*, 12 August. Available at: http://www.zdnetasia.com/corruption-slowing-india-s-e-govt-growth-62044787.htm (accessed on 9 June 2010).

Press Release. 2006. 'Microsoft Recognises Excellence in E-Government Services', *Press Release*, 6 September.

Rajalekshmi, K. G. 2007. 'E-governance Services through Telecentres: The Role of Human Intermediary and Issues of Trust', *Information Technologies and International Development*, 4 (1): 19–35.

Revenue Department. 2012. 'Policy Note 2004–2005, Chapter IV, Survey and land Records and Maintenance'. Available at: http://www.tn.gov.in/policynotes/ archives/policy2004-05/revenue2004-05-4.htm (accessed on 24 February 2012).

Saxena, K. B. C. 2005. 'Towards Excellence in E-Governance', *International Journal of Public Sector Management*, 18 (6): 1–12.

Schiller, D. 2000. *Digital Capitalism*. Cambridge, Mass: The MIT Press.

Sreekumar, T. T. 2007. 'Decrypting E-Governance: Narratives, Power Play and Participation in the Gyandoot Intranet', *The Electronic Journal on Information Systems in Developing Countries*, 32 (4): 1–24.

Thomas, J. C. and G. Streib. 2003. 'The New Face of Government: Citizen-initiated Contacts in the Era of E-Government', *Journal of Public Administration Research and Theory*, 13 (1): 83–102.

Walsham, G. 2010. 'ICTs for the Broader Development of India: An Analysis of the Literature', *The Electronic Journal on Information Systems in Developing Countries*, 41 (4): 1–20. Available at: http://www.ejisdc.org/ojs2/index.php/ ejisdc/article/viewFile/665/317 (accessed on 9 June 2010).

Welch, E. W., C. Hinnant and M. J. Moon. 2004. 'Linking Citizen Satisfaction with E-Government and Trust in Government', *Journal of Public Administration Research and Theory*, 15 (3): 371–391.

7

Intellectual Property Conundrums
and the State in the Era of the Digital

The era of the digital has presented the present intellectual property (IP) regime with a number of intractable problems. As the digital 'copy' circulates in ever larger numbers, protection has become a virtually impossible task. However, that has not dented any number of initiatives aimed at creating 'enclosures' around the digital—from the European Directive aimed at protecting databases and database services, to the Digital Millennium Copyright Act in the USA that outlaws the circumvention of any technological protection measures and the moves in India to provide a legislative basis for software patenting. While we will deal with issues related to software patenting in this chapter, it is important to recognise that the digital as a means of production, is much larger than say, the universe of convergent media that typically is identified with the digital, and includes products and processes across sectors that are imprinted by the digital. For example, genomic databases, such as Structural Genomix and the Lucknow-based human DNA bank in India, maintain biological information in digital format whereas the UIDAI maintains personal information in digitised formats. Both types of data can be commodified and they often are. Human biological information, just like personal information, is of course, a key commodity that is the object of assiduous efforts at patenting today. As Eugene Thacker (2006: 94) reminds us:

> The perspective of political economy can be useful … for fields such as genomics, proteomics, and bioinformatics can in many ways be understood as sets of techniques for producing, distributing, exchanging, and making use of biological information. That biological information may be in material form (e.g., plasmid libraries, cell cultures) or in an immaterial form (e.g., online databases), and it may be used, applied, or consumed in a range of contexts (e.g., drug development, genetic tests, DNA fingerprinting, etc.).

With the export and domestic digital markets contributing to growth in the Indian economy, there are moves by the Indian government to strengthen its commitments to digital copyright and software patenting.

There are, of course, obvious issues related to the 'enclosure' of digitised information, although additionally, there are issues with what is being digitised and what is not, and how values are being assigned in that process of selection.

The Politics of Software Patenting

An issue that has been of concern to IP activists and others in India are the moves by the Indian government to include software patenting, beginning with its inclusion in the Patents (Amended) Act 25 June 2002. This move was to be expected given that software patents have been agreed to by nearly half of the members of the WTO. In fact, software patents have been granted in the USA at least from 1982 and as Besson and Hunt (2004) have pointed out between 1982 and 1999, at least 130,650 patents were granted.

> These industries, including the computer, electrical equipment and instruments industries, are also found to account for a major share of the growth in patenting in recent years.... Some researchers have suggested that firms in these industries may patent heavily in order to obtain strategic advantages, including advantages in negotiations, cross-licensing, blocking competitors, and preventing suits.... In principle, strategic patenting can arise whenever individual products involve many patentable inventions and the cost of obtaining patents is sufficiently lo.... Firms may acquire large numbers of patents so that even if they have an unsuccessful product, they can hold up rivals, threatening litigation. Innovative firms may acquire 'defensive' patent portfolios to make a credible counter-threat. The outcome may involve the cross-licensing of whole portfolios, where firms agree not to sue each other and those firms with weaker portfolios pay royalties.

Given the positioning of India as a global software and IT hub, it was to be expected that sooner rather than later, there would be moves to strengthen software protection via recourse to a number of IP mechanisms, including copyright and patents. Indian software companies, such as Infosys, are committed to software patenting. While the Patent Act (1970) does specify that some inventions, including 'a mathematical or business method or a computer program *per se* or algorithms' (p. 3, Section 3K) *cannot* be patented, this formulation leaves room for interpretation and would seem to suggest that a programme that is integrated into a device *can* be patented. The term 'per se' can be deployed in different ways and its use in this context has generated some controversy. A software programme may not be patented, although it would suggest that if a software programme or for that matter, algorithm has a 'technical effect', it can be patented.

The Patent Amendments Ordinance (2004) put forward the view under Section 3, that patents could include '(k) a computer programme per se other than its technical application to industry or a combination with hardware; (ka) a mathematical method or a business method or algorithms'. The clearest support for the patenting of algorithms is found in Draft Manual of Patent Practice and Procedure (2008) issued by the Patent Office. For example, Section 4.11.10 notes the following:

> A mathematical method is one which is carried out on numbers and provides a result in numerical form (the mathematical method or algorithm therefore being merely an abstract concept prescribing how to operate on the numbers) and not patentable. However, its application may v·²ll be patentable, for example, in *Vicom/Computer-related invention* [1987] 1 OJEPO 14 (T208/84) the invention concerned a mathematical method for manipulating data representing an image, leading to an enhanced digital image. (Draft Manual of Patent Practice and Procedure 2008: 74)

Each of these amendments can be viewed as attempts by the government of India to harmonise its IP laws with international laws, such as the WTO-administered Trade-related Aspects of Intellectual Property Rights (TRIPS).

From a reading of the Annual Report 2008–2009 of the Office of the Controller General of Patents, Designs, Trade Marks and Geographical Indications (2009: 9–11) it is impossible to say whether algorithms have begun to be granted patents, although that could well be the case as the top five software companies that have applied for patents during this period include Samsung India Software Operations (205 patents), Infosys Technologies Ltd. (81), Tata Elxsi Ltd. (14), Tata Consultancy Services (14) and Rajendra Kumar Khare (5) and foreign applicants include Qualcomm Incorporation (252), Nokia Corporation (173) along with other firms.

Under Chapter XVI: Working of Patents, Compulsory Licenses and Revocations, the 2002 Act does lay out the terms of the patent—the 'general principles applicable to the working of patented inventions' (The Patents Amended Act 2002: 11, Clause 83):

> (c) that the protection and enforcement of patent rights contribute to the promotion of technological innovation and to the transfer and dissemination of technology, to the mutual advantage of producers and users of technological knowledge and in a manner conducive to social and economic welfare, and to a balance of rights and obligations

However, there is a feeling that the government will not be in a position to revoke patents, except in the case of a national emergency and critical products, such as patents for drugs. Since issues dealing with software patenting cannot be considered an 'emergency' issue, it would seem that the government is bound to be less predisposed to software patenting. However, in the context of moves to legitimise public sector software (see Chapter 8), the government could well be persuaded to explore the merits of opposing software patents, given that public sector software innovation may be curtailed by pre-existing patents. Additionally, small- and medium-sized companies in India that do not have the resources to negotiate with patent holders, will not be able to strengthen their own indigenous capacities in software development. However, echoing the contested nature of this issue, Adithya Banavar (2010: 98) in an article that contrasts software patenting in the USA and India suggests that the term 'per se' allows software patenting that is in the interest of nascent, local, industry.

> In India, it has been sought by legislative mandate to bar all business patent methods and bar patents that relate to software *per se*. The words are clear and unambiguous. India's software industry is in its initial phase and therefore, there is perhaps a need for allowing the patentability of software.

An article by Evans and Layne-Farrar (2004) in the *Virginia Journal of Law and Technology*, 'Software Patents and Open Source', also takes a pro-patent perspective and suggests that the threat of 'patent thickets' has not materialised. Their research, incidentally, was supported by Microsoft.

The general view, however, is that software patenting should be disallowed, given that there is still a lack of clarity on how such an exclusive right actually results in creativity (Office of the Controller General of Patents, Designs, Trade Marks and Geographical Indications 2009). In fact, as it is clear in the US context, a plethora of patent infringement-related litigations and counter-litigations by the major software companies has led to an impossible situation. The End Patents Coalition has calculated that an average of 55 software litigations are filed each week, that it costs on average US$4 million per litigation and that close to US$11.4 billion is wasted on software litigation each year (Asay 2008). In 2009, Microsoft alone was involved in contesting 50 pending patent infringement cases, while the company had filed multiple infringement cases against rival firms. While the EU was not able to push through its 2005 Software Patent Directive, it remains on their agenda and is currently involved in exploring the establishment of an international patent treaty—the United Patent Litigation System that would supersede national systems. Grosche (2006: 308) has argued that

> ... copyright with some adaptations to software has proven to be a workable and internationally accepted forms of providing incentives for innovation

in the software sector (rather than in patent litigation). Based on algorithms and abstract ideas of which it has always been recognised that they cannot be monopolised in a reasonable way, software is a phenomenon too different to allow for further 'muddling through' by imposing the complex and expensive patent system onto a new field in which it is either opposed, ignored—or abused, and where both U.S. and European courts have tired in vain to reach legally consistent, let alone convincing solutions.

Grosche's observations need to seen in the context of the granting of patents for 'business methods' as for example, the 'one-click-only' online shopping patent granted to Amazon.com in the USA. One of the better argued articles on software patenting is by Stephen Lindholm (2005). He provides a comprehensive introduction to some of the key issues related to software patenting. While Lindholm does not take an anti-software patent line, he acknowledges that a set of bad practices, including the lack of available information on the content of software patents have effectively stymied 'invention', and affected 'disclosure, commercialisation, and designing around' (p. 86). Blanket licensing of enormous patent portfolios instead of individual patents effectively shuts out smaller production that do not have the capital to buy such portfolios from companies such as IBM. Even designing around patents—a typical way in which innovation takes shape, can be difficult, because there is little knowledge available on the scope of a software patent.

> It is probably the case that competitors must design around patents before the patented design achieves a wide install base to have a chance of introducing superior designs to the market. When patents on network effect technology are instead revealed late, competitors have no power to design around them. (p. 90)

Lindholm, however, reserves his strongest criticism for the lack of software patent 'marking' that is standard practice for other types of patents. The marking would allow disclosure of the scope of the patent.

> Unfortunately, it is hard for the public to figure out which software patents cover which products. In areas like chemical engineering, it is relatively to search in the patent libraries to find relevant patents. In mechanical engineering, the patent numbers are marked on the products themselves. Software patents do neither. They are nigh impossible to find in the patent libraries, and few companies mark their software with their patent numbers. (p. 128).

Some of the more considered responses to software patenting have come from activist scholars in India, namely those associated with the Alternative Law Forum and the Centre for Internet and Society, both based in Benguluru, and members who belong to the F/OSS community. Pranesh

Prakash from the Centre for Internet and Society has argued that software patents do not make sense from both legal and practical perspectives. The legal perspective echoes the point made above by Grosche, while the practical reasons include the reality of curbs to innovation and creativity via patent gridlocks, long terms for patents, the opacity of software patents, and the barriers it presents to FOSS. As Prakash (2010a) categorically states:

> The patenting of software helps three categories of people: (1) those large corporations that already have a large number of software patents; (2) those corporations that do not create software, but only trade in patents/sue on the basis of patents ('patent trolls'); (3) patent lawyers.

Liang et al. (n.d.: 4) make the point that software patents are a stronger method of protection than copyright 'because the protection extends to the level of the idea embodied by the software and injuncts ancillary uses of an invention as well'. Dubey (2010: 4–5) reinforces this position:

> Unlike copyright that protects only the final work, software patent protect the imitation of features, elementary ideas. Software patents, by allowing its holders to claim even elementary ideas, constitutes an extremely powerful monopoly-creating instrument as the holder of patent can prevent the selling of all software implementing the patented idea—whatever the application domains can be!

Liang et al. have also argued that the flexible, public interest–based nature of copyright protection in India has served Indian industry well, but that these gains can be offset by patent protection, that for example, places obstacles in the way of 'interoperability'—a major concern in the context of the Indian government's vast investments in e-governance and interest in the development of public sector software.

Recursive Publics

While there are pressures for the Indian government to liberalise software patenting, as a relatively strong state and given its own interest in supporting F/OSS and public sector software, the state simply has to contend with multiple nay-sayers, including many knowledgeable and software-politics literate senior civil servants within the government who are inclined to support software policies that are primarily in the national and public interest. The Indian government also has to contend with publics who are, on occasion, better informed than the government on matters related to IP and software. F/OSS advocates throughout India make up what Christopher Kelty (2005, 2008) has described as 'recursive publics'. Software programming is typically made through recursive practices—meaning repetitive processes that result in the ironing out of dead ends. Today, the F/OSS community not only consists of programmers but also those who have intimate knowledge of the various layers—the technology, the legal layer and protocols—and who use this knowledge to construct a social imaginary for software use that is different from mainstream understandings. Kelty (2008: 10–11) has argued that such recursive publics are involved in a reorientation of power and knowledge in our times through their capacities to build, modify, subvert, control and adapt ideas, processes and infrastructures.

> The 'reorientation of power and knowledge' has two key aspects that are part of the concept of recursive publics: availability and modifiability (or adaptability). Availability is a broad, diffuse and familiar issue. It includes things like transparency, open governance or transparent organisation, secrecy and freedom of information, and open access in science.... Modifiability includes the ability to not only access—that is, to reuse in the trivial sense of using something without restrictions—but to transform it for use in new contexts, to different ends, or in order to participate directly in its improvement and to redistribute or recirculate it those improvements within the same infrastructures while securing the same rights for everyone else.

The role of these recursive publics in India cannot be underestimated precisely because there is a critical mass and they do, to some extent, get backing from both central and state governments.

The Political Economy of IP in the Era of the Digital

The State in India has the ultimate authority to regulate the digital, including its protection. This is by no means, a straightforward process as it has to be seen to be balancing out its public interest with the interests of national and global private interests, supra-national organisations involved in IP and governments, such as the USA, who are consistently involved in lobbying the Indian government for stronger enforcement measures and tighter IP laws with little space for exemptions. The International Intellectual Property Alliance (IIPA) that represents seven trade bodies in the USA, linked to core copyright industries including the Business Software Alliance, the Motion Pictures Association of America, the Recording Industry Association of America along with others, works closely with the USTR in compiling the annual Section 301 reviews used by the USTR to name, and if need be, levy trade sanctions against countries that are seen to be habitual transgressors. The IIPA has, for example, recommended that India be placed on the Section 301 Priority Watch List in 2010 for the lack of enforcement, inadequate legislation and barriers to market access for US-based cinema, entertainment and business software industries. The IIPA (2010) report specifically recommends that the Indian government pass the copyright amendment bill in line with World Intellectual Property Organization (WIPO) Internet treaties (WIPO Copyright Treaty and WIPO Performances and Phonograms Treaty) that are anti-piracy—optical disc piracy, retail piracy, camcording piracy, pirate printing and photocopying of books, Internet and mobile device piracy and signal theft and public performance piracy. In terms of legislation, it recommends protection for 'temporary copies' stored in a computer RAM, protection for technological protection measures against unlawful circumvention (in line with the Digital Millennium Copyright Act [DMCA]) and what they term to be 'overly broad' exceptions including '(a) a broad "private copying" exception;... (d) an overbroad exception permitting the performance of films in educational contexts and in "clubs"; (e) an overbroad exception with respect to reproduction of books by libraries' (IIPA 2010: 45–46). What is clear from such recommendations is that the intent is not only to strengthen protection of their core copyright industries, but also restrict access to knowledge and limit 'fair use' that are anti-public and whose enforcement is not in the interests of the Indian government. These restrictions are highlighted in the two WIPO treaties that are meant to strengthen copyright in the era of the digital. What is clear is that both treaties treat copyright policy in the age of the Internet and cyberspace as a matter of ensuring the protection of all manner of electronic commercial transactions and the flow of electronic signals to the neglect of creating policy out of a more thoughtful understanding of the many possibilities that are inherent to the digital. These include the reality of distributed knowledge and collaborative creativity, new types of licensing such as the GNU and Creative Commons licensing, new types of user-generated context through social networking technologies and online publishing, among other new initiatives that are linked to strengthening the digital commons and digital public domain. Clause 99 from a WIPO (2005: 23) document on copyright clearly ignores the need to protect the digital commons and instead, highlights the need to protect the copyright status quo.

> The two WIPO treaties offer adequate responses to the challenges of digital technology, and particularly to the Internet. They establish the indispensable legal conditions at the international level for the use of the digital network as a marketplace for the products of cultural and information industries, and they

regulate the copyright and related rights aspects of electronic commerce in a way that they maintain the existing balance of interests in this field and also leave sufficient freedom for national legislation. It is certainly due to this that, at the end of 1997, which was the deadline for signing the treaties, there were no less than 51 signatories of the WCT and 50 of the WPPT.

However, Pranesh Prakash (2010b), in a response to the IIPA document, has argued that

> ... given that more than half the countries of the world are not signatories to either of the WIPO Internet Treaties (namely the WIPO Copyright Treaty and the WIPO Performance and Phonograms Treaty), calling them 'international standards' is suspect. That apart, both those treaties are TRIPS-plus treaties (requiring protections greater than the already-high standards of the TRIPS Agreement). India has not signed either of them. It should not be obligated to do so.

Making the Indian Copyright Act WIPO Copyright Treaty (WCT) Friendly

India's real and projected involvement in the global digital economy and its collaboration with its key partner, the USA outweighs civil society recommendations. The protectionist moves in the USA, exemplified by restrictions to outsourcing of government IT and back office projects by the government of Ohio, USA (Shivapriya and Harsimran 2010), is seen as a potential blow to India's 3-million employee strong, US$50 billion outsourcing industry. What is interesting is the US-India Business Council's response to this move, including stronger implementations of the IT Act, better tax breaks for US companies, stronger corporate governance, better labour reform, advantageous spectrum allocation for US companies competing for 3G spectrum allocations among other sops for US industry in India. The moves by the government to make its Copyright Act (1957) Digital Rights Management (DRM) friendly has been supported by the industry, including the Federation of Indian Chambers of Commerce and Industry (FICCI). The Bill was introduced in the Rajya Sabha and has been referred to Parliamentary Standing Committee.

> The proposed Bill seeks to amend the Copyright Act, 1957 to bring it in conformity with World Intellectual Property Organisation's WIPO Copyright Treaty (WCT) and WIPO Performances and Phonograms Treaty (WPPT). The WCT deals with the protection for the authors of literary and artistic works such as writings, computer programmes, original databases, musical works,

audio-visual works, works of fine art and photographs. The WPPT protects certain 'related rights' of the performers and producers of phonograms. (The Standing Committee 2010)

The Copyright (Amendment) Bill, 2010, (http://prsindia.org/uploads/media/Copyright%20Act/Copyright%20Bill%202010.pdf, accessed on 25 September 2010) explicitly states the following:

> 65A.(1) Any person who circumvents an effective technological measure applied for the purpose of protecting any of the rights conferred by this Act, with the intention of infringing such rights, shall be punishable which may extend to two years and shall also be liable to fine. (12)

However, the amendments do provide recourse to legitimate reason for circumvention and fair use—although the IIPA has deemed such exceptions to be over generous. The Bill related to the Amendment of Section 52 of the Act expressly states for example that '(t)he storing of any work for the purposes mentioned in this clause, including the incidental storage of any computer programme which is not itself an infringing copy for the said purposes, shall not constitute infringement of copy' (10). There are two interesting dimensions to these moves to make Indian copyright law WCT compliant—(a) since India is not a signatory to the WCT, it really is not required to amend its copyright laws, so it begs the question as to why it is taking this particular route, (b) it is doing this without providing blanket prohibitions—an issue that has upset the IIPA and others. As Perry (2010) has observed:

> The Indian Bill, cognisant of personal use of materials, provides for several refined exceptions in the new s.52 of the Copyright Act, including transient and incidental storage of works due to technological necessity (for example the cache servers of internet service providers), reproduction of judicial proceedings, legislation, recitation of 'reasonable extracts', educational, electronic storage of held works by non-profit public libraries, and others. The Bill also provides for more specific exemptions for encryption research, lawful investigations, authorised security testing, requited for national identification, national security.

The Indian government has not only harmonised most of its IP legislations in line with TRIPS and other legislations, they have invested in the creation of modern IP infrastructures, in IP education, the institution of a Copyright Enforcement Advisory Council, special copyright police cells and supported IP raids (see Thomas 2006, 2010). Whether or not all this has resulted in less piracy is debateable. A number of scholars including Lawrence Liang (2005), Ravi Sundaram (2009) and others (see Chapter 9 in this book) have argued that digital piracy should not be discussed primarily as an economic loss to the core copyright industries which is how it is habitually portrayed in the media, but as an activity and process that does contribute towards economic and cultural gains, access to knowledge within new global circuits resulting in new social imaginaries. In other words, digital piracy does have the potential to democratise and level the playing field in terms of access to knowledge. As Liang (2005: 16) has observed:

> The figures of illegality pose fundamental questions to our neat categories of the liberal public sphere, where citizens interact through constitutionally guaranteed rights, as the exclusive mode of understanding the world of law and legality. The status of these transgressors as the 'not quite' and yet 'not quiet' citizens creating their own avenues of participation in the multiple worlds of media, modernity and globalisation demands that we ask fundamentally different questions of the relationship between law, legality, property (tangible and intangible) and that which we call the public domain.

The State and Traditional Knowledge: Traditional Knowledge Digital Library (TKDL) and the Politics of Digitisation

Apart from cultural piracy, the issue that has created anxieties for the Indian state is the protection of traditional knowledge, an issue that in the context of the digital has led to interesting responses from the state. This section is based on an article that I had written in the International Communications Gazette (Thomas 2010).

The compilation of a 30 million page database—the TKDL—by organisations related to the Government of India and the granting of access to this database to 34 EU countries as part of an agreement with the European Patent Office (EPO) on 2 February 2009 is a significant milestone in the efforts towards the global recognition of 'prior art' inherent in traditional knowledge. In 2010, agreements have been signed with the US Patent and Trademark Office (USPTO) and the United Kingdom Patent and Trademark Office (UKPTO). Already 36 patent applications have been rejected by the EPO, given evidence of 'prior art' and senior managers at the TKDL are confident that 21 more patent applications will be rejected (Rediff 2010). The eight-year TKDL project, the result of a collaboration between the Council of Scientific and Industrial Research (CSIR), the National Institute of Science Communication and Information Resources (NISCAIR), the Ministry of Science and Technology, the

Department of Ayurveda, Yoga and Naturopathy, Unani, Siddha and Homoeopathy (AYUSH) and the Ministry of Health and Family Welfare, contains among other content, 54 textbooks on ayurvedic medicine, nearly 150,000 entries based on ayurvedic, *unani* (system of Islamic medicine) and *siddha* (ancient South India medical system) medicine and over 1,500 postures in yoga that have evolved over many millennia including the *Yoga Sutras* of Patanjali that are over 2,000 years old. The protection of India's traditional knowledge from cultural and bio-prospectors intent on patenting India's vast cultural and biological knowledge contained in its many and diverse traditions—from yoga to traditional medicine, was the primary motive behind the compilation of this database. During the ensuing decade, the Indian government had been involved in expensive litigations in US courts over patents given to traditional medicinal and food plants from India—turmeric (Udgaonkar 2002), *neem, basmati* rice and yoga positions, the last popularised by the California-based yoga guru Bikram Choudhary.

> In 2002, the US-based Bikram Choudhary wrote a book and copyrighted Bikram Yoga which, he claimed, was a scientifically designed routine of 26 asanas completed in 90 minutes in an environment with temperatures up to 115 Fahrenheit (46 degrees centigrade). He even sent notices to yoga studios to stop using the same routine as it infringed on his copyright. In 2005, it led to a legal battle between Choudhary and the Open Source Yoga Unity (OSYU), an organisation of studio owners and yoga teachers. (Srivastava 2007)

In fact, in 2007 alone, 130 patents and 1,000 trademarks were given to yoga postures and products in the USA (Hodge 2009). Yoga is a multi-million dollar business. According to Sharma (n.d.: 12):

> Yoga has now started attracting big business and companies including Ford Motor, Pfizer and Clairol are pursuing well-heeled yogis with advertisements and it is difficult to measure its business potentiality with its growing popularity observed in many parts of US: (i) Guests at Resorts Atlantic City Casino Hotel take part in a yoga class; (ii) Rodney Yee, Yoga teacher, endorses advertisement for 'Vitasol' promoting consumer food products; (iii) Development of Yoga tourism and Yoga vacation: Kripalu Center for Yoga and Health develops as the biggest yoga retreat center in US with accommodation for 450 people; (iv) development of Yoga studios; and (v) Oprah Winfrey shows on Yoga.

The TKDL, available in English, German, Japanese, Spanish and French will provide examiners evidence of 'prior art' when confronted with patent applications related to Traditional Knowledge (TK). Plans are also afoot to create a South Asian Association for Regional Cooperation (SAARC)–wide database on traditional knowledge modelled on the TKDL (see Padma 2005).

For the moment, the key impact of the TKDL is its contribution to standard-setting with respect to the documentation of the TK. Its classificatory system is novel and it is clear that the TKDL is a model that can be replicated by other countries. In fact, a number of countries from around the world, including South Africa, Nigeria, Malaysia and Thailand, are interested in replicating the TKDL. SAARC is also interested in exploring a South Asia–wide TKDL. In March 2011, WIPO and the Indian Council of Scientific and Industrial Research (ICSIR) co-hosted a conference in New Delhi titled 'The International Conference on the Utilization of the Traditional Knowledge Digital Library as a Model for Protection of Traditional Knowledge' at which delegates from 35 countries discussed the possibility of developing their own digital databases on traditional knowledge. Already, according to V. K. Gupta (n.d.), who is the director of the TKDL, this evidence of 'prior art' is proving to be a deterrent against bio-piracy.

> The impact of the TKDL is already being felt at the EPO. Since July 2009, the EPO's TKDL team has identified 215 patent applications relating to Indian medicinal systems for which third party TKDL evidence has been filed. In two such cases the EPO has already reversed—on the strength of TKDL evidence—its earlier intention to grant the patents. In one case the applicant modified the claims submitted and, in 33 other cases, the applicants themselves withdrew their four to five-year-old applications upon presentation of TKDL evidence—a tacit admission of biopiracy by the applicants themselves.
>
> It is expected that in the coming months some 179 cases that are currently in the balance will either be rejected by the EPO or withdrawn by the applicants themselves. A recent study by a TKDL expert team at the EPO shows a sharp decline (44%) in the number of patent applications filed concerning Indian medicinal systems, particularly in relation to medicinal plants.

The TKDL's Traditional Knowledge Resource Classification (TKRC) System is modelled on WIPO's International Patent Classification (IPC) System. Chidi Oguamanam (2008: 501) describes the benefits of the TKRC system thus:

> The Indian initiative on the classification of traditional knowledge within the IPC has resulted in a detailed and improved IPC structure relating to traditional medicine. This includes the 2003 decision by the IPC Union to expand the classification of medicinal plants by about two hundred sub groups via the creation of a brand new group (A61K36) and, perhaps most importantly, the linkage of IPC with the TKRC through a concordance table prepared by India.

While there is certainly merit in expanding the global universe of knowledge, the question as to what will become of this knowledge in the context of global efforts to commercialise ideas into IP offers no easy answers. While the TKRC, as Oguamanam has observed, has vastly improved the scope and depth of the IPC, one can argue that classifications abstracted from context can result in a demeaning of practices, to a lessening of its aura and a negation of its meanings and aesthetics. Surender Kaur Verma (2004: 766) in an article that explores the viability of *sue generis* systems of the TK, makes the point that for many holders of the TK:

> ... (it) holds a sacred value which they would not part with for money. They want to safeguard their knowledge from plunder. Mere digitisation of published or known information to ease the work of patent examiners cannot resolve the question of how holders of TK should be rewarded for their care and feeding of ideas.

This line of thinking is also reflected in the questions raised by Worcman (2002):

> Will digitizing the culture or history of these collective entities in fact include the communities in the process of formation and diffusion of their knowledge? Or will the digitization process simply reproduce the western conception of storing in 'museums and libraries' what those in the west deem to have cultural value?.... It is undeniable that when the oral traditions of a community without a written language are recorded, that community's history will be preserved. But preserved for whom?

The TKDL, however, does present us with an opportunity to discuss larger issues related to nomenclature. Is the multi-accentuality of the term 'traditional knowledge' problematic and an obstacle to understanding and clarifying the worth of traditions in a context in which Big traditions are given precedence over Little traditions? In India, the TK is the preferred term that is used to cover all traditions—from that of the Big traditions associated with ayurveda and yoga to the Little traditions of the Irulas and other groups throughout India. Would it make sense to dis-inter the notion of the traditional and reintegrate it into categories that reflect contemporary traditions in India—dominant traditions, small and large 'living' traditions, traditions on the edge, reinvented traditions? And would such a categorisation enable a clearer understanding of, advocacy and commitment to the TK? While from a personal point of view, my sympathies lie with traditions on the edge, I do sympathise with and recognise the efforts undertaken by the government and organisations in India to protect the TK, including that allied to the dominant traditions, from commercial interests outside of the country. At the very same time, it is equally important that one acknowledges that there are equally rapacious exploiters of dominant traditions within the country who probably have a lot to gain from protecting its IP.

The establishment of the TKDL project is to a large extent the result of cross-party political will, but also more significantly, a reflection of the national accent on computerisation and the digital, enshrined in its numerous IT policies. As a result of this emphasis, projects related to computerisation are now ubiquitous and cut across multiple sectors in India. Most, if not all, government sectors have either been computerised or are currently in the process of becoming digitised. India's culture too is being digitised and while it is a necessity in some case, it is linked to the need to preserve and protect vanishing/under-threat knowledges, such projects are also linked to a nationalist imaginary that is fuelled by pride, distinction and civilisational superiority. India's continuing tryst with Hindu nationalism has resulted in the valorisation and historicising of numerous Hindu traditions. This includes the re-writing of its social and cultural history and the elevation of selective traditions, for example, astrology, Vedic studies and *vashtu* (tradition of spatial ordering based on the laws of nature), to academic status. If the public, global face of the digital in India is that of the software industry, call centres and e-governance, its private face includes the cataloguing of knowledge and development of databases across multiple sectors—in education, the environment, science and history—a trend that is, of course, replicated on a far larger scale globally, as for instance, in the Human Genome Project and the United Nation's Global Resource Information Database.

There is, it would seem, a global imperative to enumerate and catalogue the world's knowledge in databases. In United Nations Educational, Scientific and Cultural Organization (UNESCO) parlance, this is known as 'digital heritage'. In India, apart from the TKDL, there are dozens of public initiatives related to digital archiving including the Digital Library of India, Kalasampada, Nalanda Digital Library, Archives of Indian Labour, National Science Digital Library, the Mobile Digital Library and the Down the Memory Lane Project funded by the Ministry of Culture among numerous other initiatives (see Das et al. [2005] and Mittal and Mahesh [2008]). Mention must also be made of non-governmental efforts to create the TK bio-registers at a local levels aimed at creating databanks related to seed and agricultural practices. There are numerous NGOs and movements involved in such efforts, including the Deccan Development Society, The Green Foundation, the Gene Campaign, Kerala Sastra Sahitya Parishad, Community Biodiversity Registers, the MSSRF and the SRISTI/Honey Bee Network Project (see Gene Campaign: 2010). A key objective of SRISTI is the creation of a global registration system that facilitates 'prior art' searches and the identification of knowledge holders who require compensation for the use of their knowledge by third parties. This database currently contains 70,000 items on innovations in TK. However, as Dasgupta (2005) has observed, despite major investments in digital libraries in India, there remain hurdles including the following:

> While undertaking digitization activities the Information and technical professionals have to face multiple problems and barriers in the Indian context:
>
> 1. Lack of policy framework at the national level.
> 2. Technological problem of obsolescence in terms of software and hardware and difficulty in upgrading the same as a recurring need.
> 3. Non-availability of cost beneficial new technological advancement.
> 4. Lack of multiple Indian language OCR facilities.
> 5. Non-standard technical activities, data description and transmission characteristics.
> 6. Non-availability of well-trained personnel with necessary skills to fully participate in the new environment.
> 7. Lack of proper preservation policy to sustain digitization efforts and digital libraries.
> 8. No IPR policy for content development of digital information for research and decision making purposes.
> 9. No well thought out views on the various aspects of sustainability and long-term availability of digitized material.

A key issue that continues to remain contentious is the role of the state in the creation of databases, such as the TKDL. Who ought to be the ultimate authority and power-broker when it comes to defining and deciding on a TK database? Who should have final ultimate authority when it comes to matters, such as the sourcing and archiving of traditional knowledge? And more importantly, who decides what this archived information will be used for and who will have access to this knowledge? Is it the state or the community that owns this knowledge? If the state does get involved in such projects, what criteria should it use for selecting the TK? This is a problematic issue, given that it is not always the case that IK (Indigenous Knowledge) belongs to any given community. It is often the case that IK resides in an individual. Christian (2009: 13) raises this issue in a research report on the digitization of indigenous medicinal knowledge in Nigeria.

> Although, traditional medicinal knowledge is generally conceived as being communal in nature, undoubtedly, there are aspects of traditional medicine knowledge which usually resides in an individual as opposed to a group or the community ... it is incorrect to assert that the knowledge and skills possessed by native healers are in public domain. This belief ... is flawed because native healers, as a matter of fact rarely reveal the secrets of medicinal or herbal remedies which they individually posses.

Is the commodification of TK the only reason for its digital archiving or can there be equally valid, non-property reasons for engaging with traditional knowledge in the era of the digital? A critical issue in all this is of course, the nature of access. If the documenting of TK is primarily to ensure that patent offices have access to TK, should this objective be prioritised at the expense of other equally valid objectives, such as the need to protect the environments and peoples that are responsible for TK? And should the one priority be divorced from the other? Rikowski (2008: 17) has raised some general questions related to digitisation.

> When we see digital projects gathering pace rapidly, we need to pause, and think and question. What is being gained from any one such project? Is digitisation always worthwhile? Does it necessarily mean that our information resources are being preserved and utilised more effectively? To what extent are commercial digital projects gathering pace and how is this likely to develop in the future (given that profit is the driving factor)? Could digitisation mean that few, if any, hard copies are available in the future? Could it mean that increasing amounts of material will not be available in the future, as technology changes, and the material is not transferred to the new medium?

Arun Agrawal (2002: 290–92) uses the term 'scientisation' to describe the processes of 'particularisation, validation and generalisation' that are mechanisms used to invest traditional knowledge with 'scientific' truth (p. 291). As Agrawal has observed, this approach is based on an instrumentalist logic and it begins:

> [With the] demand ... that useful indigenous knowledge be separated from those other knowledges, practices, milieu, context, and cultural beliefs in combination with which it exists. Only the forms of indigenous knowledge that are potentially relevant to development, then needs attention and protection. Other forms of knowledge, precisely because they are irrelevant to the needs of development, can be allowed to pass away.... Successful particularisation is the first necessary step in the creation of any database. (p. 290)

It can be argued that the digital archiving of TK unfortunately fixes TK as immutable knowledge when in fact, TK is dynamic and is updated constantly in the light of the experiences of local communities.

Sita Reddy (2006), in an article on the ownership of traditional knowledge, mentions the resistance to the TKDL from the *shuddha* (pure) ayurvedic practitioners who were not consulted as opposed to those who are content to make ayurveda competitive in the global market. Their resistance based on exclusivist logic, reflects both an opposition to the disarticulation of traditional knowledge, but also the intent to preserve the constancy of hierarchical tradition. As Geoffrey Bowker (2000: 660) has cogently remarked:

> It is clear, in general, that as we create worlds of electronic information which reflect our political economy in all its contradictions, is should be no surprise if the policies that get read out of these worlds should help us shape the world in the image of that political economy—again in all its contradictions.

Conclusion

Issues raised in this chapter, inclusive of the politics of software patenting, moves to amend India's Copyright Act in line with the WCT and the State's role in projects such as the TKDL highlight the State's complex and ambivalent stance on digital IP. The Indian State, while being pressured by the IIPA and the US government to tighten its IP laws in a digital era, is also involved in deploying the digital to protect its traditional knowledge from a variety of bio-prospectors. Whether or not it is able to protect the country's larger public interests is anybody's guess, although it is vital that civil society–state partnerships are forged in the making of IP policies in the era of the digital.

References

Agrawal, A. 2002. 'Indigenous Knowledge and the Politics of Classification', *International Social Science Journal*, 54 (173): 287–297.

Asay, M. 2008. '$11.4 Billion Wasted On Software Patent Litigation...and Counting', *The Open Road*. Available at: http://news.cnet.com/8301-13505_3-9882152-16.html (accessed on 23 September 2010).

Banavar, A. 2010. 'Patenting of Computer Related Inventions: A Look at Bilsky and its Acceptability in the Indian Scenario', *Journal of International Commercial Law and Technology*, 5 (2): 90–98.

Bessen, J. and R. M. Hunt. 2004. 'An Empirical Look at Software Patents', Working Paper No. 03–17/R, March. Available at: http://www.researchoninnovation.org/swpat.pdf (accessed on 15 September 2010).

Bowker, G. 2000. 'Biodiversity Datadiversity', *Social Studies of Science*, 30 (5): 643–683.

Christian, G. E. 2009. 'Digitization, Intellectual Property Rights and Access to Traditional Knowledge in Developing Countries—The Nigerian Experience', pp. 1–35, *IDRC*, December, Ottawa. Available at: http://idl-bnc.idrc.ca/dspace/bitstream/10625/41341/1/129184.pdf (accessed on 11 October 2011).

Das, A. K., B. K. Sen and C. Dutta. 2005. 'Digitization of Scholarly Materials in India for Distance and Open Learners', pp. 1–11, Paper presented at ICDE International Conference, 19–23 November, New Delhi.

Dasgupta, K. 2005. 'Digitisation, Sustainability and Access in the Indian context', Paper presented at the World Library and Information Congress: 71st IFLA General Conference and Council—'Libraries: A Voyage of Discovery', 14–18 August, Oslo, Norway. Available at: http://archive.ifla.org/IV/ifla71/papers/132e-Dasgupta.pdf (accessed on 26 September 2010).

Draft Manual of Patent Practice and Procedure. 2008. 'The Patent Office, India'. Available at: http://ipindia.nic.in/ipr/patent/DraftPatent_Manual_2008.pdf (accessed on 8 September 2010).

Dubey, N. 2010. 'Copyright vs. Patent—The Great Debate', *PSA, ENewsline*, April. Available at: http://psalegal.com/pdf/E-Newsline-April-201004262010121808PM.pdf (accessed on 24 September 2010).

Evans, D. S. and A. Layne-Farrar. 2004. 'Software Patents and Open Source: The Battle over Intellectual Property Rights', *Virginia Journal of Law and Technology*, 9 (10): 1–28.

Gene Campaign. 2010. 'A Review of the Documentation of Indigenous Knowledge (IK) Associated With Biodiversity in South Asia', Gene Campaign, New Delhi. Available at: http://www.genecampaign.org/Focus%20Area/PROJECT/Analysis%20of%20IK%20Documentation.pdf (accessed on 14 October 2011).

Grosche, A. 2006. 'Software patents—Boon or Bane for Europe?', *International Journal of Law and Information Technology*, 14 (3): 257–309.

Gupta, V. K. n.d. 'Protecting Indian Traditional Knowledge from Biopiracy'. Available at: http://www.wipo.int/export/sites/www/meetings/en/2011/wipo_tkdl_del_11/pdf/tkdl_gupta.pdf (accessed on 14 October 2011).

Hodge, A. 2009. 'India Acts to Keep Tradition Safe for All', *The Australian*, 24 February. Available at: http://www.theaustralian.com.au/news/india-acts-to-keep-tradition-safe-for-all/story-e6frg6t6-1111118941896 (accessed on February 24 2012).

IIPA. 2010. 'India, International Intellectual Property Alliance (IIPA) 2010 Special 301 Report on Copyright Protection and Enforcement'. Available at: http://www.iipa.com/rbc/2010/2010SPEC301INDIA.pdf (accessed on 24 September 2010).

Kelty, C. M. 2005. 'Geeks, Social Imaginaries and Recursive Publics', *Cultural Anthropology*, 20 (2): 185–214.

———. 2008. *Two Bits: The Cultural Significance of Free Software*. Durham and London: Duke University Press.

Liang, L. 2005. 'Porous Legalities and Avenues of Participation', *Sarai Reader: Bare Acts*, pp. 6–17. Available at: http://www.altlawforum.org/intellectual-property/publications/articles-on-the-social-life-of-media-piracy/Lawrence-%20Porous%20legalities%20and%20avenues%20of%20participation.pdf/view (accessed on 24 September 2010).

Liang, L., A. Sethi and P. Iyengar. n.d. 'Briefing Note on the Impact of Software Patents on the Software Industry In India', *Sarai.net*, pp. 1–11. Available at: http://www.sarai.net/research/knowledge-culture/critical-public-legal-resources/whysoftwarepatentsareharmful.pdf (accessed on 24 September 2010).

Lindholm, S. 2005. 'Marking the Software Beast', *Stanford Journal of Law, Business and Finance*, 10 (2): 82–128. Also available at: http://lindholm.jp/proj/marking-pub.pdf

Mittal, R. and G. Mahesh. 2008. 'Digital Libraries and Repositories in India: An Evaluative Study', *Program: Electronic Library and Information Systems*, 42 (3): 286–302.

Office of the Controller General of Patents, Designs, Trade Marks and Geographical Indications. 2009. 'Annual Report 2008–2009'. Available at: http://ipindia.gov.in/cgpdtm/AnnualReport_English_2008_2009.pdf (accessed on 8 September 2010).

Oguamanam, C. 2008. 'Local Knowledge as Trapped Knowledge: Intellectual Property, Culture, Power and Politics', *The Journal of World Intellectual Property*, 11(1): 29–57.

Padma, T. V. 2005. 'Digital Library to Protect Indigenous Knowledge', *Science and Development Network News*, 10 January.

Perry, M. 2010. 'Towards Legal Protection for Digital Rights Management in India: Necessity or Burden?', *Social Science Research Network*. Available at: http://papers.ssrn.com/sol3/papers.cfm?abstract_id=1647582 (accessed on 25 September 2010).

Prakash, P. 2010a. 'Arguments against Software Patents in India', *CIS*. Available at: http://www.cis-india.org/advocacy/ipr/blog/arguments-against-software-patents (accessed on 24 September 2010).

———. 2010b. 'The 2010 Special 301 Report Is More of the Same, Slightly Less Shrill', *CIS*. Available at: http://www.cis-india.org/advocacy/ipr/blog/2010-special-301 (accessed on 24 September 2010).

Reddy, S. 2006. 'Making Heritage Legible: Who Owns Traditional Medical Knowledge?' *International Journal of Cultural Property*, 13: 161–188.

Rediff. 2010. 'Bio-Piracy: India Wins Case Against 15 Patents', *Rediff Business*, 26 April. Available at: http://business.rediff.com/report/2010/apr/26/bio-piracy-india-wins-case-against-15-patents.htm (accessed on 26 September 2010).

Rikowski, R. 2008. 'Digital Libraries and Digitisation: An Overview and Critique', *Policy Futures in Education*, 6 (1): 5–21.

Sharma, S. n.d. 'New Patent Regime in India—Challenges and Future of the Pharmaceutical Industry', pp. 1–27. Available at: http://works.bepress.com/cgi/viewcontent.cgi?article=1003&context=shashi_sharma (accessed on 3 November 2010).

Shivapriya, N. and J. Harsimran. 2010. 'Ohio Bans Offshoring of IT Projects by Govt Depts.', *The Economic Times*, 8 September. Available at: http://economictimes.indiatimes.com/infotech/ites/Ohio-bans-offshoring-of-IT-projects-by-govt-depts/articleshow/6515714.cms (accessed on 24 September 2010).

Srivastava, S. 2007. 'Lotus in The Muck', *Outlook India.com*, 25 June. Available at: http://www.outlookindia.com/article.aspx?234960 (accessed on 3 November 2010).

Sundaram, R. 2009. 'Revisiting the Pirate Kingdom', *Third Text*, 23 (3): 335–345.
Thacker, E. 2006. *The Global Genome: Biotechnology, Politics and Culture.* Cambridge, Mass: MIT Press.
The Standing Committee. 2010. 'The Standing Committee on Human Resource Development Invites Suggestions on the Copyright (Amendment) Bill, 2010'. Available at: http://164.100.47.5/newcommittee/press_release/press/ Committee%20on%20HRD/Press_release_of_copyright_amendment_ bill__10.pdf (accessed on 25 September 2010).
Thomas, P. N. 2006. 'Interpreting IP Contestations in India', in P. N. Thomas and J. Servaes, (eds), *Intellectual Property Rights and Communications in India,* pp. 174–189. New Delhi: SAGE Publications.
————. 2010. 'Traditional Knowledge and the Traditional Knowledge Digital Library: Digital Quandaries and other Concerns', *International Communications Gazette*, 72 (8): 659–673.
Udgaonkar, S. 2002. 'The Recording of Traditional Knowledge: Will It Prevent Bio-Piracy', *Current Science*, 82 (4): 413–419.
Verma, S. K. 2004. 'Protecting Traditional Knowledge: Is a Sui Generis System an Answer?', *The Journal of World Intellectual Property*, 7(6): 765–805.
WIPO. 2005. 'WIPO National Seminar on Copyright, Related Rights and Collective Management', WIPO/Republic of Sudan, Khartoum. Available at: http:// www.wipo.int/edocs/mdocs/arab/en/wipo_cr_krt_05/wipo_cr_krt_05_1a. pdf (accessed on 24 February 2012).
Worcman, K. 2002. 'Digital Division is Cultural Exclusion. But Is Digital Inclusion Cultural Inclusion?', *D-Lib Magazine* (online), 8(3). Available at: http:// www.dlib.org/dlib/march02/worcman/03worcman.html (accessed on 11 October 2011).

8

Public Sector Software in India

In early February (1–2) 2010, I took part in a South India Regional Workshop on 'Software Principles for the Public Sector, with Focus on Public Education' that was held in Bengaluru (IT for Change 2010). The workshop was jointly organised by UNESCO, e-Governance Department, Department of Public Instruction and Sarva Shiksha Abhiyan (Government of Karnataka), Karnataka Jnana Aayoga (Karnataka Knowledge Commission) and the NGO, IT for Change. A number of senior civil servants, including Dr Ajay Kumar, Principal Secretary, IT and e-governance, Government of Kerala, Mr C. Umashankar (the former general manager of Electronics Corporation of Tamil Nadu Limited [ELCOT], Tamil Nadu and F/OSS evangelist) and senior government and civil society representatives took part in this event. This was followed by a similar workshop in Jaipur (25 February) and an international event in Kochi (27–28 May). What was clearly on display during the Bengaluru meeting was the strong belief by many civil servants on the need for F/OSS-based public sector software, the breadth of government initiatives in this regard, and also the willingness of government to partner with civil society and NGOs such as IT for Change to achieve this goal. The importance of public sector software is best illustrated by the ₹200 billion investment by the Government of India in the National e-Governance Plan (see Kanungo 2010), e-governance projects and pre-existing research and development initiatives related to F/OSS supported by the IITs, the National Resource Centre for Free and Open Source Software (NRCFOSS), NIC, the Centre for Development of Advanced Computing (C-DAC) and policy initiatives such as the Ministry of Information and Communication Technology's draft policy on Open Standards for e-Governance (E-Governance Standards 2009). There is a critical, strategic reason for government commitment to public sector software. Governments tend to be among the biggest consumers and manufacturers of information and it makes infinite sense for this information to be made available to all its citizens. However, for this to happen, there has to be a commitment to standards that allow for inter-operability, both vertically and horizontally and across sectoral boundaries.

To some extent, public sector software is an aspect of the new approach to public management in India that is an outcome of internal reform as well as external pressure—such as the public sector adoption of the RTI. This new approach is based on increased efficiency, decentralisation, increased accountability, improved resource management and marketisation (Heeks 1998). One can also argue that public sector software in the context of e-governance enables the growth of the information and knowledge commons. Given that information is largely a non-rivalrous resource, the key issues in the context of its public provisions are access, affordable use and relevant content. The 'tragedy of the commons', to use a phrase popularised by the biologist Garrett Hardin (1968) to describe the pressures of over population-led over-grazing of cattle on common pastures, is not applicable to the information commons, given that your consumption and mine of any given digital resource does not deplete it in any way. There is however, a tragedy of the anti-commons that can be blamed on a market-based, profit-driven drives to enclose intellectual property, thereby restricting innovation and creativity. As Michael Heller (1998: 677) has observed:

> A *tragedy of the commons* can occur when too many individuals have privileges of use in a scarce resource...A *tragedy of the anticommons* can occur when too many individuals have rights of exclusion of a scare resource. The tragedy is that rational individuals, acting separately, may collectively waste the resource by underconsuming it compared with a social optimum.

The Public Sector in India

Public sector software needs to be viewed in the context of India's commitment to public sector-based development. Given the scale of issues that faced the Indian nation at its Independence—poverty, unemployment and lack of development, planned development was seen as an answer. This led to the institution of the Planning Commission in 1950 and growth based on successive FYPs. The Indian State through its public welfare projects subsidies lives and livelihoods for the majority of Indians—literally millions of people. Additionally, employment in the public sector in 1981 was in the region of 15.5 million, '68 per cent of the total employment in the organised public and private sectors' (Tata Institute of Sciences 2008). While economic liberalisation in the 1990s has led to disinvestments in the public sector, public sector expenditures continue to grow. Public sector projects, such as the MGNREGA, that guarantee 100 days of employment for the rural poor in public works projects and the Public Distribution System that facilitates the purchase of subsidised grains and oils, enables vast sections of the Indian population to stay alive. In this sense, the public sector is involved in creating equity, justice and a level playing field in variety of sectors, including education, health, agriculture, manufacturing and industry. It is, of course, well known that the public sector in India is plagued with corruption, lack of accountability and politicisation—issues that have been exposed through movements such as the RTI (see Thomas 2010). The strength of public sector policies is that it is intentionally directed towards the welfare of the most under-privileged sections of the population, which in the case of India, runs into many millions. The objectives of public sector software are explicitly linked to furthering access and affordable use of software by the majority of people in India. As the country commits itself to the digital, public sector software will ensure that the fruits of this revolution that is currently being enjoyed by segments of the Indian population will also be made available to populations who otherwise, will not be linked to the informational revolution. Notwithstanding issues related to increased possibilities for the state to extend its surveillance capacities—the positive freedoms associated with public sector software should not be discounted. The fact that public sector software does have the potential to unleash creativity and innovation through collaborative learnings, applications and co-creation is an important positive freedom associated with this software. It can also, in the context of the RTI, be leveraged by ordinary people to reform governance and make the public sector accountable to its publics.

Defining Public Sector Software

As described in the Public Software Centre (n.d.) website:

> Public Software being publicly owned, allows for its free sharing as well as modification by all. It thus allows the freedoms that Free and Open Source Software (FOSS) allows. Hence in most cases public software and FOSS are synonymous. However there is an important distinction. While FOSS essentially requires the freedoms of the individual user to use, study, share and modify the source code, in addition to this, public software emphasises its 'public good/public interest' nature and vests on government the responsibility of ensuring that basic software required for negotiating the digital world is freely available to all. FOSS is premised on principles of freedoms of ownership on products of collective labour—essentially a polical economy model that is applicable as an exemplar for society's processes of production—in most areas of knowledge production and certainly in the digital space, where such collaboration has a

revolutionary new context and possibilities. Thus FOSS celebrates a 'negative right' that all have the right to use, study, modify, distribute software (share the fruits of collective labour). Public Software on the other hand is organised on public goods principles, that certain goods whose production may not offer sufficient incentives for the private sector and whose availability is important to all in society, need to have an alternate model of production and distribution. Public Software thus emphasises the 'positive right' of citizens—that basic software for negotiating digital society is their entitlement. It concerns the public sector and its role and obligations to society.

Public sector software is an increasingly important issue for governments throughout the world. As government's in the UK, Germany, France, the Netherlands, Denmark, South Africa, Brazil along with numerous other countries have increased investments in e-governance, there have been complementary moves to explore the most efficient inter-operability standards, cost-effective software solutions and ways to strengthen 'universal and affordable access'. There is a belief that open source software and open standards ensure greater transparency, interoperability, independence and flexibility leading to sustainable, long-term solutions. The fact that public sector software based on open standards advances modular solutions is again a significant reason for government investments in open solutions. Modular solutions need to be seen against that dominant reality of bundled software that is an aspect of vendor lock-ins. K. D. Simon (2005: 23) explains the benefits of modularity:

> Modularity allows components to be loosely coupled or interchanged independent of one another. A user can select many different, small companies to from an OSS solution. The components are not directly linked to one provider or developer. Instead, users can obtain these components from various sources located all over the world.... Modularity is one of the primary reasons that OSS is closely connected to open standards.

Private sector firms too, such as IBM, Oracle and Sun Microsystems, have invested in open standards and such moves have hastened the government towards adoption of open standards. In 2009, Tim Berners-Lee, often described as the father of the World Wide Web, was invited by the then prime minister of Britain, Gordon Brown, to explore possibilities to unlock and make publically available, literally hundreds of public data sets for public use. As Chatfield and Crabtree (2010: 44–45) describe it, Whitehall civil servants were exposed to the cultural politics and convictions of an open source enthusiast.

> Most Whitehall computers run on a heavily encrypted network called the 'government secure intranet'. But Berners-Lee, used to his own laptop,

demanded wireless internet access. He also wanted his team to use an open source project management tool, called Basecamp. But the biggest bone of contention came over Microsoft Word. Much government work is done by civil servants emailing Word documents back and forth. Yet Berners-Lee refuses, on principle, to use Word, which is a proprietary rather than an open source format. On one occasion, one official recalled, Berners-Lee received an urgent document in Word from one of the most senior civil servants—and refused to look at it until a junior official had rushed to translate it into an acceptable format.

In the UK, there are moves to speed up the adoption of open source software on public sector IT systems, save on licensing fees and avoid proprietory software lock-ins (see Allen 2009: 8). What seems to be the trend is not the complete marginalisation of proprietory software, but openness to the need for mixed systems in e-governance. In the case of India, for example, the networking of public libraries using the e-Granthalaya software developed by the NIC is based on Microsoft technology:

[and it] runs on a Windows platform in client/server mode over a local area network or on stand-alone system...Version 3 is being developed in collaboration with the Microsoft Corporation as a development partner.... The e-Granthalaya software is being distributed free of charge to all Government libraries, including public libraries in India, under NIC's e-Governance support role. (Matoria et al. 2007: 52)

While a mixed approach is favoured by a number of governments, there is increased wariness of proprietorial software that stems from a virtual monopoly that vendors such as Microsoft continue to exert throughout the world. A number of governments have experienced the lock-ins that are a result of the deployments of proprietorial software in e-governance projects and there is a growing consensus that the software used to generate, manage and process 'public' data needs to be publically owned and operated. Ghosh et al. (2008: 23) describe the effects of such lock-ins that can be the result of the procurement of proprietory software:

A one-time, presumably competitive acquisition of a proprietory system for web server administration can result in a requirement that all future additions to the web site must be made with the same proprietory system. This not only limits the future choice of the public administration that acquired the software in the first place; it forces citizens, businesses and other future contractors developing additions to the public website to become customers of the vendor of the original software acquired by the public administration.

If standards are controlled by any given vendor, it can result in a lack of compatibility between existing hardware, operating systems and file formats that have been deployed in e-governance, e-administration and e-government initiatives. While inter-operability remains an issue within national territories, it can be an even more complex issue in the context of supra-national states, such as the European Union where member states use different standards. This can lead to higher transactional costs and inefficiencies in information flows.

Bountouri et al. (2009: 205), in an article on 'metadata interoperability in public sector information', highlight the various levels that can be affected and that are a consequence of differing standards/protocols and heterogeneity in software applications:

> Syntax—heterogeneities caused by the differences between protocols, encodings and languages used by information sources (i.e. query languages, data formats etc.);
>   Schema—heterogeneities coming from the implementation of different data models, data structures and schemas;
>   Semantic—heterogeneities produced by semantic conflicts arising from the fact that the meaning of the data can be expressed in different ways and with different interpretations; and
>   System—heterogeneities arising from different hardware platforms, operating systems and networking protocols.

These concerns are being addressed in India, although it is not clear to what extent progress has been made at these four levels. The National Informatics Centre is involved in exploring standards for e-governance, and 'metadata and data standards for application domains' is one of five areas, inclusive of network and information security, quality and documentation, localisation and language technology standards and technical standards and e-governance architectures that they are currently working on.

Their concerns need to be seen in the context of the flexibility required to 'mash' data that can lead to the public sector delivering innovative solutions to public problems. The issue of whether such data mash-ups should be based on public–private partnerships remains an issue, given legal issues with IP, ownership of data as well as political and economic issues. The publics involvement in mash-ups is best illustrated by the example from the UK where public data—3,000 data sets to be precise, have now been released to the public, increasing the potential for crowd-sourcing initiatives. There are, however, 'new' issues that have emerged in the context of user-generated content based on the Ordinance Survey maps and other data sets that have been released to the public. Michael Batty et al. (2010: 39), from University College London, refer to some of these challenges:

> While new Web and mobile-based geospatial services and applications will provide clear benefits to users, there are still ethical and social factors that are not yet fully understood or addressed. There are issues concerning user

generated and 'open' data, ethics and privacy issues with regard to the handling of data, and these will have a bearing on the development of location-based information and services. In particular, the privacy issues around broadcasting personal location information, particularly within social networks, will potentially have unintended consequences beyond the simple usage and value that these applications provide.

The other key question of concern is the extent to which adding different layers of data, which independently are each within the bounds of confidentiality imposed by the data provider and by Government, lead to breaches in confidentiality when added together.... [They note that studies have demonstrated] the measures that are already being taken in the public sector to limit the amount of geographical information provided in individual-level datasets and to create secure environments for data analysis, in recognition of the perceived high risk of disclosure of confidential data on individuals.

Dependency, Risk and E-Governance

The issue of dependency that was discussed in the context of media imperialism and the New World Information and Communication Order (NWICO) and that was rather hastily marginalised in the wake of the euphoria over the multi-ways flows in the brave new world characterised by cultural globalisation, has been resurrected, although this time around, the struggle is not about Cold War politics, but involves objectives shared by governments in the developed and developing world. Dependency in the context of e-governance does have major security implications, given that any vendor's control over public data sets can compromise a nation's sovereignty. Dependency has been a characteristic feature of global software, given the monopoly that vendors such as Microsoft have enjoyed for more than two decades.

The issue of informational dependency in the context of the 21st century, however, is qualitatively different from media dependency in the 20th century. In the context of convergent, informational capitalism characterised by the informationalisation of all productive and life processes, dependency can have serious consequences for any government. Federspiel and Brincker (2010: 41) employ the German political theorist Ulrich Beck's notion of the 'Risk Society' to understand current anxieties related to software standards in Denmark, a country that on 1 January 2008 passed a resolution that supported open standards for all public sector software. As they point out:

> Bearing in mind Beck's definition of risk, software lends itself to risk analysis: The software market transcends national states—in fact, national states are apparently

quite unable to regulate or control this market. The software market produces and delivers products on which the public sectors are completely dependent. This is particularly evident in countries like Denmark where the public sector has undergone digitalisation. Finally, one cannot insure against data losses, malfunctioning electronic filing systems, or breakdowns in communication infrastructures, the consequences if which are difficult to quantify and thereby compensate in monetary terms. Therefore, the risks associated with software may be characterised as incalculable.

Beck's understanding of 'risk' is based on the various environmental hazards facing the globe in the context of late modernity and in a situation characterised by the globalisation of risk best illustrated by catastrophes, such as Chernobyl, and the relative powerlessness of the state to deal with the intended and unintended consequences and risks associated with progress and growth. Beck (1999: 25) describes the change in the power of the nation-state thus:

> The national state is a territorial state; its power is grounded upon controlling the membership, defending the borders, laying down the laws for a particular place. The world society created by globalisation cuts across national state boundaries, not only economically, but through a multiplicity of social circles, communication networks, market relations and lifestyles, none of them specific to any locality.

The network society's investments in the establishment, maintenance and harmonisation of data flows—economic, political, cultural and social—certainly contribute to the strengthening of faith in the ability of global capitalism to contribute to growth and progress. However, this hope and certainty is offset by issues related to the security of data flows and the inability to control these flows, given the 'uncontrollable' nature of the digital. In this sense, as Cottle (1998: 8) has observed, the 'nature of contemporary "risks" for Beck are historically unprecedented in terms of their spatial and temporal reach, their potential catastrophic effects and, importantly, their invisibility'. While there is no denial of the tremendous contributions by the services sectors to growth in India, how to manage this growth without endangering the security and sovereignty of the nation is an issue that is of concern to the Indian government. E-Governance has already begun to generate vast amounts of data on the public, and public sector software is a way of ensuring that this data is managed primarily in support of the national interest. While the draft National Policy on Open Standards in e-Governance (E-Governance Standards 2009) does acknowledge security concerns in clause 4.7, its specific objectives as outlined below support the national interest:

The National Policy is designed to ensure appropriate Information Technology adoption that promotes the interests of the nation with level playing field to all. In particular, it aims at the following:

3.1 Promote innovations and entrepreneurship in e-Governance at grass root level of the society, spread across the geographical limits of the country.
3.2 Ensure availability of multi-lingual e-Governance services.
3.3 Ensure reliable long term accessibility to public documents and information
3.4 Ensure cost effective e-Governance services.
3.5 Provide larger spectrum of choice of solutions and flexibility to users of e-Governance systems by avoiding vendor lock-in.
3.6 Provide better and fair opportunities to all vendors in e-Governance eco system by enhancing interoperability. (1)

One can argue that public sector software mitigates the risk of 'organised irresponsibility'. Here again Ulrich Beck's (1997: 29) suggestion for the need for a 'relations of definition' is useful because it refers to the role played by 'rules, institutions and resources' in the mitigation of such risks. The following four questions can be applied to understanding risk not only in terms of e-governance but all 'development' projects supported by the state and the private sector in the context of contemporary India:

(1) Who-that is, what social agency and authority establishes in what way how harmless or dangerous products and their side-effects are? Does the responsibility lie with those who create and profit from the risks, or with those who are currently or potentially affected, or with public agencies? (2) What type of knowledge or unawareness of causes, dimensions, agents and so on is consulted or acknowledged here? Who bears the burden of proof? (3) What is considered 'sufficient proof' and this, of course, must be answered in a world where all knowledge of hazards and risk moves in the presuppositions of probability theory. (4) Where hazards and destruction are recognised and acknowledged, who decides issues of liability, compensation and costs for the affected parties, and who rules on appropriate forms of future monitoring and regulation?

Public Software Challenges

While there are, at any given time, a number of e-governance initiatives in India that are powered by public sector software solutions, such as NRCFOSS/C-DAC's Linux-based Bharat Operating System Solutions (BOSS), there are inter-state variations in the deployment of such solutions. While the southern states, particularly Kerala and to lesser extent, Tamil Nadu and Karnataka, have adopted such solutions, along with Gujarat, Orissa, West Bengal and Assam, a number of states in North and Central India have yet to follow suit. The Government of Assam's Information Technology Policy (*The Assam Gazette* 2009: 1216–1217), for example, specifies the F/OSS as the basis for public sector software:

3.12   FREE AND OPEN SOURCE SOFTWARE POLICY:

(a) The Government would promote use of Free and Open Source Software (FOSS) in all the departments and State agencies, bodies and authorities.

(b) The State Government would promote manpower development and training in use of FOSS, especially in day to day office works.

(c) The State Government would promote imparting training on FOSS in schools and colleges.

(d) Entrepreneurs/companies using FOSS for application/website development would be given preference over those using third party packaged applications.

(e) All source codes customized developed for any State Government body shall be duly archived in a repository, and shall be made available freely to other Government departments.

(f) The Government departments and bodies would ensure that Open Document Format (ODF) is adhered to in creating and storing editable documents, data and information and all applications developed by the respective departments adhere to ODF and other Open Standards and are largely independent of Operating Systems (0s) and web browsers.

(g) The Government departments and bodies would ensure that any generic hardware procured has support for multiple Operating Systems (OS) such as Unix, Linux, OpenSolaris and other open source platforms.

The example of Kerala is well known and, to a large extent, the commitment to public sector software is the result of political will by both major political parties. Kerala, for example, is home to a number of passionately committed civil servants and civil society activists to the values of free and open source software solutions. The F/OSS-based IT@School project in Kerala has, for example, led to ICT-enabled education in 8,000 schools in the state and has been involved in the training of 200 master trainers and 5,600 IT coordinators (selected from teaching staff). The public-owned software has been bundled into a single CD for a one-point installation—not achievable in the context of the use of proprietary software. While the lack of awareness of F/OSS-based solutions does exist, more formidable issues are the pre-existing lock-ins and tie-ups that dominant software players such as Microsoft have with the state governments in India. In the state of Maharashtra, for example, the Department of Education and Microsoft have entered into a contract whereby Microsoft will set up IT academies and train teachers at no cost to the state and in which, curriculum design will also be handled by Microsoft. Trade bodies, such as NASSCOM and MAIT, have also played a role in trying to water-down the Draft Policy on Open Standards for e-Governance by lobbying for multiple standards and royalty encumbered standards (see IT for Change 2010a). At the Bangalore workshop on Software Principles for the Public Sector, a resource paper (IT for Change 2010b) included examples of software deployment that does not adhere to public sector principles. Among the nine examples, there was the following example of software-use in the context of the MGNREGA in Andhra Pradesh.

> AP's NREGA application has been developed by the private sector at 'no cost' to the Government. However, in not taking ownership of the software source code (a mistake often done in e-governance application development), the department is dependant on one vendor for servicing and/or enhancements. Also the Government cannot share this application with other state governments, who could have used it for NREGA in their states with some customisation, since it is in any case a central government schemes with common procedures and processes. In the present situation, every state government would need to pay license fees to the vendor for using the software, which fees may also go up as number of per state users go up. Significantly, the most important part of 'intellectual property' vested in this application actually came from the government officials who discussed and laid out requirements and processes, and tested software, in an intense process over many months. The corresponding 'technical expertise' required to design and develop the application is relatively trivial and easily available as a commodity from the market. However, now the whole IP of the application is owned by the private vendor who can make a lot of money out of it, selling it to other public agencies. *This case is not unique. We think what has happened in this case is true of much of e-governance application development going on in the country.* (Emphasis in the original.)

This example clearly illustrates the dangers of risk associated with private sector access to public data sets, including documents and databases that cover a wide variety of domain areas. Control over domain-specific data can lead to its commercial exploitation and compromises in privacy and security resulting in digital and other divides. It can be argued that the payment of license fees, lack of access to the source code, lack of competition, inability to innovate or reuse software is, from a public perspective, a case of 'organised irresponsibility'. The decision to use a Windows-based software platform for the nation-wide Aadhar Unique ID project, despite prior promises to the contrary is another example of the politics of a Janus-faced state and the influence of a major software vendor. 'The Unique Identification Authority of India (UIDAI) mandates that all "middleware" used in Aadhaar must be vendor neutral. However, by using software that is only Windows-compliant, UID applications have already established a clear vendor lock-in' (Kurup 2010).

One of the major issues facing the public sector software movement is the fact that they are involved in both 'reacting' and 'responding' to the reality of multiple standards and issues with inter-operability in e-governance projects and the politics of resistance to change at government levels, as well as proactively lobbying for a more focussed, intelligent and centralised approach to public sector software development in India. The silo approach to departmental management affects the sharing of content and this is a major concern in India where consanguineous government units act as if they are unrelated. The lack of standardised UNICODE compliant fonts for example, has led to compatibility issues. This is a key issue in the context of e-governance, given that the intent is to deliver e-governance in the language spoken by the common man—a challenge in the context of immense language diversity (500 languages, 216 mother tongues, 10,000 dialects, 22 constitutionally recognised languages). Kewal Krishnan (n.d.: 6) from the NIC, highlights some of the issues with standardisation related to language:

> Storage standards, font standards, inputting standards, transliteration/Roman equivalent, Sorting order/sequence for Indian languages, OCR standards, Standards for Website and Email, Local search engine standards, Availability of all constitutionally recognised Indian languages in all Operating Systems, Strategy for conversion of data from ISCII to UNICODE.

While there are a number of initiatives in India that are looking to deliver on free software Unicode typefaces, much more work needs to be done in this regard. The lack of training in F/OSS and resistance to F/OSS in the public sector are also issues that public sector software enthusiasts have to contend with.

At the end of the meeting in Bengaluru, held in February 2010, there were general areas of agreement related to public software:

- Ownership issues of process/source code—PS should be government-owned, and this ownership should be meaningful and well-documented. Involvement of private players is welcome insofar as ownership of source code was not vested with private agencies.
- Technological issues—Unicode fonts, geographical standards, language standards, etc. need to be developed for free and open use, and mandated by policy.
- Wider community should be involved along with domain experts, technology experts to develop and customise PS.

- Need shareable data between government departments—availability of all public software on a single platform/portal for use across departments and states.
- Approach to issues of software, the method of functioning of agencies such as NIC and CDAC and others, issue of hierarchy and power, etc. need to change. (IT for Change 2010a: 14)

Conclusions

The emphasis on public sector software by the Indian government illustrates the State's commitment to information futures in India in which majority of people have access to maximum public data flows in a language of their choice. While there are plans afoot to deliver e-governance via localised 'Common Services Centre', the equivalent of tele-centres, it is anybody's guess as to whether or not such centres will facilitate access for all Indians, irrespective of caste, gender, class and other markers of identity and status. To belabour a point that I have made in a number of my writings on the media in India (see Thomas 2010), such reforms can only lead to social change if they are complemented by other social reforms. While disintermediation effects certainly need to be celebrated, endemic asymmetries can and do lead to a reinvention of power and privilege in the context of network societies. The politics of access and affordable use, in other words, also need to be dealt with. However, and despite such concerns and continuing issues with the reputation of the Indian state as a habitual recalcitrant, whose interests are at varying odds with millions of its citizenry, public sector software clearly reveals that the Indian State is indeed complex, multifaceted in its response and commitment to the welfare of its citizenry. Despite its many shortcomings, it is also capable of supporting the project of substantive democracy.

References

Allen, A. 2009. 'Open Software "Best for Taxpayer"', *Supply Management*, 14 (5): 8.

Batty, M., A. Crooks, A. Hudson-Smith, R. Milton, S. Anand, M. Jackson and J. Morley. 2010. 'Data Mash-Ups and the Future of Mapping', *JISC Technology and Standards Watch*, September, pp. 1–45. Available at: http://www.jisc.ac.uk/media/documents/techwatch/jisctsw_10_01.pdf (accessed on 29 September 2010).

Beck, U. 1997. 'Global Risk Politics', *The Political Quarterly*, 68 (B): 18–33.

Beck, U. 1999. 'Beyond The Nation State', *The New Statesman*, pp. 25–27, 6 December.

Bountouri, L., C. Papatheodorou, V. Soulikias and M. Stratis. 2009. 'Metadata Interoperability in Public Sector Information', *Journal of Information Science*, 35 (2): 204–231.

Chatfield, T. and J. Crabtree. 2010. "Mash the State", *Prospect Magazine*, 167 (February): 42–46.

Cottle, S. 1998. 'Ulrich Beck, "Risk Society" and the Media: A Catastrophic View?', *European Journal of Communication*, 13 (5): 5–32.

E-Governance Standards. 2009. 'Draft National Policy on Open Standards for e-Governance'. Available at: http://fosscomm.in/OpenStandards?action= AttachFile&do=get&target=Policy_On_Open_Standards_V2.pdf (accessed on 28 September 2010).

Federspiel, S. B. and B. Brincker. 2010. 'Software as Risk: Introduction of Open Standards in the Danish Public', *The Information Society*, 26 (1): 38–47.

Ghosh, R. A., R. Glott, P-E. Schmitz and A. Boujraf. 2008. 'OSOR Guidelines Public Procurement and Open Source Software', pp. 1–117, *IDABC Dissemination of Good Practice in Using Open Source Software*, Unisys Belgium, UNU-MERIT.

Hardin, G. 1968. 'The Tragedy of the Commons', *Science*, 162 (3859): 1243–1248.

Heeks, R. 1998. 'Information Age Reform of the Public Sector: The Potential and Problems of IT for India', pp. 1–21, *Information Systems for Public Sector Management*, Working Paper Series No. 6. October, Institute for Development Policy and Management, University of Manchester. Available at: http://unpan1.un.org/intradoc/groups/public/documents/NISPAcee/ UNPAN015479.pdf (accessed on 28 September 2010).

Heller, M. E. 1998. The Tragedy of the Anti-Commons: Property in the Transition from Marx to Markets', *Harvard Law Review*, 111 (3): 621–688.

IT for Change. 2010a. 'South India Regional Workshop on Software Principles for the Public Sector, with Focus on Public Education', *Case Studies—Public Software*, February.

———. 2010b. 'Software Principles for the Public Sector with Focus on Public Education', Report on the Workshop, Bengaluru, 1–2 February 2010.

Kanungo, V. 2010. 'Government of India to Invest in ₹20,000 Crores on E-Governance by 2014', *e-GovWorld 2010*, 19 July. Available at: http://67.223.235.55:8081/ eGovWorld/newsupdate/opportunities-for-indian-it-companies-to-beat-global-demand-in-it-services-as-government-of-india-decides-to-invest-rs-20-000-crore-on-e-governance-projects-1 (accessed on 27 September 2010).

Kurup, D. 2010. 'Aadhaar Software Locked-in with Windows', *The Hindu*, 2 November. Available at: http://www.thehindu.com/news/national/ article863657.ece (accessed on 2 November 2010).

Krishnan, K. n.d. 'Localisation and Language Technology Standards' pp. 1–25, ppt., National Informatics Centre (NIC). Available at: http://www.panl10n. net/Presentations/Bhutan/Consultation/NIC%20India.ppt.pdf (accessed on 30 September 2010).

Matoria, R. K., P. K. Upadhyay and M. Moni. 2007. 'Automation and Networking of Public Libraries in India Using the *E-Granthalaya* Software from the National Informatics Centre', *Electronic Library and Information Systems*, 41 (1): 47–58.

Public Software Centre. n.d. 'What is Public Software?', Public Software Centre. Available at: http://public-software-centre.org/node/31 (accessed on 28 September 2010).

Simon, K. D. 2005. 'The Value of Open Standards and Open Source Software in Government Environments', *IBM Systems Journal*, 44 (2): 227–238.

Tata Institute of Sciences. 2008. 'Indian Labour Market Report', ADECCO Institute, Tata Institute of Sciences. Available at: http://www.esocialsciences.com/data/articles/Document11452009240.3434107.pdf (accessed on 29 September 2010).

The Assam Gazette. 2009. 'Information Technology Policy of Assam', *The Assam Gazette*, 4 August. Available at: http://assamgovt.nic.in/pdf/ITPOLICY-2009-Final-Gazette-Style.pdf (accessed on 28 September 2010).

Thomas, P. N. 2010. *Political Economy of Communications in India: The Good, the Bad and the Ugly*. New Delhi: SAGE Publications.

Section 4
Contested
Information Technology

The final chapter in this volume is on cultural piracy. It deals with realities of the 'copy' in networked India. While the government and cultural and informational industries have invested in law and order solutions aimed at curbing the practice of piracy, it is difficult to curb, precisely because we live in the era of the copy. This chapter argues that pirate solutions from below need to be 'weighed' in context, since they offer the means for those on the margins to encounter and participate in the digital economy and, thus, contribute to digital futures for all.

9

Piracy in the Contested City: Access, Distribution and Equity

Audio-visual and software piracy are a priority global issue. This is not surprising, given the monetary value associated with cultural products, including revenues that accrue to exports of film, media and software products, and domestic consumption incomes that are worth billions of dollars. Increasing revenues related to trade in IP and moves to protect IP are core aspects of the global IP economy today. In the year 2007 alone, sales of US copyright products in non-US markets were worth US$126 billion (Siwek 2009: 17). In 2007, the value added by the core copyright industries in the USA was in the region of US$889.1 billion; 6.44 per cent of the GDP, while the value added for the total copyright industries has been calculated at US$1.52 trillion or 11.05 per cent of the GDP (IIPA 2009a). These industries have consistently led economic growth in the USA during a decade in which, other core industries, such as manufacturing, have faltered. While copyright industries in India do not earn as much revenues when compared to US-based industries, incomes generated in the Indian media and entertainment industry market are by no means insignificant and are expected to grow from US$11 billion in 2009 to US$25 billion in 2011 (CII 2009).

Combating piracy has also become a major concern in India. Speaking at the Federation of Indian Chambers of Commerce and Industry (FICCI) FRAMES 'Business of Entertainment' Conference, US–India Business Council (USIBC) President, Ron Somers (2009), introducing an industry-led study on cultural piracy in India, observed, 'that the Indian entertainment industry loses some 820,000 jobs and about $4 billion each year to piracy'. Bollywood, an industry that has consistently fed off and copied scripts from Hollywood and, thus far managed to stave off copyright claims, is now under pressure. The report by Rhys Blakely in the *Australian* (2009) on the out-of-court settlement by the Indian film company, B. R. Films to Twentieth Century Fox of an amount of US$200,000 for the film *Banda Yeh Bindaas Hai* (This Guy is Fearless), an illegal remake of the Oscar winning *My Cousin Vinny*—the very first payment of its kind for the copying of a Hollywood film—does suggest that Bollywood will find to harder to tread the copy-route in the future. This is a turnaround from what used to be the norm even as late as 2003, when the romance novelist Barbara Taylor Bradford lost her bid to take the Indian Sahara TV to court for basing their 260-part television series *Karishma-Miracles of Destiny* on her novel *A Woman of Substance*. Rachana Desai (2005: 270), who is on the side of the rights owners, believes that claims against Bollywood will bring about some equity in an industry that is dependent on the cheap copy rather than on investments in local screen writers.

> Hollywood is script driven, while Bollywood is star driven. In other words, because directors know that they can get away with copying a tried-and-true American script, they are less willing to invest money in Indian screenwriters. Big name actors are paid astronomical amounts, while the writers are given meagre sums to 'Indianize' Hollywood films.

Piracy, in other words, works at a variety of levels—it includes cannibalising within and between cultural industries to external cannibalising that is often referred to as 'cultural piracy'.

While piracy and the liberalisation of global film and television imports has been an enduring concern at the USTR's office, the advent of digital copy technologies, the inability to devise foul-proof encryption technologies and the negative economic impact of the 'copy' on a variety of digital media industries has led to the re-doubling of efforts aimed at curbing media and software piracy. The moves to frame cultural piracy with terrorism in the post 9/11 period has intensified the global mediation of the cultural pirate as a terrorist. Today there are any numbers of global, regional and national state–private sector initiatives aimed at curbing trade in pirated media products. The Indian government has attempted to harmonise its many IP legislations with global requirements, invested in the modernisation of IP offices throughout the country, encouraged state-level enforcement measures, including the setting-up of special police units to combat piracy, supported anti-piracy training at different levels and established joint industry–state initiatives aimed at curbing piracy. Global initiatives range from technological solutions, such as digital rights management systems to enforcement initiatives to lobbying for more stringent penalties for those who violate the terms of copyright. Private media consortiums, such as the IIPA that includes key, apex copyright industry bodies like the Business Software Alliance, the Motion Pictures Association and the Recording Industry Association of America along with four other trade associations, are involved in a variety of 'enforcement' initiatives throughout the world, including in India. The Recording Industry Association of America's random suits against 40,000 file sharers in the USA is just the latest initiative to influence world consciousness on the matter of paying for downloaded and shared music in an era in which the technologies of the copy are ubiquitous, and entire generations have got used to and are comfortable with free downloads of music and film. The moves by various states in India, including Tamil Nadu, Karnataka and Maharashtra, to include cultural pirates in the purview of Acts, such as for example, in Tamil Nadu, the Tamil Nadu Prevention of Dangerous Activities of Bootleggers, Drug-Offenders, Forest Offenders, Goondas, Immoral Traffic Offenders and Slum Grabbers Act, 1982, places cultural pirates in the company of those who are generally considered to be low forms of criminal life. These attempts to negate and criminalise cultural piracy make sense from the perspective of the dominant economy that is based on proprietorial flows of culture, knowledge and capital. However, whether or not this approach makes sound sense in a global context characterised by multiple circulations of capital, culture and knowledge, mediated by formal and informal economies, is yet to become a legitimate question in need of an answer in policy circles.

While predatory pricing certainly is a factor that contributes to cultural piracy, another issue that is absolutely central towards understanding this phenomenon relates to the fact that the digital indeed is a revolutionary mode of production based on the 'copy' that can be harnessed by both Microsoft in Seattle and the cultural pirate sitting in the anonymity of home in different parts of the world. The IP critic Siva Vaidhyanathan (2004: xiv) describes the core contestation that is at the heart of this battle.

> As distributed information systems gain prominence and importance, the reaction to them grows fierce. Distributed systems tend toward anarchy. Centralised systems tend towards oligarchy. The space between these models is shrinking, offering no middle ground, no third way.... One of the chief challenges of the twenty-first century will be to formulate ethics, guidelines, habits, or rules to shape an information environment that provides the freedom liberal democracy needs as well as the stability that commerce and community demands.

While Vaidhyanathan's solution may hold good for the USA, how to democratise information, knowledge and culture in a context characterised by multiple economies, multiple politics and multiple equity deficits, remains an issue for countries, such as India.

This chapter attempts to theorise cultural piracy from a number of angles. As against the dominant trend to dismiss piracy as little more than intellectual and monetary theft or as a means to launder ill-gotten wealth, it argues that piracy is this and more, that it offers us a window to explore the spaces and places of uneven globalisation, presents lessons on the value and worth of alternative distribution systems and the morality of everyday practices, provides us with insights on the democratic potential of the copy, and gives us a vision of another access to information, knowledge, culture and ideas. It argues that there is a need to recognise the variety of cultural practices in the modern city that constantly short circuits the project of modernity imposed by global and national capital. The need to comprehend the layered city where the border between the legal and illegal is constantly shifting in spite of the structures and rules of Capital is a task that is only beginning to be explored by critical theorists of the cultures and political economies of urbanity and the city. The ponderous, heavy-handed, 'law and order' response from the dominant copyright industries, that is not based on an understanding of the nature of creativity within the network society, does suggest that they are out of touch with the sources of creativity and flows of life in the real world.

The Control Paradigm

An understanding of 'pirate modernity' (Sundaram 2001) is not of course, on the agenda of countries like the USA. Their goals are to increase IP-related revenues and to make environments safe for circulations of 'legal' cultural products. One can argue that this approach is based on a profound and ultimately futile misreading of complexity, a familiar attitude adopted by this hegemony in other contexts too, such as the wars in Iraq and Afghanistan. This inability to grasp the reality of alternative circulations of culture, understand the multiple reasons for the growth of cultural piracy or implement alternative approaches to dealing with IP infringement is a major blind spot for the dominant copyright industries. This global reality is as true of cities located in the developed as well as in the developing world. Ravi Sundaram's (2009b: 338) description of the nature of contemporary piracy is the stuff of nightmares for both governments and their cultural industries.

> Postcolonial piracy is typically a post-liberal (if not a post-Marxist) cultural effect. Piracy destabilises contemporary media property and, working through world markets and local bazaars, both disrupts and enables creativity, and evades issues of the classic commons while simultaneously radicalising access to subaltern groups in the Third World. Post colonial piracy works more through dense local networks of exchange and face-to-face contact, rather than individual online downloads.... Piracy ... occupies a field the edges of which move all the time, margin to centre, international to local.

To the dominant cultural industry, cultural piracy is a relatively straightforward matter of unscrupulous foreigners ripping off creators of culture. Piracy is seen in terms of black and white, good versus bad, the legal versus the illegal and right versus wrong. This attitude is best exemplified in the US government's annual global survey of media piracy through the office of the USTR. This initiative involves naming countries that habitually transgress IP and using the threat of trade sanctions against these countries to bring them to heel. While the threat of Section 301 sanctions against habitual offenders is a stick that it is used often to bring recalcitrant offenders in line, rewards are given to countries that comply. As is stated in the 2009 IIPA India report (2009a: 50):

> India currently participates in the Generalized System of Preferences (GSP) program, a U.S. trade program that offers preferential trade benefits to eligible beneficiary countries. One of the discretionary criteria of this program is that the country provides 'adequate and effective' copyright protection. In 2008, $3.96 billion worth of Indian goods entered the U.S. under the duty-free GSP program.

The trade benefit to India is an important motive for contemporary efforts to extend copyright protection and curb piracy. However, cleaning the Augean stables of piracy in India is bound to be a complex task, given the fact that *the* key cultural industry in India, cinema, responsible for both export and domestic revenues, has thrived on its links to the informal economy. In fact, as Pendakur (2003) has observed, the film industry in India was recognised as a legitimate and legal industry by the State only as late as 1998. Its links with the underworld, the mafia and as the space for money laundering is too well known to be recounted here (see Sethi 2009 and Pendakur 2003). This history characterised by complex and illegal investments in the Indian film industry, provides the background to the current efforts to clean it. However, this is by no means, an easy task. Athique (2008: 713–714), in a study of piracy as it relates to the film industry in India, describes the gaps between official anti-piracy policies and the specific reality of cultural production in India.

> The complex relationship between the Indian film industry and the underworld, between the official and informal economy in India, and between media technologies and global trade, all serve to illustrate how the dynamics of cultural production in a developing country highlight the proprietary nature, and limited worldview, of intellectual property rhetoric. The regimes that are currently being implemented to further commodify and control cultural production, and to ensure that digital technologies remain under centralised control, were not developed with the operating conditions of Indian cinema in mind.... The

rhetoric on piracy, legitimacy and sovereignty provided by Hollywood despite its ready availability and its evangelical black-and-white world-view, may therefore prove to be less than satisfactory in articulating the challenges facing Indian media in the new world economy.

The reasoning that underlies the dominant political economy of copyright is based on a theoretical construct that privileges the primacy of profits, property, authorship, reason and morality. At the heart of what is an economic argument is the belief that IP is an entirely reasonable arrangement based on sound morals that contributes to growth and prosperity. At a surface level, the reasons for and the morals underlying the pro-copyright argument seem valid enough. After all, creativity needs to be rewarded. A professional writer and musician (irrespective of the existence of prior knowledge in his/her areas of specialisation) need compensation for his/her creativity and protection for the symbolic and cultural capital created through labour. One can argue about the relative merits of individual and collective forms of creativity, although it is important to acknowledge that both forms exist, that it is important to explore adequate compensatory mechanisms. The Creative Commons Project, although critiqued for its individualist approach, nevertheless remains an example of another solution to issues related to IP compensation. While one can celebrate the subversive nature of cultural piracy vis-à-vis the dominant copyright industries, one needs to also acknowledge that piracy affects 'cultural labour' in general, including the fortunes of the traditional musician as well as the marginal writer. Whether it is in Peru, Nigeria or India, traditional musicians face similar issues related to the copy. The English scholar, Brian Larkin (2005: 114) who writes on copyright issues in Nigeria, in an interview with Anand Taneja at Sarai-CSDS, Delhi, articulates this unease while at the same time acknowledging the complex effects of piracy.

> I worry about piracy in Nigeria because it has affected the Nigerian music industry, really hurt people's ability to live their lives, and make music.... But piracy also has had a powerful effect in that it shifted people back into supporting live performances, it renewed patron-client relations, i.e., music that is not commodified by sale through cassettes.... At the same time piracy facilitates access to media in Nigeria.

It is this double-edged nature of piracy that makes it a fascinating topic for study. Piracy is not by any means resistance, although it certainly is the basis for access. While the Hollywood-inspired 'piracy is terrorism' just does not account for the complex nature of piracy, it is important for us to acknowledge that organised crime has played a major role in controlling the overseas distribution circuits of Bollywood film, invested in its production and controlled piracy circuits from Dubai to Karachi. Pirate products have contributed to the closure of film theatres all over India, although it has also contributed to home-based family viewing (see Leena 2004).

The Individual Author

The edifice of copyright law is constructed on the modernist, socially evolved presumption of the 'authorship' of 'natural man', meaning that the author of an expression that is unique and original, is entitled to investing it with property rights. Martha Woodmansee and Peter Jaszi (1994), in an edited volume on the construction of authorship, trace the relationship between 'genius', the individual author and the law to the era of the 'Romantic' poets in the UK, in particular, William Wordsworth and Samuel Coleridge who privileged individual creativity at the expense of collaboratory knowledge, an understanding that has continued to define 'copyright' even in the era of the digital characterised by examples of co-creativity as diverse as Wikipedia and Open Source Software. A specific understanding of creativity, in other words, is at the core of modern copyright law. The first modern copyright law, the Copyright Act of 1710, was instituted during the reign of Queen Anne in the UK, when the commercial viability of printed texts was beginning to interest the attention of latter-day IP pirates. Copyright was basically an agreement between the creative artist and the state. This contract ensured that the State, in exchange for the temporary protection of, and reward for creative endeavour (provided the copyright owner kept his or her mouth shut on matters related to State and faith), would eventually return this creative expression to the public domain. To reiterate, copyright was conceived as a social contract—between the rights of the creator of a work and the public domain, in which the immediate, short-term grant of monopoly rights and the protection of the moral and monetary interests of the creator was balanced out against the long-term interest of social cultural policy and the public domain. While it is relatively uncomplicated to understand the need for 'authorial' copyright when the 'business of expression' was the sole source of income for an individual artist, it is less so in the context of mass reproduction characterised by the commercialisation of production, in a context in which the ownership by the author of his/her expression has migrated to, and become a pecuniary categorical imperative of modern, global corporations. Today, 'authorship' does not accrue to either the individual or to the collective authors of traditional texts, software and other cultural products—but to their corporate employers. In other words, in the space of the last 200 years, and especially during the last two decades, the world has seen a rapid dismemberment and downgrading of the moral rights of the author to the extent that today, this right does not exist in TRIPS parlance.

The dilution of Article 6*bis* is a case in point. *Article 6bis* of the Berne Convention for the Protection of Literary and Artistic Works (Paris Text 1971, see Berne Convention 1999) remains a primary text in the area of copyright and has provided the basis for a number of derivative national and international texts on copyright. While it did advance proprietorial understandings of copyright and was adopted by the Uruguay Round of GATT, there was one Article that was rather unusual—Article 6*bis*. Article 6*bis* (1) affirms the following that:

> Independently of the author's economic rights, and even after the transfer of the said rights, the author shall have the right to claim authorship of the work and to object to any distortion, mutilation or other modification of, or other derogatory action in relation to, the said work, which would be prejudicial to his (*sic*) honour or reputation.

This clause is universally known as the 'moral clause' since it affirms the continuing rights of the author (paternity and integrity), independent of the subsequent sale of this work to private, corporate interests. In an otherwise pro-corporate document, this was an almost redemptive clause.

Two subsequent rulings on IP—the prescription of minimum IP rights in the global trade environment and TRIPS that came into effect on 1 January 1995 and now reflects the WTO's stance on Intellectual Property Rights (IPR) have legitimised the efforts made by corporations, governments and trade organisations to commoditise and corporatise IPR at the expense of individual innovators/creators. The overview of the TRIPS Agreement states clearly that with 'the exception of the provisions of the Berne Convention on moral rights, all the main substantive provisions of these conventions (WIPO, Paris, Berne) are incorporated by reference and thus become obligations under the TRIPS agreement between TRIPS member countries' (World Trade Organisation 1999). In the context of the USA, where proprietorial understandings of IPR are conceived and honed, '(there) is' as Fred Greguras has noted, 'no one championing the expansion of moral rights in the U.S'. 'Authorship', however, continues to be a problematic concept, particularly so in the context of the new, digital technologies of reproduction. Digital technologies have unfixed the singular location, fixed materiality and objectivity associated with products related to the previous generation of technologies. The network society has problematised 'creativity' as the domain of the individual and as Johanna Gibson (2006: 140) has argued:

> In a networked society, the expression can no longer exist independently of the cultural and ideological experience of knowledge creation. It is part of the cultural practice of the society. Therefore, the commercial system of intellectual property necessarily must come to grips with the networking of information and the critical nature of access to the means of communication and knowledge development for all citizens. In that the language for expression is shared, our individual subjectivity is built upon the collective subjectivity of that shared meaning. It is built on the creation of selves.

It is not too difficult to understand the overwhelming pressure to impose proprietorial versions of the IPR, given contemporary projections of Net-based incomes, of the e-economy, multimedia futures and knowledge bonanzas. It would seem that the domestication of Napster, the company that was the ultimate nightmare to the futures of convergent industries such as Time-Warner, Bertelsman, Sony, Vivendi and EMI, had to be complemented by legal moves against the 40,000 file sharers in the USA. Both are victories for supporters of the proprietorial economy and those who believe in the singular morality of the IP.

The philosopher Richard Rorty (1996: 9) has observed that '(moral) universalism is an invention of the rich' and that 'moral idealism goes along with economic success', meaning, that such positions are more often than not, the creations of a people who are/were well-endowed in monetary and material terms and who are/were secure, politically, socially and in terms of their prospects within metaphysical futures. Such people often are the keepers and interpreters of knowledge. They are the one who, in terms of history, posed the big questions of life and systematised the answers to it, more often than not, investing these answers with particular inflections and divesting it of all traces of multi-accentuality. These secure people believed that their sense and interpretation of the moral community ought to be identical with the biological community, meaning that 'the' moral community be nothing less than universal, the morality for all people. The many mutinies being waged by the not-so-secure communities—from Seattle to Brazil, to India, can, in the light of this reality, be seen as an attempt to privilege other moralities. In other words, following on from this statement, one cannot expect those who live in less secure environments, in circumstances that deny life chances, to be partial to the interests conveyed by dominant forms of moral universalism and much less, to articulate understandings of moral universalism. Or to put it more bluntly, a moral universalism rooted in the redistribution of wealth—of land and property and the inviolability of bio-diversity will not exactly get enthusiastic support from the ranks of the WTO or for that matter, from the established keepers of moral order. There is just too much at stake in this business of morals.

The Pirate City

I had, in an earlier article on everyday resistance in the city (Thomas 1996: 11), flagged the need to critique familiar markers, such as the concept of 'community'.

> Is there a need for us to subject terms that have been emptied of their referential meaning to a healing process, what Godway and Finn (1994: 3) echoing Gayatri Spivak refer to as a catachresis—by putting the received version of 'community' into question, disrupting the taken-for-granted knowledges of its realization and value, so that a gap can appear—an absence, an abyss, an aporia ... where certitudes must be abandoned and creativity and change ... are possible?

A number of contemporary scholars in India including Ravi Sundaram (2009b), Lawrence Liang (n.d.) and others from outside, including AbdouMaliq Simone (2006), Brian Larkin (2004), Rafael Sanchez (2008), have attempted to disrupt the familiar narrative of the city and cultures in the city, described often in terms of black and white, legal and illegal, and have attempted to create another basis for its understanding beyond the straightjacket views favoured by both the Right and Left. In this narrative, the urban pirate and Pentecostal squatter, the holder of a tenuous land deed and indeed, the Kafkaesque State are implicated in the negotiation and shaping of the city, in spite of the project of planned modernity that is a feature of contemporary cities.

Solomon Benjamin's (2007) essay entitled 'Occupancy Urbanism' refers to the complex nature of land tenure in India that defies easy characterisations and the social history of land that continues to be contested even in an era of the planned city. Using Bangalore and Delhi as examples, he proposes:

> The concept of Occupancy Urbanism as a way to read the everyday city and its spaces of politics. The city is understood as an intense dynamic that is being built incrementally via multiple contestations of land and location. The concept poses the urban 'frontier' as an oppositional site rather than accepting it as a definitive edge of 'capital'. This site, built around; and, economy and complex local politics, is shaped by multi-dimensional historicities embedded in daily practice. It offers an unexpected resilience, stakes an unpredictable

claim that cannot be uprooted via narratives of maps, modernity shaped by 'Mega' projects, civil society, economic imperatives, or the rubric of 'development'. Nor does it accept the nature of 'resistance' shaped by explicit purpose and organisation as viewed in 'social movements' or NGO-centric 'deep democracy', or reactions reduced to 'tactics' in confrontation with 'strategies'.

'Space', in this sense, echoing de Certau (1984: 117) 'is a practiced place'. While Benjamin's characterisation of land tenure in Bangalore city encourages us to read the city in terms of a fluid complexity based on a flexible conception of land ownership, it also points to the city within the city that orders time and space, and opportunities within its own logic. An example of this contestation over land is a report in the *Hindu* (2009b) of moves to evict cobblers and their bunks in Chennai city by the Chennai Corporation. The Madras High Court ruled that since the scheme was established and funded by the central government, 'it was neither open to the respondents to evict the cobblers from the bunks nor remove the bunks or refuse to renew their licenses' (p. 3). At the same time, whether or not the city within the city is beyond modernity or is itself an expression of modernity in the margins, needs further exploration. After all, the state is intensely involved in most aspects of this project and it remains in many respects the apex of modernity.

Benjamin, in other words, argues that for all the planning that goes into the making of cities, they are intensely layered and fiercely resistant to the constant moves to bring it into line with the project of the modern city. Officially sanctioned arson is often responsible for the torching of slums located at the heart of cities in India, although such displacements are countered by the setting-up of other informal habitations in the centres and peripheries of the city. The fact remains that Indian cites are based on an 'idiom of urbanity' that is peculiarly Indian. This idiom, as Ananya Roy (2009: 81) has argued, is legitimised by the State that is involved in fixing and un-fixing the boundaries of the legal and illegal, formal and informal, thus, enabling a regime of control, especially over the ownership of land. In other words, planned development is but a moment in the deeply illegal city that, for example, grants the flagship Indian software company, Infosys, hundreds of acres of land expropriated from marginal farmers. In this sense, the State in India, in Sen's words, is:

> ... a deeply informalised entity, one that actively utilise(s) informality as an instrument of both accumulation and authority...the Indian city is made possible through an idiom of planning whose key feature is informality, and yet this idiom creates a certain territorial impossibility of governance, justice and development.

The lawyer, Lawrence Liang describes the 'legal' means used by the state to legalise illegality by referring to the Karnataka Industrial Areas Development Act's expansion of the 'doctrine of "eminent domain" (the absolute authority of the state to acquire land) to fit the demands of a land hungry information industry'. Is it any wonder that piracy thrives in an environment characterised by the fickle and arbitrary exercise of power and expropriation? In fact, the environment of piracy also offers ample scope for law enforcers to make money. There are cases of police attached to Video Piracy Cells being arrested for corruption (see *The Hindu* 2009a) and a senior Inspector General's wife, owner of Riyan Studio in Kochi, Kerala, being charged for the production of fake VCDs (*Indian Express.com* 2006).

A Reflexive Understanding of Piracy

For our purposes, the city as a complex entity is an entry point for an understanding of cultural piracy. Contemporary forms of cultural piracy while being linked to global distribution chains, nevertheless are realised in the cities of the world. It is urbanity, the uneven flows of city life and the constant battles to redraw the lines between the legal and the illegal that is part of the framework for cultural piracy in modern cities from New York to Mexico City, Kano to Chennai and Shanghai. As cities implode and are unwilling or unable to cope with the demands made by multiple migrants placed at different levels on the socio-economic ladder, transgressions of the 'dominant legal' along with instances of the 'informal' become a parallel spaces where life-worlds for increasingly large numbers of people are validated. In this sense, the use of the term 'piracy', as AbdouMaliq Simone (2006: 361) has argued in the context of a study of two pirate towns in Africa—Johannesburg and Douala—should be used 'flexibly, even heuristically, as a way of talking about and then intersecting diverse urban practices concerning the pursuit of livelihood and opportunity' and as a 'tactic to draw attention to both long-term and emerging dilemmas faced by African urban residents trying to make do—making do in cities where the chronic sense of crisis necessitates more extraordinary actions in order for households and individuals to stay afloat'.

Michel de Certau (1984: 95), in his classic text *The Practice of Everyday Life*, has observed that in spite of the totalising city:

> Urban life increasingly permits the re-emergence of the element that the urbanistic project excluded...Beneath the discourses that ideologize the city, the ruses and combinations of powers that have no readable identity

proliferate; without points where one can take hold of them, without rational transparency, they are impossible to administer.

De Certau's description of a city within a city does suggest that these are mutually exclusive enclaves. That is not necessarily true as in most parts of the world, the informal and the formal economies are closely linked to each other. The roadside vendor and maid, mechanic and carpenter, fish merchant and, indeed, video pirate may exist at the edges of the formal economy, but they certainly negotiate with the formal economy in their everyday lives. The space of the gated community may be secure but the environment of the gated community certainly is not (see for example, Monterescu 2009). Similarly, those who live lives in the formal economy are linked in so many ways to the informal economy. Miller et al. (2005: 222), in their study of Global Hollywood, make the point that film distribution is implicated in a circuit that includes both the legal and the illegal:

> Local networks have always been embedded with global ones. Contemporary international media distribution maps onto the extra-legal movements of capital, people, goods and services: piracy does not simply invert the conventional circuits of the 'authentic' commodity through social space. Extra-legal movements may be symmetrical, asymmetrical or interdependent with the circuits of 'authorised' cultural trade, part of continually shifting alignments between legal and pirate economies.

Ravi Sundaram's descriptor 'pirate modernity' describes in some ways, the failure of the city to inscribe all its inhabitants within its dominant spaces characterised by the economy, politics and leisure. Perhaps, this is doomed to be a futile project, given the impossibility of such totalising embraces in the context of ever-expanding cities. There are many gradations and intensities of pirate modernity in different urban environments throughout the world. The relative crisis of infrastructures dictates the intensity and extensity of alternative economic systems. The collapse of the dominant infrastructure in Kano, Nigeria, as Brain Larkin (2004: 291) observes, has led to the emergence of 'pirate infrastructures' providing a variety of services and acting as 'a powerful mediating force that produces new modes of organising sensory perception, time, space, and economic networks'. While it is tempting to describe these spaces and opportunities in the language of resistance, for most people, these are the means of primary survival. These economic networks thrive on distributing and circulating both the legal and the illegal and arguably facilitate the consumption of products that otherwise would be beyond the reach of the majority of city-dwellers. In the knowledge economy, the exchange value invested in informational products, for example, Microsoft's Windows operational system, is high relative to local incomes and this is particularly the case in a country like India, where the price of Windows-based software packages can range from ₹6,000 (US$121) to ₹17,000 (US$351), prices that are equivalent to or more than the average monthly salary of an average city dweller. Piracy enables access. In fact, there is much to be gained by revisiting Walter Benjamin's (1992) key text, *The Work of Art in the Age of Mechanical Reproduction*, in which he describes successive technological revolutions that have enabled the copy and, thus, severed the aura and sense of art as unique tradition.

> That which withers in the age of mechanical reproduction is the aura of the work of art ... the technique of reproduction detaches the reproduced object from the domain of tradition. By making many reproductions it substitutes a plurality of copies for a unique existence. And *in permitting the reproduction to meet the beholder or listener in his own particular situation, it reactivated the object reproduced*. These two processes lead to a tremendous shattering of tradition which is the obverse of the contemporary crisis and renewal of mankind. (Author's emphasis.)

The relationship between cities and consumption varies tremendously. Quoting from a study by Edensor, Mark Jayne (2006: 163) describes the diversity, sensuality, complexity of place and space in Indian cities, with its multi-variant sound-scapes, smell-scapes, movement-scapes as examples of the many ways in which the city is produced, reproduced and 'brought to life'. The pirate city, in this sense, can be described as an antidote to 'Late capitalism' that 'has rendered street life predictable, marked by sensual deprivation, with difference reduced to commmodified sameness. The destruction of the functional and cultural diversity of the street had thwarted human contact, the desire or difference and the need to wallow in the obscure and confusing'. Given the contexts of the city in both the North and the South, characterised by massive divides in the consumption of space and place, malls and gated communities on the one hand to multiple street lives on the other, the pirate city is the 'other' on our door step that we either refuse to acknowledge and ignore.

Piracy and the Distribution of Popular Culture

An under-theorised area in the context of cultural piracy is access and the modalities of access engendered through alternative practices of distribution. Pirate access needs to be explored against the reality of dominant media control. Vertical and horizontal integrations by media giants today enable control over every aspect of cultural flows—from the inception of an idea, to its production, distribution, exhibition and consumption. This is as true of transnational companies such as News Corp. as it is of national companies such as Reliance in India. The Reliance Anil Ambani group's Adlabs and related companies already have the advantage of vertical integration—with their involvements in production, co-production, post-production, distribution and exhibition in the film industry, major investments in digital cinema, horizontal integration including FM radio operations in 45 circles (Big 92 FM) along with involvement as a DTH and Internet Protocol TV operator/provider, not to mention its major interests in telecommunications. As Sevanti Ninan (2006: 3), the Indian media critic has observed:

> Anil Ambani's trajectory as a future media moghul is to produce entertainment content, put in place a variety of distribution networks, and then leverage the synergies that can be created between the two. Make a film at Adlabs, process it there, distribute it here and abroad ... show it in theatres you own, put it on your DTH platform as pay per view, play its music on your FM stations.

Adlabs film exhibition chains are both domestic and external, and include more than 200 cinemas across Malaysia and East, mid-West and West Coast USA. Their 2006 acquisition of the highly successful domestic television production firm Synergy Communications (producers of the Hindi version of 'Who Wants to be a Millionaire') has given them another important stake in domestic television.

Alternative cultural distribution not only ruptures distribution monopolies, but also offers insights on the ways in which social networks and interest groups are harnessed in the making of niche markets. Kate Eichorn's (2006) study of the illegal copy book trade 'U of T Copy' in Toronto suggests that the spaces for alternative distribution systems are as much a part of the environment in a developed, modern city, as it is in a Third World city. Olatunde Lawuyi's (1997), study on video marketing in Ogbomoso, Nigeria, explores the relationship between the Baptist work ethic, mercantilist Islam and video marketing through video clubs, and Brian Larkin's (2004: 309) research on Hausa video in Nigeria shows the way in which the structures and practices of video piracy, including its distribution and marketing, provides the model for the highly successful, 'legal', Hausa video industry.

> Because the new Hausa videos are dubbed using the same machines as pirate films, because they rely on the same blank cassettes and are distributed through the same channels, piracy has created the aesthetic and technical horizons for nonpirate media ... the parallel economy has migrated onto centre stage, overlapping and interpenetrating with the official economy, mixing legal and illegal regimes, uniting social actors, and organising common networks. This

infrastructure creates its own modes of spatiality, linking Nigeria into new economic and social networks.

Similarly, a study by Srinivas (2003: 53) on the distribution of Hong Kong martial art films in the Indian B-circuit reveals the 'license' used by distributors in Andhra Pradesh, involved in the 'translation' of these films into the local imaginary through the creation of links (often fictitious) between unfamiliar actors and familiar ones—Bruce Lee's daughter, Jackie Chan's guru, etc., thus, helping to create an audience for such films. While B-circuit distribution mainly involves 'legal' films, the study clearly shows the ways in which distributors use creative, culturally grounded means to establish alternative distribution circuits. Srinivas' findings validate the study by Jeffrey Himple's (1996) on film distribution in La Paz, Bolivia that clearly reveals that difference is inscribed and reinforced through film distribution as films move from the centre in La Paz to the smaller neighbourhoods on its margins. However, as he points out: 'Distribution is also driven by commercial interests that reveal a prosperous Aymara cholo-mestizo bourgeoisie. This alternation maps the city as a space of mutual antagonisms, rather than neat oppositions, between parallel Western and Ayamara middle classes.' Piracy, in the case of cinema, offers access to popular culture to all those who live in the city, from the settled classes to migrants and those who live on its margins. In this sense, piracy is a complex phenomenon that reflects popular negotiations within the cities of today and is more than just about the illegal copy. As Lobato (2007: 118) observes in an article on the distribution of what he terms 'subcinema', piracy is also an 'informal and non-legal distribution system', an 'entrepreneurial activity' and a case of non-resistant media.

Conclusions

The city is the site for cultural production, including the processes related to the production, circulation, consumption and appropriation of pirated cultural goods. Unlike the physical city that is bounded, the pirate city can be described not only in terms of the city within the city, but also in terms of the localities and spaces where everyday practices are validated. Cultural piracy, in this sense, needs to be studied not in terms of an aberration, but as enactments of specific forms of 'city'(zen)ship linked to the varied and uneven terrain of opportunities for self-fulfilment in neighbourhoods that exhibit varying levels of ties with uneven globalisation. At the very same time, the city needs to be seen as a site characterised by shifting boundaries between the legal and the illegal through transactions that involve the state, the market and multiple economies. Ravi Sundaram (2009a: 81,175) in his book *Pirate Modernity* comments on the tactics of piracy in Delhi.

> The pirate city threw up a dizzying complexity of production sites, tenure, work practices, and agglomeration.... Small, flexible sites of production and circulation contributed most to this new morphology, feeding into political patronage at the local level, raising demand for 'regularisation' and infrastructure.... Pirate urbanism's tactics avoided visibility, except in local political mobilisations or financial arrangements with lower officials. The lack of visibility helped pirate media urbanism exploit the expanse of Delhi, connecting through mobile telecom infrastructures.

There are multiple circuits and circulations of the symbolic in the city, and spaces where ideas and knowledge are appropriated and used. Such appropriations are by no means acts of resistance, but everyday practices that inform the daily business of life. A one-size-fits-all approach to cultural piracy, grounded in a law and order solution is inappropriate, precisely because the city in its many guises, places and spaces reflects many accommodations between the legal and the illegal. In this sense, the solutions advocated by the USTR and copyright industry lobbies are pointless because the technologies of the copy are ubiquitous and have become an essential aspect of everyday life. Our cities reflect the reality of uneven globalisation and the digital copy really adds another dimension to life in the contested city.

The reality of cultural piracies suggest that despite efforts to institutionalise, streamline and structure India's tryst with IT via policies enacted by the government and investments made by the private sector, the digital remains a contested entity, a site for claims and counter-claims in a revolution that is still unravelling and is 'unfinished business'.

References

Athique, A. 2008. 'The Global Dynamics of Indian Media Piracy: Export Markets, Playback Media and the Informal Economy', *Media, Culture and Society*, 30 (5): 699–717.

Benjamin, W. 1992. 'The Work of Art in the Age of Mechanical Reproduction', *Illuminations*, pp. 211–244. London: Fontana.

Benjamin, S. 2007. 'Occupancy Urbanism: Ten Theses', *Sarai Reader 2007: Frontiers*, pp. 538–563.

Berne Convention. 1999. 'Berne Convention for the Protection of Literary and Artistic Works (Paris Text 1971)', p. 1. Available at: http://www.law.cornell.edu/treaties

Blakely, R. 2009. 'Bollywood Pays up for Plagiarism', *The Australian*, p. 12, 8 August.

CII. 2009. 'Confederation of Indian Industry', July 2009. Available at: http://www.cii.in/menu_content.php?menu_id=224

De Certau, M. 1984. *The Practice of Everyday Life*. Berkeley, Los Angeles, London: University of California Press.

Desai, R. 2005. 'Copyright Infringement in the Indian Film Industry', *Vanderbilt Journal of Entertainment Law and Practice*, Spring: 259–278.

Eichorn, K. 2006. 'Breach of Copy/Rights: The University Copy District as Abject Zone', *Public Culture*, 18 (3).

Gibson, J. 2006. *Creating Selves: Intellectual Property and the Narration of Culture*. Aldershot, Burlington: Ashgate.

Greguras, F. 'Copyright Clearances and Moral Rights', pp. 1–7. Available at: www.batnet.com (accessed on 11 August 2010).

Himple, J. 1996. 'Film Distribution as Media: Mapping Difference in the Bolivian Cinemascape', *Visual Anthropology Review*, 12 (1): 47–66.

IIPA. 2009a. 'India, IIPA 2009 Section 301 Special Report'. Available at: http://www.iipa.com/rbc/2009/2009SPEC301INDIA.pdf

———. 200b. 'IIPA Press Release', July. Available at: http://www.iipa.com/pdf/IIPACopyrightIndustriesReport2003-2007PressRelease.pdf

Indian Express.com. 2006. '3 top cops, CM star in Kerala's piracy musical', *Indian Express.com*, 9 December.

Jayne, M. 2006. *Cities and Consumption*. New York and London: Routledge.

Larkin, B. 2004. 'Degraded Images, Distorted Sounds: Nigerian Video and the Infrastructure of Piracy', *Public Culture*, 16 (2): 289–314.

———. 2005. 'Brian Larkin Interviewed by Anand Taneja', in *Contested Commons/ Trespassing Publics: A Public Record*, pp. 110–115, The Sarai Programme, New Delhi.

Lawuyi, O. L. 1997. 'The Political Economy of Video Marketing in Ogbomoso, Nigeria', *Africa: Journal of the International African Institute*, 67 (3): 476–490.

Leena, B. S. 2004. 'These Pirates Are in Trouble', *Business Standard*, 9 December.

Liang, L. n.d. 'The Other Information City'. Available at: http://www.t0.or.at/wio/downloads/india/liang.pdf (accessed on 24 February 2012).

Lobato, R. 2007. 'Subcinema: Theorising Marginal Film Distribution', *Limina*, 13: 113–120.

Miller, T., N. Govil, J. McMurria, R. Maxwell and T. Wong. 2005. *Global Hollywood 2*. London: BFI Publishing.

Monterescu, D. 2009. 'To Buy or Not to Be: Trespassing the Gated Community', *Public Culture*, 21 (2): 403–430.

Ninan, S. 2006. 'The New Moghuls', *The Hindu Online*, 8 October. Available at: http://www.hindu.com/mag/2006/10/08/stories/2006100800070300.htm (accessed on 11 August 2010).

Pendakur, M. 2003. *Indian Popular Cinema: Industry, Ideology and Consciousness*. Cresskill, NJ: Hampton Press Inc.

Rorty, Richard. 1996. 'Who Are We?: Moral Universalism and Economic Triage', *Diogenes*, 44 (5): 1–15.

Roy, A. 2009. 'Why India Cannot Plan Its Cities: Informality, Insurgence and the Idiom of Informality, *Planning Theory*, 8 (76): 76–87.

Sanchez, R. 2008. 'Seized by the Spirit: The Mystical Foundation of Squatting Among Pentecostals in Caracas (Venezuela) Today', *Public Culture*, 20 (2): 267–305.

Simone, A. M. 2006. 'Pirate Towns: Reworking Social and Symbolic Infrastructures in Johannesburg and Douala', *Urban Studies*, 43 (2): 357–370.

Sethi, A. 2009. 'The Currency of Character', *Seminar, 598: Circuits of Cinema*, pp. 64–68.

Siwek, S. E. 'Copyright Industries in the U.S. Economy: The 2003–2007 Report', pp. 1–23. Available at: http://www.iipa.com/pdf/IIPASiwekReport 2003-07.pdf (accessed on 11 August 2009).

Somers, Ron. 2009. 'Piracy in India's Entertainment Economy Causes Huge Losses to Indian Economy', PR Newswire. Available at: http://www.prnewswire.com/news-releases/piracy-in-indias-entertainment-industry-causes-huge-losses-to-indian-economy-57149602.html (accessed 24 February 2012).

Srinivas, S. V. 2003. 'Hong Kong Action Film in the Indian B Circuit', *Inter-Asian Cultural Studies*, 4 (1): 40–62.

Sundaram, R. 2001. 'Recycling Modernity: Pirate Electronic Cultures in India', *Sarai Reader: Old Media/New Media Ongoing Histories*, pp. 93–99.

———. 2009a. *Pirate Modernity: Delhi's Media Urbanism*. New York and London: Routledge.

———. 2009b. 'Revisiting the Pirate Kingdom', *Third Text*, 23 (3): 335–345.

The Hindu. 2009a. '4 police Personnel Suspended', *The Hindu*, 6 February.

———. 2009b. 'Authorities Cannot Remove Bunks Set up for Cobblers', *The Hindu*, p. 3, 11 August.

Thomas, P. N. 1996. 'Communication as Everyday Resistance: Economic Migrants, Popular Culture and 'City'zenship', *Media Development*, 2: 10–14.

Vaidhyanathan, S. 2004. *The Anarchist in the Library: How the Clash between Freedom and Control Is Hacking the Real World and Crashing the System*. New York: Basic Books.

Woodmansee, M. and P. Jaszi (eds). 1994. *The Construction of Authorship: Textual Appropriation in Law and Literature*. Durham/London: Duke University Press.

World Trade Organisation. 1999. 'An Overview of the Agreement on Trade-related Aspects of Intellectual Property Rights (TRIPS Agreement)', pp. 1–20. Available at: http:// www.wto.org/wto/intellec (accessed on 21 August 2006).

Index

About the Author

Pradip Ninan Thomas is Associate Professor and Co-Director of the Centre for Communication and Social Change at School of Journalism and Communications, University of Queensland, Australia. A leading academic in the area of communication and social change, Thomas is also on the advisory boards of a number of international institutes including the India Media Centre at the University of Westminster.

He is Chair of the Participatory Communications Section, IAMCR, and on the editorial committees of a number of journals, including *Media Development, Journal of Creative Communications, Communication for Development and Social Change, Journalism and Communication Monographs* and the *International Journal of Press/Politics*. In 2010, he was involved in a study of communication rights movements in India.

Thomas has published more than a hundred articles on communication, many in refereed journals including the *International Communications Gazette, Info, Global Communications and Media, Economic & Political Weekly, Telematics & Informatics, Asian Journal of Communication, Media Development* and *Communication for Development and Social Change.*

He has authored and/or co-edited a number of books, including:

- *Who Owns the Media: Global Trends and Local Resistance*/2001/ Zed-Southbound
- *Intellectual Property Rights and Communication in Asia: Conflicting Trends*/2006/SAGE
- *Indigenous Knowledge Systems and Intellectual Property in the Twenty First Century: Perspectives from Southern Africa*/2007/Codesria
- *Strong Religion/Zealous Media: Christian Fundamentalism and the Media in India*/2007/SAGE
- *Political Economy of Communications in India: The Good, the Bad and the Ugly*/2010/SAGE
- *Negotiating Communication Rights: Case Studies from India*/2011/ SAGE